THE SKILLS
OF
MANAGEMENT
SECOND EDITION

W. DAVID REES

D1331855

ROUTLEDGE

First published in 1988 by
Routledge
11 New Fetter Lane, London EC4P 4EE

© 1988 W. David Rees

Typeset by Pat and Anne Murphy,
Highcliffe-on-Sea, Dorset.
Printed and bound in Great Britain by Mackays of Chatham Ltd, Kent

British Library Cataloguing in Publication Data

Rees, W. David.—2nd ed.
  The skills of management.
  1. Management
  I. Title
  658.4   HD31
  ISBN 0-415-00425-X pbk

THE SKILLS OF MANAGEMENT
Second Edition

Contents

Preface to Second Edition

Perhaps the best way of explaining the rationale for this edition is to liken the writing of the book to the production of a motor car. Car design has to take place within a changing environment — particularly in the technological and market areas. However, if a car is to be produced at some stage the design has to be frozen so that production can start — even though opportunities for improvement continue to emerge. However, note is taken of these opportunities for further improvement so that they can be incorporated into the next model. This is just the process that has taken place with this book. Also — just as with car production — there is all the information about the performance of the product after it has been launched. The most important source of information in this respect has been discussions about the content with mature students who are in managerial jobs.

The overall framework of the book has been retained but all chapters have been amended — some of them being quite substantially expanded. This has been for a variety of reasons, particularly because of changes in the environment in which managers have to operate. New material has become available — often contributed by mature students and I have enlarged some areas where the previous explanations were too short.

More emphasis has inevitably been placed on the pressure for greater cost-effectiveness — in both the private and public sectors. A related issue is that of managing in a context of chronic high unemployment. These developments have been examined to see what changes they have caused, both in the way organisations operate and in their structure. The rise of the flexible firm is one of the new topics that is included. Explanation and comment on quality circles is also given.

Account has been taken of legal developments — particularly those changes in employment law likely to affect the individual manager. These include the law relating to discrimination in employment. More attention is given to the role of women and a new section has been included about assertiveness training — which is of relevance to both sexes.

Other areas that have been expanded are the explanation of the technique of role set analysis, and relevant aspects of theory relating to organisation behaviour and motivation. A section has been added on the dangers of over-involvement in the job and managerial stress. The basics of job evaluation are explained in the new Chapter 7 as is the likely impact of the changes in the law relating to equal pay on pay structures. A section on the role of the manager as coach and trainer has been included in Chapter 10. The dangers of looking at departmental activity in isolation from the rest of an organisation are illustrated with particular reference to industrial relations, and the implications of the reduced role of trade unions are also examined.

These of course are just the changes in the book — the basic core survives and is seen as being strengthened by these additions. The aim remains to provide managers and students of management with a text that is useful and interesting yet rigorous. Care has again been taken to express ideas in an intelligible language and the fund of illustrative examples has been enriched.

W. David Rees

Acknowledgements

Acknowledgements are primarily due to the countless number of students who, in different classes, have allowed me to test out my ideas and have contributed both ideas of their own and many invaluable illustrative examples which appear in this book. The classes have been on a wide variety of courses — primarily within the Polytechnic of Central London's Centre of Management Studies. Particular thanks are due to the students on the MA in Manpower Studies course and also to the many managers from the Plessey Company who have come to the Polytechnic for training. I have gleaned innumerable valuable ideas from my colleagues and from employees of the Bass Group and the London Borough of Hackney. Mention should also be made of the students I have met at the Royal College of Nursing — particularly those who first prompted the idea of my writing the book.

There are also some individuals from whom I have received particular help. These include Reece Evans, formerly of the Bass Group, and Bob Lee of Britvic-Corona. Janey Rees gave me many useful ideas and much constructive comment which have strengthened the book. Help has also been received from Bill Ball, Robin Evans, the late Tom Howell, Jill Porter, Jonathan and Sarah Rees, Angela Rice, Billie Sayers, Bob Walker and Leslie Willcocks. Enormous thanks are due to my wife, Christine, who helped across the whole range of the activity — from the conceptual and creative to the grammatical — and who lived through it all. The book is much stronger because of her help. Thanks are particularly due to Liz Kennedy for her help, and to numerous managers who have discussed the content and contributed ideas and examples. Especial thanks are due also to Sue Lloyd-Evelyn who undertook market research, typed the various drafts and converted all the manuscript into a coherent form.

Introduction

For nearly 20 years I have been teaching management subjects at the London Management Centre, which is part of the Polytechnic of Central London. In that time I have always been at a loss for an appropriate basic book to recommend either to students studying management on professional, undergraduate and other courses or practising managers. After some prompting from student groups, I have now written such a book. Over the years I have become fascinated with the way in which people in widely different organisations and countries seem to be grappling with the same basic issues and problems. Consequently I have been able to identify a core of basic issues that match the syllabus requirements of a wide range of courses as well as being relevant to the practising manager. One of the great weaknesses with existing books, particularly those aimed at students, is the lack of practical examples. I have been able to draw on the contributions made by practising managers in hundreds of classroom discussions to provide appropriate practical examples to illustrate the relevant theoretical concepts. Because of this, it has been possible to make the book relevant, with a sound integration of theory and practice.

It is increasingly recognised that people who train as specialists are likely to accumulate considerable managerial responsibilities in the course of their career. Consequently the syllabuses of many professional and specialist courses have been adapted to include management. Few people start off as managers. Organisations usually have some sort of departmental structure. The normal career progression is to start off as a specialist and then acquire responsibility for supervising or managing other specialists. Even business studies graduates usually find that they have to be placed in a specialist job despite the general nature of the training they have received. If that is the pattern, it is just as well to prepare people for what is to come. If the specialism requires training why not also the management aspect? Many people, however, do not have the benefit of training in this area, and it is hoped that this book may be of assistance to them as well as to those who are pursuing a specific course of study.

I have discussed the distinction between administration and management in Chapter 3. These terms tend to indicate significantly different approaches, if only in emphasis, and the distinction deserves attention. However, I have not spent time on what I see as the rather sterile distinction between supervision and management. I have used the term 'management' generically so as to incorporate supervision. My scepticism of the value of this distinction has been reinforced when I have run management courses for different levels within the same organisation. At one stage, for example, I was involved in running management courses simultaneously at three different levels in the Health Service. These were for ward sisters, middle managers and senior nursing officers. The, perhaps heretical, conclusion I came to was that the basic problems facing the people employed at these different levels were very much the same. Status might demand that course syllabuses be written up differently and indeed there would be some genuine differences. However, it was the common nature of problems rather than their difference which was the more noticeable. The same reasoning can apply to management syllabuses on examination courses. Any introduction to the basic concepts is going to have to cover much the same general ground, whether it be on a Business Educational Council, undergraduate, professional or postgraduate course.

The range of topics covered includes general management concepts and the management of people. The range does not extend to areas such as finance, marketing and work study. These areas are not only outside my own particular area of competence, but are also areas where there is likely to be considerable variation of responsibility between managers. The knowledge required of an accounts section leader is likely to be quite different from that required of a production supervisor in these areas. What I believe I have done is to identify a range of topics that is of relevance to all persons studying or involved in management. The scope of managerial responsibility is potentially so wide that the coverage cannot be exhaustive. However, no person with management responsibility can escape the need, for example, to consider such issues as defining his objectives, organising his time, delegation, motivation and employee relations.

In writing this book I have taken into account the needs of managers and students in and from countries other than Britain. I have for a long time been concerned that teaching and writing should be such that it is comprehensible to people from other countries without detracting from its value to British students. The avoidance of long words when short ones will do is very much in keeping with the theme of the chapter on communication. It means that readers, whether from Britain or from overseas, do not have to translate unnecessary jargon in order to understand the concepts that are contained in the book.

The actual topics included in the book are based on the needs of both British and overseas readers. In considering the needs of overseas readers I have been able to capitalise on my own experience. This has included lecturing in management at the University of Guyana and the Mara Institute of Technology, Malaysia, my period as External Examiner at Ngee Ann Polytechnic, Singapore, and running management training programmes for Pertamina, the National Oil Corporation of Indonesia. My exposure to different countries and different nationalities has led me to the conclusion that the bulk of the material in this book is about skills that are needed in a wide range of cultures. Material has been included about the problems faced by managers coping with other cultures, but this can be as much an issue for British managers as for those from other countries.

I have also taken account of the changing nature of the societies in which we live. High levels of unemployment, new technology and changes in social and political conditions all mean that managerial behaviour has to adapt to a changing world to be effective. One final point regarding style, which perhaps in itself underlies the changing social scene: the pronoun 'he' is used throughout the book in a generic sense and covers the feminine as well as the masculine gender.

1

Managers and their Background

INTRODUCTION

Management may be defined as 'getting work done through others'. Many people embark upon their careers without expecting to become involved in management. Nevertheless, they may well find that they gradually accumulate managerial responsibilities. Such people may find that, although they may be designated as specialists, a critical and increasing part of their job is the management of other people. In other cases people may be promoted from a specialist job and given the title manager. They may still be required to make a specialist contribution. The difference between these two sets may be that the recognition of the managerial element by employer and employee is gradual in the first instance and more sudden in the other. The actual balance of the activity may be much the same in both instances.

Whatever route people take into management, they still need to discharge their responsibilities effectively. They are much more likely to be effective if they clearly recognise the range and nature of the responsibilities they have acquired. Having identified their responsibilities, the next step is to develop the skills that are necessary to handle them. This first chapter is about the essential first step of identifying the manager's role. The particular topics that are covered are: the route most people follow to management, the dilemma of specialist-managers, the appointment of managers and the problems of maintaining balance between specialist and managerial activity.

HOW PEOPLE BECOME MANAGERS

The structure of organisations is usually such that most of the employees are engaged on a specialised activity. The number of general jobs involving, for example, the co-ordination of the work of a number of different specialist departments tends to be very limited. One is tempted to ask just how many truly general management jobs there are. It may be that in private firms there are few, if any, apart from that of managing director. The entry into organisations is, I would argue, essentially into specialised activity. People may be engaged at a lowly level in a specialised department. Alternatively they may have advanced specialist skills — that they have acquired either by experience or training, or by a combination of both. This specialist background is the pedigree of the vast majority of managers. This can be demonstrated by probing into the background of almost anyone you know who has managerial responsibilities. Engineering managers come from the ranks of specialist engineers. Bank managers will have previously been engaged in specialist banking activities. Ward sisters or nursing officers will inevitably have a professional nursing qualification. A head teacher will have a teaching qualification. Football managers are invariably ex-professional players. Small business entrepreneurs are usually running a business based on their initial technical skill — for example, in the building trade or as a motor mechanic. In the main I am sure that this is not just how things are but how they should be. Figure 1.1 shows, in a rather simplified form, how specialists become managers.

The amount of time spent on managerial activity is indicated by reading off the level of the shaded area on the vertical scale on the left hand side of the diagram. The balance of activity, much of which may be of a specialist nature, is calculated simply by subtracting the managerial element from 100 per cent. Initially a specialist may be employed 100 per cent of the time on specialist activity. This may well be after professional training as an accountant, engineer or whatever. The competent specialist may gradually acquire minor supervisory responsibilities — perhaps quite informally. For example, this could be helping newcomers with their job. After five years of competent performance it would not be unusual for a specialist to be promoted. Given the structure of organisations, this usually involves an element of managerial responsibility. An engineer could become

2

Figure 1.1: The managerial escalator

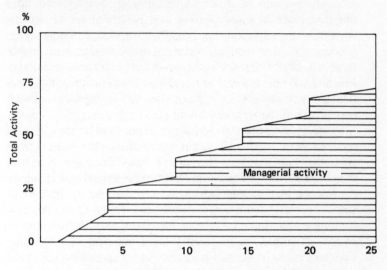

Years of employment (excluding full-time training)

a section leader or a bank cashier an assistant officer. After a further five years there could be a further formal promotion, either within the same or another organisation, which could have been preceded by a certain amount of accumulation of managerial responsibility on an informal basis. People tend to be carried along this 'escalator' and may finish with most or even all of their time on the managerial side of the axis. The exact course of progress will vary widely from one person to another. However, the escalator-type progression is a very common way in which people become managers. The managerial activity may well be in a specialist context, but the crucial change is that the former specialist may have to spend most of his time managing other specialists, rather than engaging directly in specialist activity himself.

THE CONFLICT BETWEEN SPECIALIST AND MANAGERIAL ACTIVITY

The possession of specialist skills is normally an asset and in many cases quite indispensable. If the person who manages in a specialist environment does not understand it, he will be under a great and perhaps insurmountable handicap. Management does not take place in a vacuum but in a particular set of circumstances — usually requiring specialist knowledge. This may be necessary so that instructions are sensible but also to inspire respect in others. However, this specialist pedigree of a manager is at the root of many of the problems that confront him, particularly the danger of getting the wrong balance between specialist and managerial activity.

Some of the problems which are likely to arise may now be obvious. A person may have embarked on a career and acquired specialist skills that he is increasingly less able to use. A person may have an emotional commitment to his specialist area, and a confidence in that area which may be backed up by several years' formal training. Conversely the commitment to, and training and aptitude for, the managerial side of the job may all be low. It would not be unusual for a manager in a specialist environment to have had his training in his specialism measured in years and his training in management measured in days. Few managers have a formal management qualification and the managerial content in specialist courses is usually small or non-existent. The lack of emphasis on management training was confirmed by a study undertaken for the Confederation of British Industry and the British Institute of Management published in 1987. One of the findings was that, 'It is estimated that UK managers receive an average of about one day's formal training per year. This figure hides a wide average. The majority of managers receive no formal training.'[1,2] This inexorably creates the temptation for managers to adjust the balance of their activity so that they concentrate on what they like doing and what they feel equipped to do, at the expense of the managerial aspects of their job. This dilemma can sometimes be revealed by the job titles people use. A colleague of mine, who used to do manpower advisory work in the civil engineering industry, found that the approach of the senior man on site was often indicated by whether he used the title 'site engineer' or 'site manager'. Job titles can be revealing in many other occupations as well — for example the choice of the term 'buyer' or 'department manager' in a department store. It could even be that the use of the term 'headmaster' indicates a traditional orientation around teaching rather than the management of other teachers.

Why do people proceed up a career escalator that may not

particularly appeal to them? The answer is that, given the structure of most organisations, this may be the only way for them to gain promotion. The acceptance of an increasing amount of managerial responsibility may be the only way in which employees can increase their pay, status and authority. A further pressure to take promotion may be an antipathy to being supervised by any of the other people who may be appointed to the boss's job. Some people may be reconciled to this shift and be able to cope with it. Others may not be reconciled to it and/or may not be equipped to handle it. This may lead to them over-concentrating on the specialist area — either through conscious design, or more likely because they have never really reasoned it through. The problems may be compounded by the actions and perceptions of their bosses. If the boss hasn't reasoned it through either, a pattern may be created down the line. Alternatively, even if the boss has reasoned it through for himself, the appointment of subordinate managers may still be faulty.

THE APPOINTMENT OF MANAGERS

The easiest way to choose a potential manager is to look at his historical performance and appoint or reject on that basis. The danger in this approach is, however, that there may be critical differences between the duties that a person has performed in the past and those that he may be expected to perform in the future. This is over and above the problems of judging historical performance anyway. If a person is moving from specialist to mainly managerial activity it could mean that he is appointed on the basis of his specialist performance. Whilst this is a legitimate and necessary area to investigate, the person's managerial potential may be more important. Unfortunately this point may not be properly grasped and, in any case, it is so much easier to assess historical performance rather than speculate about a person's managerial potential. It is, for example, far easier to count the number of international caps that a professional footballer has acquired than judge whether he has the appropriate range of skills to manage a football club. This is no doubt why there are so many disastrous appointments to football management! Experience as a professional footballer may be vital, but there are other factors that may be vital as well — even if they are more difficult to identify — either in the job or in the person

5

applying for it. It is because of this reasoning that there is the adage in the engineering industry: 'It is easy to lose a first-rate craftsman and gain a third-rate foreman.'

The appointment of managers may prove to be a fairly random affair — the competence of the selectors may mean that it is often a question of luck as to whether the people with the right mix of skills and potential are appointed in the first place. However, the individual who finds that he has emerged through the selection system as a manager needs to address himself to the behaviour that will be appropriate, even if those appointing him did not.

An apt illustration of many of these points is provided by the case of the English test cricketer, Ian Botham. He lost form dramatically after being made captain of the English team and ultimately resigned in 1981 during the series against Australia. During the next four matches his form returned spectacularly. By the end of the series he had scored 365 runs and taken 28 wickets and was responsible, more than anyone else, for England winning. Interestingly the reaction to this example by West Indian audiences has been that they, in the past, have seen similar examples in the Caribbean. In fairness, this problem is one of trying to combine two roles rather than of simply moving from one to another. However, the issue of who should be chosen to combine such roles is still critical and in practice may necessitate great care in selection.

SPECIALIST CAREER STRUCTURES AND THEIR LIMITATIONS

The dilemma of the specialist who is forced into management is accentuated by the difficulty that organisations have in providing alternative career progressions. In some cases it may be possible to get around the dilemma by providing the opportunity for specialist career progression. However, the extent to which this can be done seems to be severely limited in practice as it frequently proves impractical to separate out managerial and specialist duties.

One attempt was made with the non-commissioned ranks in the British Royal Air Force. Separate technical and supervisory career structures were established for the 'other ranks'. Airmen on the technical side could work their way through the ranks of junior technician up to chief technician. The conventional non-commissioned ranks were retained. The theory was that those with the technical expertise should concentrate on that side leaving the supervisory tasks to those with the conventional non-commissioned officer ranks. Problems did however arise with this breakdown, in that it was a lot more difficult to disentangle the technical and supervisory roles in practice than in theory. The various levels of technicians still had to brief, instruct and control their subordinates in technical matters. These aspects could not be farmed out to a distant NCO who had no technical knowledge. The non-technical NCOs had their problems too. They tended to accumulate the residual and unpopular supervisory duties to do with parades, guards and general orderly duties. Consequently the division between the two structures was abandoned.

Some companies, such as Imperial Chemical Industries, have found that they have been able to create technical career structures for some people at least. This can provide a means of retaining high-calibre technical personnel and allowing them to concentrate on what they are good at. Another approach can be to provide specialists with administrative assistants to help the specialist get the best of both worlds.

Another instance in which there has been an attempt to develop a specialist career structure is in the nursing profession, but this also has met with only very limited success. Nurses used to have a clinical career structure, but this created problems of imbalance in that the managerial tasks tended to be ignored. Consequently, following the Salmon Report[3] in 1966, drastic changes were made in the nursing career structure. Job descriptions were introduced defining the managerial element in jobs and, once nurses moved from ward sister to the next grade of nursing officer, their jobs were exclusively managerial. Partly as a reaction to this there has been some attempt to recreate senior clinical jobs for nurses. However, it has not been possible to develop this to any great extent. The constraints are that nurses have to be managed by someone which means that the senior nurses have to be involved in managerial activity. Also the demarcation line between the medical work undertaken by doctors and nursing activities means that there is not that much scope to develop the clinical nursing role anyway. So the dilemma of many nurses is likely to remain. They will have trained at length for a job for which they have aptitude and

7

emotional commitment. In order to gain promotion they have increasingly to move away from direct clinical involvement. At least in their case, though, these often unpalatable truths are clearly recognised. The career path is clear and the use of job descriptions and training in nursing management clarifies what nursing officers should be doing.

The essential point is that there are limits to the extent to which specialist and managerial activity can be disentangled. There is undoubtedly room for much more experiment in this area. Also there is obviously a strong case for giving senior specialists as much clerical and secretarial-type assistance as is practicable. However, none of this is likely to end the dilemma of specialists having to manage. When the separation of managerial from specialist activity is suggested in group discussion on management courses as a solution to the dilemma, I often respond by asking whether the people without specialist knowledge could supervise the people present. The standard answer is 'no', whether it be a high technology industry like electronics or not. The clear implication of this is that a large part of management activity must be undertaken by specialists.

IMBALANCE IN THE JOB AND ITS CORRECTION

The pedigree of most managers is, therefore, such that there is likely to be a conflict between what they were originally trained to do and what they need to do. An appropriate starting point, for any manager concerned with assessing and developing his own managerial skills, is to ask himself whether he has got the balance right between what he is doing and what needs to be done.

There can be many reasons for the balance being wrong. These include: managers doing things just because they enjoy them, pressure from subordinates and failure on the part of managers to think about the balance between their managerial and specialist activity.

Personal preference

Frequently a manager concentrates unduly on what he simply enjoys doing. This can operate in many, if not all, managerial environments. On one occasion I was explaining this problem to a group of transport managers. They grasped the point and told me in return that not only did they recognise the phenomenon, but they had a name for it. Supervisors who insisted on driving, ostensibly to 'keep their hand in', were described by them as being 'cab happy'.

If this type of activity only happens occasionally perhaps one shouldn't worry unduly — it is when it forms a regular pattern that there is likely to be a serious problem. Sometimes however it may be a calculated strategy of having 'the penny and the bun'. The most extreme example I came across of this concerned the head of an educational institution. The gentleman who obtained this job had been attracted to it by the many tangible benefits. Once he had been appointed he announced that as he was an academic he would only undertake academic work. He deemed managerial work to be beneath his intellectual status. The position then arose that the only work he would do he wasn't given and the only work he was given he wouldn't do. Needless to say the subordinates in this case were not at all amused by this blatant contract violation — particularly as they had to do their boss's job whilst he effectively did nothing. The head did however at least provide a perfect example of how a person could get his role completely the wrong way around as far as everyone else was concerned. One has rather more sympathy for people who are sucked into management but who are concerned that, if for any reason they lose their jobs, they will have difficulty in returning to their specialist sphere unless they have kept up to date.

Pressure from subordinates

The traditions of a particular occupation may also influence a manager's behaviour. In teaching, for example, there may be considerable pressure, direct and indirect, by junior teachers, for senior teachers, or for head teachers, to concentrate on teaching. The person in a supervisory position may have to be prepared to resist the pressures of subordinates which could lead to his striking the wrong balance. Such a person may also feel that 'he should not give a job to a subordinate that he cannot do himself' — a frequently quoted maxim. There may also be the fear that, unless a direct specialist involvement is retained, the manager will become out of date and perhaps ultimately unable to manage at all. The problem is that, if a person responds to these pressures, he may make matters worse. This can happen in two ways: by interfering in the work of subordinates and also by neglecting the critical managerial aspects of a job.

The pressures by subordinates for a manager to demonstrate competence and interest in their specialist activity can be real enough. However, subordinates may also quite fail to comprehend the other aspects of a boss's job. Additionally they may resent the 'creaming-off' of the more interesting parts of the job by a boss who wants 'to keep his hand in'. This may be particularly annoying if the boss does this on a random basis so they never quite know what their job is. Situations where you have 'two cooks in the kitchen' may generate more friction than where one cook leaves the other to get on with it and puts up with any adverse comments about the lack of specialist involvement. Specialist knowledge in the work situation is a means to an end and not an end in itself. The manager is likely to be judged ultimately by his results — not by his specialist knowledge. The specialist knowledge that he requires is that which enables him to supervise others. If subordinates can do a particular job better than the manager, the manager's skill is in arranging just that state of affairs. To compete with the subordinate, and then fail, is hardly to be recommended. There is a world of difference between a manager having no specialist competence and having sufficient specialist knowledge to supervise subordinates. The latter may be quite sufficient. It would be very nice if all managers knew more about every aspect of the subordinate's job than the subordinate, but it is not very realistic — particularly with changing technology. It may also not do a great deal of good for the esteem of subordinates. The manager may have to face up to being confronted by a specialist issue that he cannot deal with. Rather than have nightmares about this, it may be that this is simply an issue where the manager reroutes the subordinate to a source where he may get the right information.

Ironically this seems to be less of a problem for those operating at the top of an organisation: managing directors are not likely to try to compete with their various specialists. It may be that the structure at the top of an organisation — with, for example, the work of various departments being synthesised by one person — makes it much clearer just what the top manager should be doing. Managers at this level seem to be able to move more easily to a different type of organisation compared with those managers who are at the middle level and managing in a very specific specialist environment. The options for this latter group may be restricted, for example, to managing similar specialist activity elsewhere, but on a larger scale. The freedom to appoint people without detailed specialist knowledge may be subject to considerable variation between different industries. Managing directors in high technology industries can perhaps only come from within that industry. Even at this level though there may be a temptation for the person at the top to devote too much of his time to his favourite area. Managing directors, for example, will invariably have started off by acquiring a specialist skill even if they have subsequently moved into a career path of running progressively larger companies.

Failure to think about the correct balance

Another reason why managers sometimes engage in an inappropriate balance of activities may simply be that they have failed to identify the fact. If the general style is for over-concentration on specialist activity an imbalance may not be easily recognised by others either, far less be the subject of constructive comment and advice.

Sometimes managers can find out the right balance by accident. One who did was the football manager Colin Addison when he was player-manager of Hereford United. He broke his leg and found that, although the team was deprived of a player, overall they benefited because of his enforced concentration on management. The gains that this concentration brought more than compensated for the loss of a member of the first-team squad. It is easy though to see why professional footballers may try and combine the daunting tasks of playing and managing. Their reputations will be as players and, if they step down a division or two, they may find that for a while they can cope with both tasks. However, there is a danger that they will fail in both directions. Their playing ability will be on the decline because of age — just as technical specialists moving up the managerial escalator will find that their technical skills are declining. Their selection and support by club directors may be such that they have limited help, and perhaps limited aptitude, for the job for which they have been chosen. Under these pressures, and those of trying to learn a new job, probably with a new club, they may 'regress' into doing what they have been historically good at. The more they try in this direction, the more may be their physical exhaustion and retreat from the key area of management. Perhaps a few player-managers can cope with this for a while; others try and fail and still others accept that they have to 'cross over the line' and concentrate full-time on management.

The example given concerning football management is meant to help explain a general problem. This is that when people are experiencing strain in the managerial part of their job they may seek to avoid this by 'regressing' into their former specialist role. This may provide a temporary refuge and restore confidence by enabling the person concerned to do what he feels good at. However, like much 'avoidance behaviour' it is likely to make matters much worse in the long term. A symptom of this may be the eagerness with which a manager insists on 'acting down' when a subordinate is away.

Training and monitoring

A key feature of any strategy for correcting imbalance in the job is for those likely to have the problem to be made more aware of it. They may manage to do this for themselves with learning taking place perhaps on a trial and error basis. However, training and monitoring of performance, as well as careful selection, can help to ensure that people don't have to learn everything the hard way — or even not learn at all. The trend towards including a management component in vocational undergraduate and professional courses is a welcome development in this respect. However, any such undergraduate training needs to be reinforced by further training once those concerned have had greater exposure to management problems. Such exposure is likely to lead to an increased awareness of what the problems really are and the concepts and skills that may assist with their resolution. Such further training is not entirely a matter of going on courses. There is a considerable responsibility for bosses to see that those who are given managerial responsibilities are also given help through appraisal, counselling and coaching. These issues are further developed in Chapter 10.

CONCLUSION

The theme of this chapter has been that, at all levels of management, managers are likely to have the task of managing particular activities when there are other things they would prefer to be doing. They will not always realise it if they neglect the managerial aspects in favour of what they like doing. The rest of the book is intended to give help to those who want to manage effectively. Chapter 2 is logically about the identification of objectives. Breaking a leg may be one of identifying priorities in a job, but there are easier ways. Regrettably, however, there are many people who never do come to identify the appropriate balance.[4]

NOTES

1. *The making of British managers*, a report for the British Institute of Management and the Confederation of British Industry into management, training, education and development prepared by Dr John Constable and Roger McCormick (BIM, April 1987), summary p. 3.

2. For a report demonstrating the lack of emphasis on management training in Britain, see Handy, Charles *et al.*, *The making of managers: a report on management education, training and development in the USA, West Germany, France, Japan and the UK* (NEDO/MSC/BIM, 1987).

3. *Report of the Committee on Senior Nursing Staff Structure* (the Salmon Report), (HMSO, 1966).

4. For a further account of the problems facing people who have moved into managerial positions, see M. Broussine and Y. Guerrier, *Surviving as a middle manager* (Croom Helm, 1983).

2

Identifying the Manager's Job

INTRODUCTION

In this chapter we consider how effectively managers use their time and how they go about, or fail to go about, identifying their jobs systematically. The specific techniques of 'management by objectives' and role set analysis are explained. The skills involved in time management are also covered.

ACTIVITY VERSUS EFFECTIVENESS

One of my own earliest observations about managers was that they tend to fall into two groups: those who define what has to be done, get on with it and then go home; and those who create a flurry of physical activity and seek to justify their positions by the demonstrable effort they put into a job, rather than by the results they achieve. The latter group also tends to be reactive in its responses, rather than innovatory. The emphasis on effort tends to combine neatly with a reactive 'management by crisis' approach. There can, perhaps, be some of this in most managers but it is still useful to consider the different approaches. Sometimes the attempts at self-justification are a combination of humour, pathos and ineffectiveness. I have in mind here such managerial games as: never going home until the managing director has left, working overtime for the sake of it, and seeking to demonstrate to colleagues that you have worked later than them. Such stratagems may or may not work in the short term. It may even be that in some cases they are necessary political ploys, given that there will be political activity in any organisation. However, the great danger is that, if a manager spends too much time simply justifying himself, he may fail actually to diagnose what he should be doing and to do it. Ultimately managers are much more likely to be judged by results than by anything else. Activity-centred behaviour is in any case much more likely to spring from incompetence and/or insecurity rather than adroit political behaviour. This type of behaviour is likely to aggravate the position of the manager in the long run rather than ameliorate it.

What is work?

One point that needs to be established at this stage is just how people define 'work'. A notion that I have repeatedly come across is that work is synonymous with physical activity. This misconception can have most unfortunate consequences, particularly in the job of a manager. One manifestation of this misconception is when shop-floor workers have applied for various white-collar positions. The mental activity of a clerk or rate-fixer or supervisor may simply not be perceived by a person used to manual work because such mental activity is not overt. A person who applies for a white-collar job, labouring under this delusion, may find out only too late that the mental activity may be far more demanding than the physical activity to which he has been accustomed.

I remember one occasion when a steelworker in a television interview referred to a particular Secretary of State and complained that 'she had never done a day's work in her life'. This is a criticism that is often levelled at people in such positions. However, whatever one thought of that particular Secretary of State, one could hardly sustain an argument that she was not hard-working. A further example, to illustrate this point, was volunteered by one of my students on a course in hospital ward management. She related an incident when she had noticed a patient fall into a coma. At the time she was the staff nurse on that particular ward and knew that this patient was on a special diet. She stopped what she was doing to try and puzzle out if the staff who would administer drip feeding to the patient would be aware of his special dietary needs. Her mental activity was soon interrupted by the ward sister, who brusquely asked her what she

15

thought she was doing, just standing there, and told her to get on with her work!

The recurring problem, of course, is that it is obvious when people are working at a physical level, but less obvious when they are engaged in what is likely to be more crucial mental activity. This is compounded by the fact that you can, of course, have staff just standing around day-dreaming and not engaged in mental problem-solving activity. Also the tradition of judging manual workers by their rate of physical activity is something which can carry over into judgements about whether managers are working or not. It may be that managers have to some extent to respond to this type of pressure by demonstrating physical activity. It may be crucial though to their effectiveness that they do not over-react to such pressure. Managers need also to make this distinction when they are assessing, and perhaps pressurising, their own subordinates.

THE IDENTIFICATION OF THE MANAGER'S JOB

Perhaps the first thing that any manager needs to do is actually to identify his job. This should be seen as a continuous process rather than a 'one-off' activity. Organisations have to change in order to survive and the jobs of managers need to alter accordingly. This is why, if a manager has a job description, it should be seen as a starting point for identifying the job rather than a definitive unalterable document. Job descriptions, whilst being useful, may also leave considerable room for interpretation as well as need updating. They also suffer from the deficiency that they usually do not give a clear indication of the priorities in a job. There are also likely to be other ways in which a manager identifies and adjusts his job. He is hardly likely to be left completely to his own devices — there will obviously be instructions from superior managers. In some cases the remit for a manager will be very specific and the problem will primarily be one of doing the job rather than of identifying what needs to be done. In other cases — perhaps where there is considerable internal and external change — the manager may need to spend a considerable amount of time defining and redefining what needs to be done. A further guide may be the way the work was performed by a previous incumbent. It would be folly to ignore the way a previous incumbent had performed a job, but perhaps equally foolish not to review his interpretation of a job nor to allow for changed circumstances. There can in any case be considerable misunderstanding about just what is done before one gets to the question of just what needs to be done. In my own experience I have found that it is usual for there to be significant surprises when the purpose and content of jobs are actually clarified. Usually the job holder will find that he is undertaking some tasks of which his 'boss' is unaware. It is also likely that there will be some tasks that he is expected to do of which he is unaware. One of the reasons for these misunderstandings is that the 'boss' may have never fully appreciated the demands of the job. Alternatively, he may have appreciated these demands at a previous time, or even have done the job at one stage, but may be basing his view on what was historically done rather than what is subsequently needed.

Short-term pressures and long-term needs

Much of a manager's time will be devoted simply to responding to pressures and demands from other people. The 'in-tray' tends to dominate the daily pattern of activity. Whatever a manager wants to do in the long term is all very well, but often cannot be contemplated until the short-term pressures have been dealt with. However, there are dangers that a manager will simply react to short-term pressures and not think out what he should be doing from a long-term point of view. Managers may also fall into a particular pattern of identifying certain short-term pressures and ignoring others. In other words, the response can be repetitive without the managers really questioning what needs to be done, even on a short-term basis.

Responding to a predetermined selection of short-term issues can become a total way of life for some managers. In some cases this may be because of the sheer pressure on a manager, in other cases because he wants to avoid certain issues. One problem with this approach is that some of the issues that are left are important; moreover, if the manager thought things out on a long-term basis then some of the short-term pressures might be reduced or eliminated. Managers have to react to some at least of the short-term pressures. However, it can be very easy to fall into a pattern of just doing this, with possibly disastrous results on long-term effectiveness. Managers need to compare what they are doing in the short term with what they should aim to be doing. This though is not always a question that managers are prepared to ask.

In a study of the way 160 managers actually performed their jobs, Rosemary Stewart observed that:

> A fragmented day is often the laziest day; the day that demands the least in terms of mental discipline, though the most in nervous energy. It is easier to pass from one subject to a second when the first requires a difficult or unpalatable decision, or sustained thought. It is easier to respond to each fresh stimulus, to hare after the latest query, than to set an order of priorities and try to keep to it. This, of course, includes knowing when the latest query has priority. It is easier to be a grasshopper jumping from one problem to another, than a beaver chewing away at a tough task.[1]

The definition of objectives

As has already been indicated, the reverse of the reactive activity-centred approach of managers is one where objectives are carefully identified and then, hopefully, achieved. A consequential benefit can be that the manager's time is allocated in proportion to the priority of a task. The reactive manager may find, assuming he ever thinks in these terms, that he has failed to match the time available to the key elements in his job. Management writers who have made historically important contributions to this issue of managerial objectives include Peter Drucker[2] and John Humble.[3] Peter Drucker appears to be the first person who used the term 'management by objectives', whilst John Humble developed the idea into a systematic method of management not just for the individual manager, but for the total organisation.

'Management by objectives' was very fashionable in the late 1960s and early 1970s, but has since declined in popularity. It was very often applied in a simplistic manner. There was also little stress in the literature on how to handle the conflicts that can emerge between individual and organisational objectives. There may also have been exaggerated expectations of what could be achieved by 'management by objectives' when all managers were required to participate in a 'total' scheme.

The crucial question for managers to ask is just why are they doing a particularly task or job. It is all too easy to say what one is doing rather than why. Answering the question 'why?' can produce surprising results. The following *Evening Standard* report, whilst not an example of a managerial job, makes the appropriate point:

Night watchmen at Westminster Council House in Marylebone Road protecting the Council's silver plate, cost ratepayers £21,000 last year. Clever economists at the Council now think that the resident caretaker may be able to handle the job alone. They have discovered that the silver was moved elsewhere years ago.[4]

Humble explains that, in his view, every manager needs to define the overall purpose of his job and then to identify the six to eight key tasks which need to be accomplished if that overall purpose or objective is to be achieved. The identification of the key tasks that are contained in a job does present some advantages over the conventional type of job description. Job descriptions can, by their length and detail, obscure the key elements in a job. Part of the Humble approach is that, if the overall objective and the accompanying key tasks are defined, then the rest of the detail can be left to look after itself. Consideration can then be given to the definition of each key task in detail. This is accompanied by the specification of the minimum acceptable standards of performance. Where possible this is quantified, particularly by the inclusion of quantitative and qualitative standards, cost limits and time deadlines. The relevant control information that is needed to see that the key tasks are being adequately performed is also specified. An example is given in Appendix I to this chapter of the way in which John Humble's approach to 'management by objectives' can be applied to the job of a financial and budget accountant in an oil company.

There are potential advantages to the individual manager in this approach. The specification of the key tasks in a job enables the manager to judge whether or not he is concentrating on those critical elements that must be undertaken properly if the overall objective is to be accomplished. Shortfalls can be identified precisely and the manager thus has a means of assessing his own performance. The manager may then begin to see the ways in

19

which a job needs restructuring or his own performance could be improved. This type of approach to the job may bring considerable motivational advantages, with the manager feeling a greater sense of ownership of the job. Motivational advantages may also accrue from improved performance. There are further advantages to be gained by internalising the discipline, so that a manager is working out what needs to be done and then assessing his own work and taking appropriate corrective action. Even if all a manager does is to define his main objective, and then to list the six to eight accompanying key tasks, this may provide the basis for a considerable improvement in performance. The listing of key tasks can make the manager ask himself whether or not he is allocating his time to these key tasks in order of their importance.

There are pitfalls with this approach but, with care, the impact of these problems can be reduced or overcome. There is a danger that those parts of the job which can be easily quantified and checked are over-emphasised. Sometimes objectives or key tasks can be difficult to define — but they should not be neglected simply because success in other aspects is easier to record. Over-enthusiasm can also be a problem — an increased sense of ownership can lead a manager to set unrealistic objectives or standards of performance for himself. A further danger is that the objectives may not have been thought out correctly or they may not be properly integrated with the rest of the activity of an organisation. It may be rather chaotic if managers take it into their heads to define their own objectives and then vigorously pursue them without proper co-ordination between them. It is for this reason that John Humble recommends the 'management by objectives' approach for a total organisation, with individual manager's objectives interlocking with the objectives for the rest of the organisation. This approach has to be reconciled in turn with another problem. This is that the very improvements that a 'management by objectives' approach may promise may precipitate conflicts of interest that will generate resistances to some of the proposed changes.

A key issue is that people may complete documents in quite a different way according to whether or not the documents are going to be used as external control mechanisms. Consequently, any documents that are shown to the boss may be carefully edited so that his control is not too tight. This will also reduce the chances of the subordinate being forced to develop the job in a way he finds unpalatable. However, these problems of editing do not arise if a manager uses the 'management by objectives' approach on an individual basis and not as part of an integrated control system.

Alan Fox[5] has very lucidly explained that, if one takes the pluralistic approach to organisations, one sees that policies that may be to the advantage of an organisation as a whole may not always be to the liking or in the interests of particular groups or individuals. If, for example, a 'management by objectives' approach indicates that labour-saving economies can be achieved, then those people who are going to be the subject of those economies may say that it will be all very well for those who remain in an organisation but what about those who are made redundant as a consequence? This means that the organisational approach to 'management by objectives' is limited by the ability of managers to resolve such conflicts. This, in my view, does not invalidate the concept of 'management by objectives' on an organisational basis, but it does set limits to it. Unfortunately some managers may fail to identify the conflicts of interest that such an approach can precipitate and so may mishandle their approach. Even where the conflicts are recognised, their resolution may require a degree of sensitivity and skill beyond the capacity of many managers, even after training. This particular drawback is less of a problem for the individual manager trying to make use of 'management by objectives' thinking — which is the focus of this chapter. It is, however, just as well that managers bear in mind some of the potential traps, whilst at the same time seeking to extract the benefits of the 'management by objectives' approach. It is necessary to have regard to the objectives of other managers and other parts of an organisation. A change in orientation to a job may precipitate conflicts of interest with the people with whom the manager has to interact — particularly subordinates. A manager may even find that this type of approach exposes internal conflicts within himself. He may establish that the job needs to be redefined in a particular direction, but the direction may not be one in which he wants to go. One of the advantages of the individual simply applying the thinking of 'management by objectives' for himself, and not as part of an organisational approach, is that he can try and identify these conflicts in private and try and resolve them in his own time and way, rather than being forced too much out into the open about it by a formal organisational approach.

The identification of the role set

An alternative or additional technique that may help a manager check whether he is using his time effectively is to identify his 'role set'. This involves charting the key people and groups with whom he has to work. The chart needs to indicate the volume of contact that is appropriate with each constituent part and also the priorities. It needs to be remembered that there may be some particularly influential members of the role set with whom contact may be infrequent but very important when it does occur. A diagram should be drawn so that the more important a member of the role set, the closer he is located to the person at the centre. Figure 2.1 illustrates the role set diagram of an assistant officer at a small branch bank in a cosmopolitan city. The assistant officer reports to the branch manager and is accountable to him for domestic banking operations.

Figure 2.1: A role set diagram

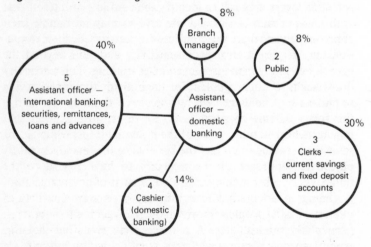

The next step is to see that the time and priority allocated to the elements in the role set are in line with what is actually needed. To do this effectively it is best for the person concerned to keep a diary of how he really spends his time over a few representative days. The actual time allocation to the individuals and groups in the role set can then be compared with what is considered desirable. Whilst this may reveal misjudgements about the proportions in the model of time allocation it may also reveal that the manager's time is not being used as wisely as it should be. It is all too easy, for example, for those who have easy physical access to a manager to claim a disproportionate share of his time. Managers may also prefer spending their time with some individuals or groups because their social and/or professional company is found to be more enjoyable than that of other individuals or groups. Role set analysis may demonstrate the need for the manager to make a conscious effort to give an appropriate share of his time to those people who work outside his department or to clients or other people who are external to the organisation. It may be found particularly necessary to spend time 'building bridges' with individuals or groups with whom one tends to be thrown into conflict rather than just taking the short-term solution of avoidance.

In estimating the amount of time that other individuals or groups require of your attention it is necessary to remember that one can allocate too much time, as well as too little. Subordinates can feel 'over-supervised' and those in senior positions to oneself may have as their objective not to spend too much time with you! However having said this it is obviously potentially damaging to spend less time with one's boss in particular than he deems appropriate. It is also necessary to consider what time one needs for oneself — particularly for reflective thought. Diary analyses by managers usually reveal that it is very difficult for them to arrange periods when they can engage in concentrated work or reflective thought without interruption. Such time may however be essential if one is to do long-term thinking about a job. Appropriate refinements to the 'role set diagram' are to allow a percentage of time for oneself as well as for 'others' who will invariably take up a share of one's time.

Amongst the benefits that can be obtained from this method of analysis is that it may show whether or not a job is viable as currently structured. There may be so many individuals and groups the manager has to interact with that the job may be impossible. Alternatively the manager may be tackling his job in an inappropriate way. One example of this was the manager who, it emerged, was trying to deal directly with his subordinate subordinates instead of just with his immediate subordinates. Whether any problems are organisational or of the manager's own making there may also be health implications if the manager has a pattern of interaction which is just too much to cope with.

The emphasis in this section has so far mainly been about working out appropriate time allocations. It is necessary to spend some time working out just what the priorities are in terms of the individuals and groups with whom one has to interact. An interesting example of the application of this type of thinking concerns a change in strategy announced by the former Commissioner of London's Metropolitan Police, Sir Kenneth Newman, in 1987. Faced with the dilemma of limited resources to deal with an increasing amount of crime, he reviewed the allocation of resources to the various types of crime. He judged that the public were particularly concerned about acts of violence against the person, such as sexual assault and mugging, and in comparison with these crimes, less concerned about car thefts. Consequently he adjusted the deployment of police resources in line with what he believed the public priorities to be. A blunt way in which the individual manager can identify priorities is to ask himself who is in the position to do him the greatest damage? The leader of an architectural group, when asked to do a role set analysis on this basis, likened it to the theory of 'damage limitation' — which is one way of viewing it. The value of doing this is to see that those who can do one the greatest damage are top of the list in getting their share of the time. It is also of value, as will shortly be explained, in working out what to do if one comes under conflicting pressures.

Establishing the order of importance in the role set is not always as easy as it seems. One training officer gave the example of how he mistakenly thought the most important member of his role set was the managing director of a company he once worked for. The training officer had numerous differences of opinion with his immediate boss and sought to overcome the bad working relationship by going 'over the head' of his boss, the company secretary, to the managing director. The company secretary became aware of this and as a counter measure started giving bad reports of the training officer to the managing director. Consequently the more the training officer went to the managing director the greater the number of bad reports there were of him. The managing director, faced with a choice, understandably preferred to accept the view of the more strategically placed company secretary. Ideally of course he should not have allowed the training officer to bypass the company secretary but that is what actually happened. Eventually the training officer, prompted by good advice from other colleagues, came to realise that the most important person in his role set was the company secretary. In the end he did what he should have done in the first place, in his particular case, which was to work on improving his relationship with his immediate boss! This illustrates the important point that it isn't the most senior person in an organisation who is necessarily the first in importance in one's role set. The view senior people have of you may well be important but it is necessary to work out whose word they take into account when forming their opinion of you! It isn't however just people of high status who may be in a position to inflict 'damage' on a manager. Often people in low status positions, but who control important, and perhaps scarce services, can do the same. So too may those who control access to important information or who act as 'gatekeepers' to senior managers.

Informal members of role sets may also need to be identified, assessed and handled in terms of their importance. A failure to do this effectively allegedly contributed to the enforced resignation of President Reagan's Chief of Staff, Donald Regan, in 1987. The informal member of the role set was said to be the President's wife, Nancy Reagan, and press reports suggested that on one occasion Donald Regan 'put the phone down on her'. It was also suggested that Donald Regan relied too much on his relationship with the President and not enough on the other powerful political figures in the role set. The other members may not have been individually as important as the President but collectively their influence was considerable, especially if it was reinforced by the views of the 'First Lady'. The extent to which these reports are true or untrue is unimportant as far as the basic point is concerned — the need for careful identification of the role set and appropriate responses based on that analysis.

A further way in which the concept of 'role set analysis' can be developed is by taking the marketing approach of actually asking the individuals and groups in one's role set just what their expectations are of you in the way you do your job. Care however has to be taken about who you approach and the manner of the approach. One of the problems can be to arouse expectations that cannot be met. As a minimum though one should reflect on just what the expectations are of you by the other individuals and groups in your role set. This may reveal a variety of misunderstandings about what you expect from others and what they expect from you.

What also may be revealed is that some of the expectations are contradictory. This may happen if the manager is given incompatible tasks, or if the sheer volume of work he is expected to do is unrealistic. The most practical way of handling such a dilemma is often for the manager himself to try to gauge what the real priorities are amongst the welter of instructions he is given. He will also need to be sensitive to changes in organisational priorities. A production supervisor in a car factory may need to pay more attention to the need to meet production quotas when demand is high and more attention to quality standards when the demand for cars is slack.[6] Those senior to the manager may be reluctant to admit that the various requests are in conflict. Therefore, the reality may be that the individual manager has to work out what the real priorities are at a given time. To do this the manager may need, as in the car factory case, to judge just what the priorities are with others in the role set and the ways in which they may be changing. In an ideal world one would work only in organisations where job demands were compatible and all legitimate expectations could be met. However, as we live in an imperfect world it is just as well to have a method of resolving contradictory pressures. It is also as well to recognise that when changes in priorities occur it is often politically too difficult for policy makers to say that a certain priority has been abandoned, or even downgraded. The most one may get is an admission that a certain objective has been 'put on the back burner'. However, managers ignore these shifts in priority at their peril as otherwise they may be failing to adjust their pattern of activity to a new scale of priorities. The ways in which this issue can arise in public sector organisations, and its various effects, are considered in the next chapter.

The last point to make in this section is that what has been explained is a progressively more sophisticated method of gathering data and developing insight about how to identify one's job. After all this has been done it is up to the manager to evaluate and synthesise the material and stamp his own personality on the job. There is more to identifying a job than working out what those in strategic positions want of you — but it is, to say the least, prudent to take that into account before then adding that essential indregient — one's own personality.

TIME MANAGEMENT

When he has clarified his overall objective, key tasks and role set, it may also be appropriate for a manager to consider how effectively he uses his time. One view of the manager's job is that the only real resource is his time. There appear to be enormous variations in the ways in which managers either use their time effectively or squander it. Consequently this topic deserves specific attention. Issues of particular importance are the identification of priorities, the logical sequencing of work and the need for managers to avoid wasting other people's time.

Identifying priorities

The reactive or grasshopper manager may fail in his management of time in the first instance by failing to identify the priorities in his job. The priorities of a job need to be established quite consciously. To do this it may be necessary to write them down and then either to rank the priorities over a particular time period or to group them into bands of varying urgency. Even the well-organised manager will find that he has to react to some extent to the short-term crises and pressures that he meets in his day-to-day job, but he should have as a constant reference point a clear grasp of the priority issues that are accumulating and which merit attention.

The identification of the priorities in a job may reveal fundamental issues about the appropriate balance of activity. Some interesting examples of this at an organisational level concern police and medical work. The police have consciously looked at the balance between crime detection and crime prevention. The same type of issue arises with medical work in trying to strike the right balance between health cure and health care.

Finding the time to think about the job may itself constitute a problem, particularly for the manager who is already heavily involved in 'firefighting' activities. However, unless he somehow finds the time to think his way through to a more rational pattern of activity, he is unlikely to be effective. One of the problems in organisations is that managers find that they have to cope with so many interruptions that it is difficult to find time to think in a concentrated and systematic way about the job. It may be necessary to do this away from one's normal place of work or

27

to use a secretary or other person as a screen to prevent interruptions. It may also be necessary to have a clear idea of who those people are who make unproductive claims on one's time with a view to reducing the time spent with them. It is one of the ironies of organisational life that so often the people with the most time to waste are those who insist on spending long periods telling you how busy they are.

Establishing the priorities in a job may well involve a careful look at the conflict between what a manager prefers to do and what he actually needs to do. This is a necessarily recurring issue in this book. I found that I had to face up to much the same issue when I was an undergraduate student preparing for my examinations. The subjects which I enjoyed revising were those at which I was good but where the scope for improvement was consequentially least. After much anguish I decided that I really had to spend most of my time working on those subjects which I liked least, but where the potential for improvement was greatest. The personnel policies of organisations unfortunately don't always help people take a balanced approach in their job. In one local authority building department all the charge-hand craft-workers were upgraded to be general trades supervisors. The idea was sound enough in principle — which was to avoid having a charge-hand craft-worker on every site where craft-workers of that particular trade were working. Unfortunately the idea was poorly implemented. There was no attempt to select who should be upgraded and who should not. Neither was there any attempt to train the newly appointed general trades supervisors either in management or in the technical aspects of the new trades that were nominally under their control. Consequently most of the newly appointed general trades supervisors were too frightened to supervise craft-workers in trades other than their own. This meant that, for example, the person who had previously been a charge-hand bricklayer spent nearly all his time with the bricklayers and rarely tried to supervise the craft-workers in the other groups such as the electricians, plumbers and carpenters.

Sequencing work

Once the priorities of a job have been clearly identified, it is then necessary to consider whether or not they need to be tackled in a particular sequence. This may be particularly necessary if time may run out. The domestic example, which illustrates this point, is that it is more appropriate for people pressed for time in the morning to get dressed before they eat breakfast. It is much more practicable to run down the road for the train fully clothed but with breakfast unfinished rather than the other way around.

The need for careful sequencing was brought home to me by the simple but apt examples of two van drivers. One driver would look at the first address and drive off and then look at the next address and so on. In the course of a day he was likely to retrace his route several times. The other driver would spend about an hour each morning planning his route so that, although he started his deliveries later, he covered his route with the minimum mileage. Another issue that needs to be taken into account is the need to give time for ideas to be mulled over. It is not just the speed at which issues are dealt with that is important, but also the quality of any decisions. Some managerial judgements are likely to be all the better if preceded by reflective thought. The thought may not even need to be conscious as ideas can suddenly fit into place after subconscious mental activity. Students can also find this when answering examination questions. A difficult question that is put on one side whilst an easier one is tackled may appear much simpler when it is read for the second time a while later. However, the manager needs to recognise the difference between mulling over difficult issues, so that an appropriate decision is eventually taken, and procrastination.

Saving other people's time

Attention must also be given to the need to avoid wasting other people's time as well as one's own. Preparation for discussion or interviews means that the time of the other people is likely to be saved as well as any work being more effective. Prior preparation is particularly important if one has to chair a meeting, as will be explained in more detail in Chapter 13 on meetings and chairing. Let it suffice at this point to give the example of a local government body where 23 people from different parts of London were called to a meeting that had to be aborted because it had not been properly planned. One's potential to waste the time of colleagues can, therefore, be even greater than the potential to waste one's own.

In planning one's activity it is also necessary to recognise that people meet social as well as work needs whilst they are doing their job. An over-planned approach to the job may be too inflexible, and it can also make life dreadfully dull. Additionally it may be necessary to spend some time maintaining working relationships by a certain amount of social conversation. There are obviously limits to the extent to which this should be done, but it could be foolish to ignore this aspect. Managers also need to pace themselves at work and it may be necessary to have some periods in the working day when they relax a little. A final point that needs making is that at times the volume of activity confronting a manager can seem quite overwhelming. But he cannot tackle everything simultaneously. A careful assessment of just what has to be done, and in what order, may help the manager cope far more than if he rushes in and does the first thing that comes to hand without having a clear idea of the total picture.[7]

CONCLUSION

There have been two interlocking themes in this chapter. One is whether the individual manager is simply going to be dictated to by events, or whether he is going to develop a strategy for influencing events, as well as being influenced by them. The other is whether the manager is going to seek to justify himself by looking busy or by his results. It is to be hoped that readers will opt for exerting some influence over events and will try and justify themselves by their performance rather than by mere activity. Good management is like good medicine — the starting-point is accurate diagnosis. One would not think much of a doctor who prescribed treatment before he had diagnosed the patient's condition. Sadly this approach can be all too common in management. Managers can implement prescriptive action before they have defined their objectives or the problem areas. A diagnostic approach needs to be taken to the total job as well as to the individual problems that present themselves. There needs to be conscious resistance to action for action's sake or the adoption of prescriptive solutions just because they are fashionable. If a manager is able to take this approach he is likely to find that the gains are not just confined to improved performance in the immediate job. The development of this type of approach is likely to develop the habit of diagnostic thinking, the identification of scope for initiative, and the acceptance of responsibility. The manager who does this is preparing himself for further promotion as well as cultivating a positive approach to life in general.

NOTES

1. Rosemary Stewart, *Managers and their jobs* (Pan Piper, 1970), p. 154.
2. Peter F. Drucker, *Practice of management* (Heinemann, 1955).
3. John Humble, *Improving business results: the definitive work on management by objectives* (McGraw Hill, 1967). See also John Humble, *Management by objectives in action* (McGraw Hill in association with the British Institute of Management, 1970).
4. *Evening Standard*, London, 10 January 1977.
5. Royal Commission on Trade Unions and Employers' Associations, *Industrial sociology and industrial relations*, Research Paper No. 3, Alan Fox (HMSO, 1965).
6. Joan Woodward, *Industrial organisation: theory and practice* (Oxford University Press, 1965), pp. 171–2.
7. For a more comprehensive account of time management read H. Reynolds and M. E. Tramel, *Executive time management* (Gower, 1981).

APPENDIX I: EXAMPLE OF MANAGEMENT BY OBJECTIVES

Financial and budget accountant in the London office of a USA-based medium-sized oil company.

1. *Job title:* Financial and budget accountant (London).
2. *Overall objective:* To assist the financial controller in ensuring that financial and budgeting documents required by management and by statute are provided within deadlines to appropriate standards and that London Office achieves timely financial arrangements.
3. *Position in organisation:*
   (a) Responsible to the financial controller, London Office.
   (b) Directly supervising all work allocated by the financial controller by:
      (i) instructing and overseeing selected staff and delegating work as is considered appropriate;
      (ii) ensuring that the company's standards as to technical quality are met;

31

      (iii) ensuring completion of assigned work within budget established by general manager, London Office.

4. *Limits of authority:*
   (a) Can engage, within budget, any staff as required.
   (b) Cannot sign contracts with clients or joint ventures on behalf of the company.
   (c) Can delegate any work for which the F & B accountant retains ultimate responsibility.

Key tasks	Standards	Control information
1. *Statutory information*		
(a) Submit statutory accounts for the UK subsidiary.	Once a year. To be passed by external auditors as showing a 'true and fair view'.	Auditor's report
	Receipt by company registrar within the statutory time limit.	Receipt document from registrar.
(b) Meet close deadlines for double-entry book-keeping for Tunisia, Netherlands, UK, Spain and N. African subsidiaries.	Monthly submission of every transaction within ten days after the end of the month concerned.	Receipt by USA Head Office through computer. Edit and validation checks performed there on 10th of every month.
(c) Submit to bankers full profit and loss account and balance sheet for UK subsidiary.	Receipt of each of the ten banks once a quarter 45 days after 31 March, 30 June, 30 September and 60 days after the statutory accounts date of 31 December.	As per loan agreement. Non-receipt will incur penalties.
2. *Budgets*		
(a) Revise for internal purposes capital and operating expenditure budgets for exploration and development in Europe, Africa and the Mediterranean.	Quarterly, within 20 days following a quarter's end (see 1(c) for dates).	Liaison with general manager (UK) in creating budgets. Completed budgets signed off by the exploration and general managers of the division. Corporate deadlines established by head office.

Continuation

(b) Draw up in line by line detail (e.g. +50 sub codes in the P&L code) the general and administration budget for the year for UK subsidiary.	To be completed by 31 August preceding the accounting year budgeted for (January–December).	As per corporate deadline. Receipt acknowledged by head office.
(c) Submit annualised budget to joint venturer, the North African General Petroleum Company, to run from July to June (joint venturer's financial year).	By 26 June, before the exploration advisory committee meeting at which it will be discussed with the joint venturer.	As per concession agreement with NAGPC and North African government. Receipt acknowledged by same.

3. *Forecasting*

(a) Prepare a three-month cash forecast for all projects based in Europe, Africa and the Mediterranean, and submit to head office.	Send to head office by 20th of the month preceding the relevant three-month period.	Receipt acknowledged by head office.

4. *Management information*

(a) Prepare authorisation for expenditure report showing actual capital expenditure against budgeted for each project past and future in London division.	Monthly: project-based stats report. Submit within 20 days after month concerned.	Receipt acknowledged by general manager, production manager and explorations manager in London office.

5. *Management of financial arrangements*

(a) Ensure, through others, that financial agreements and requirements are held to deadlines. Specifically:—		
(1) as operator: to meet sub-contractors' normal credit terms.	Avoidance of additional charges.	As per joint venture contract(s).

Continuation

(2) as non-operator: to follow accounting procedures as per joint operating agreements, liaise with others with working interests in order to meet the financing of the operator when required.	Avoidance of fines for non-payment or default. Avoidance of cancellation of agreement(s).	As per joint venture contract(s).
(b) As operator: negotiate with North African General Petroleum Company for recovery of costs incurred in seismic surveys and exploration.	Produce invoices quarterly. Make available NAGPC 30 days before scheduled meeting. (Negotiation from exception report.)	Recovered costs as per instructions and expectations of general manager, London Office.

3

The Manager and the Organisation

INTRODUCTION

Managers have to operate in the situations in which they find themselves. They may have a long-term aim to alter the situation they are in or to transfer to another one, but that may be little help in dealing with their immediate problems. Complaining about the situation as it is may invite a riposte similar to that of the soldier depicted in the famous Punch cartoon sheltering from shell fire during the First World War — 'if you knows of a better 'ole, go to it'. In other words, one has to make the best of things as they are, at least in the short term, and not as one wishes they were. The nature of the problems will be greatly influenced by the type of the organisation in which a manager works. In turn, the nature of that organisation will be influenced by the environment in which it exists. Managers will find that they have to work in a great variety of different situations. If they move to another organisation, or to a different part of the same organisation, they may find that the behaviour that was previously appropriate is quite inappropriate in their new position. They may also find that the situation they are in changes and this may also necessitate change in their managerial behaviour. It is therefore important that managers carefully assess the situations which they are in with a view to matching their behaviour with the circumstances.

In this chapter some of the basic organisation theories are explained. The key factors which can determine the structure of an organisation are examined. These include the impact of technology, size, the need to identify the critical function, and national culture. The problems involved in integrating the work of different departments are considered. So is the importance of 'role' in determining people's behaviour and the need to distinguish between personality and role behaviour. The final section is an area that is attracting an increasing amount of attention. This concerns the differences in the ways in which private and public sector organisations operate.

THEORIES OF ORGANISATION

The historical approach to management was that it consisted of a set of principles which were capable of definition and universal application. This was the approach of writers such as F. W. Taylor[1] and Henri Fayol[2] at the turn of this century. The views of such writers became known as the Classical School of organisational thought. The common collective view was that work could be so organised that the objectives of organisations could be accomplished with great efficiency. Organisations were viewed as the product of logical thought concerned largely with co-ordinating tasks through the use of legitimate authority. Employees were seen as rational beings whose interests coincided with those of the organisations in which they were employed. They were also seen as being capable of working to high levels of efficiency provided they were properly selected, trained, directed, monitored and supported. Indoctrination and coercion would be used if necessary to achieve a rational approach by employees. This was presumed to lead to employees behaving exactly as they were told. Great emphasis was also placed on the need for the careful and detailed explanation of organisational structure.

Later the limitations of the classical writers became apparent, particularly their simplistic approach to people. The Hawthorne experiments conducted at the Western Electric Company in Chicago in the 1920s and 1930s revealed that groups can have a powerful effect on the way that organisations work and that people didn't always do what employers wanted or act in a way that they considered to be rational. The existence of informal networks and working relationships was also observed.[3] This led to the evolution of the Human Relations School of organisational thought with which Elton Mayo in particular was associated. The work of industrial sociologists has subsequently emphasised the need to view organisations as social entities. As has already been explained in the previous chapter, it is also necessary to recognise that there can be considerable conflict between the objectives of the organisation and those of the individuals employed in it. As is also explained in Chapter 12 informal and formal employee organisation can also lead to the sharing of power in organisations so that there are limits to the authority of management.

A further school of thought which has emerged has been the Systems Concept of Organisations. This views organisations as dynamic organisms with interconnected parts. Each part is dependent on integration with related parts if objectives are to be accomplished. Each part however has to operate in an environment which influences what the employees in that section want to achieve and are capable of achieving. The approach taken in this book is consistent with this view of organisations.

It will be seen that organisational theory has gradually evolved. The formulation of one school of thought has facilitated the testing of that approach with actual organisational behaviour and the development of further schools of thought. The valid aspects of a particular approach have then been capable of being integrated with later views. The approach of the classical writers, in particular, needs to be seen in this light. It would be foolish to decry the work of writers such as Taylor and Fayol. Apart from its pioneering nature, much of what they had to say about organisations is still worth considering. However, their principles of organisations need to be seen as possible guidelines rather than definitive works. The variety of managerial and organisational situations is such that it is impossible to set down universal principles. In any such list, the 'principles' are platitudinous or have clear exceptions.

It is also necessary to have some understanding of the various approaches to management so that one can understand the views that colleagues have about the way in which organisations should work. Such approaches may be reinforced, or be caused, by cultural background. People tend to have beliefs and make value judgements about the ways organisations should operate. Even if these are never formally expressed, they may nevertheless be held with considerable conviction. Hopefully such views will match the situations that arise. However, there are likely to be occasions when they don't, and it may be as well to recognise when a situation demands particular organisational arrangements which are in conflict with the beliefs of colleagues. It may even be appropriate to reflect on one's own ideology and the extent to which it is appropriate to the current situation.

Mechanistic and organic structures

A particularly useful classification of organisational structures is the extent to which they are mechanistic or organic. The ideas of Taylor, Fayol and others in the scientific management school were, and to a large extent still are, particularly appropriate to large-scale organisations operating in stable environments. Burns and Stalker[4] have since suggested that circumstances like that lend themselves to 'mechanistic' systems. This is in contrast to more rapidly changing environments where more adaptive 'organic' systems may be necessary.

The features of mechanistic systems include: a clear hierarchy of control, a high degree of specialisation of labour, and reference upwards for the reconciliation of differences within the organisation. This type of arrangement may be entirely appropriate where there is sufficient time to prescribe organisational arrangements and procedures in this type of detail so that they match the environment in which the organisation operates. Where however the technology and market are rapidly changing it could be a recipe for disaster. A mechanistic system would simply not be adaptive, or its responses fast enough, to deal with changing circumstances. Hence the need in some situations for 'organic' systems. These are characterised particularly by greater room for initiative, and for contact, co-operation and decision-taking to be in accordance with the needs of particular situations rather than the formal organisation. These two different systems should be seen as different ends of a continuum rather than straight alternatives. Few, if any, organisations will be completely mechanistic or completely organic. However it is important for the individual manager to be able to recognise the difference between the two.

The work of Burns and Stalker was based on research into certain Scottish companies, particularly in the electronics industry, in the period 1953–7. Considerable success had been achieved in the application of scientific research findings within the Air Force in the Second World War. This had been accomplished by the creation of particular (organic) structural arrangements. The aim of the research was to investigate the extent to which such arrangements needed to be, and could be, introduced in organisations in peacetime. It is worthwhile quoting just what the the wartime experience was.

At weekly meetings (known as 'Sunday Soviets') particular operational problems would be discussed, informally, thoroughly and intimately. The scientist who designed equipment and the men whose lives and fighting efficiency depended upon it got to know one another's problems as they could have done in no other way; equipment was tailored to operational needs, needs suggested new equipment and, perhaps most important, use suggested new possibilities. The Germans, whose technical ability could not be supposed inferior, had nothing of this kind. They had a Plenipotentiary for High Frequency Techniques, in charge of research laboratories; an Air Ministry opposite number specified to him — by letter — what the Luftwaffe wanted and the specifications went out, undiscussed, to whatever laboratories were free to handle them. Not only were needs less adequately met, since they were less closely appreciated, but the new possibilities thrown up by the 'Sunday Soviet' type of contact remained unappreciated and conseqently unrealised.[5]

A particular problem found in the firms in the Burns and Stalker studies was that they often had arrangements for co-ordination between the research and development departments and production that had more in common with the German wartime procedures than the British. However, it was clear that certain types of technical innovation where know-how was diffuse and rapidly changing clearly demanded the reverse type of arrangements. I subsequently witnessed a failure of research and development for just these reasons. It concerned the unsuccessful attempt to introduce an improved version of the existing product in an engineering firm. The research staff blamed the production staff for being technically incompetent, whilst the production staff blamed the reasearch staff for being impractical, unrealistic and failing to communicate all their requirements. The company's response was not to create more organic relationships in this area (no-one was aware of this concept) but to establish three competing design teams. The view was that the best design would then be chosen for production. Not surprisingly this approach did not prove to be very satisfactory either.

A variation of this type of arrangement is the matrix structure. Essentially this involves the setting up of more or less permanent project-type groups to which people are allocated from resource centres. The line, or command, structure is retained on the resource group side but the appropriate mix of specialists can then be allocated, full time or part time, to 'product-type' teams. This arrangement is very often found necessary in high technology organisations. It is also often found in colleges. It can assist in seeing that clients' needs are properly identified and met. If you have resource groupings only, as is often the case for example in universities, the danger is that activity is focused on the development of the discipline alone without regard to the needs of clients. A feature of behaviour in many organisations though is that in any conflict between project groupings and the line structure it is the latter that usually wins. This is because of the power base of the command structure rather than because it necessarily has the better arguments.

The flexible firm

An extension of the concept of the organic organisation may be provided by the concept of the flexible firm. This has been particularly developed in Japan, where security of employment is often guaranteed only to a core of permanent employees. Other employers are engaged on a temporary basis. Potentially an organisation is more likely to be able to adapt and survive if the outer core can be shed or replaced easily. This enables the security of those in the inner core to be more easily guaranteed. Whilst people usually prefer to work in the inner core, unemployment is such in most countries that employment in the outer core may well be viewed as being better than no job at all. Consequently the competitive pressures on organisations and the lack of alternative work makes it seem likely that organisations will increasingly have this type of structure. Some of the ways in which the flexibility can be achieved are old established — such as the recruitment of part-time and temporary employees, fixed-term contracts, flexi-time, the use of agency staff and sub-contracting. However, the point that needs stressing is that employees may be more obliged to work in this way given the economic situation. Also technological developments, such as those in electronic data processing, mean that practices such as working at home and subcontracting are possible in entirely new areas. Other aspects of this approach include contracting for people to perform a variety of different jobs and even to operate at varying levels of responsibility in accordance with the fluctuating needs of an organisation. Organisations that can predict their likely pattern of activity may also offer annual hours contracts so that employees' work attendance varies with, for example, the seasonal demand for their products. In days of full employment employers were much more inclined to recruit most or all of their employees for a standard working day. A combination of economic pressures and increased imagination means that more thought is now given to recruiting some people to work at peak periods of the day only. Such arrangements could enable banks, for example, to have their counters fully manned at lunchtime, and thus overcome the problem of leaving counters vacant at peak time so that staff can have their lunch.[6, 7]

Quality circles

An organisational development that has links with the organic system and project and matrix structures is that of quality circles. This deserves mention if only because of the publicity it has received. Quality circles have been defined as:

A small group of between three and twelve people who do the same, or similar work, voluntarily meeting together regularly for about an hour per week in paid time, usually under the leadership of their own supervisor, and trained to identify, analyse, and solve some of the problems in their work, presenting solutions to management, and where possible, implementing solutions themselves.[8]

Quality circles have attracted considerable attention because of their popularity in Japan since the 1960s and the economic success of that country. Consequently they have been introduced into manufacturing and service activities in other industrial countries. The potential benefits are mainly improved quality,

41

cost savings and the improved morale created by these achieve-ments and the increased employee participation that is the essence of the process. Whilst the idea may be capable of useful application in other countries one must always be wary of attempts to transplant management practices from one country to another — as is explained later in this chapter in the section on national culture. It is also necessary to beware, as is repeatedly stressed in this book, of management panaceas that so often turn out to be simplistic attempts to deal with complex issues. It is not surprising to learn that quality circles often fail and that even in Japan only one in three work.[9] However, many apparently succeed and it may be that the concept can work in selected situations provided the conditions are right. The way in which quality circles are implemented is also crucial and the six critical factors in their introduction have been identified as:

1. Commitment by the board and senior management.
2. Involvement of middle management and supervisors.
3. Trade union support.
4. Delegation of decision-making.
5. Adequate training.
6. Use of a pilot study.
7. Monitoring.[10]

FACTORS THAT DETERMINE THE STRUCTURE OF ORGANISATIONS

There are many variables that will affect the structure and operation of an organisation. These may be within the organisa-tion, outside it, or a combination of the two. Managers need to work out which factors in their particular situation are likely to be important. These could include the impact of technology, the size of their organisation, the identification of the critical function at a given time, and culture.

The impact of technology

One of the most critical factors is that of technology. The rate of technological change can obviously influence whether an organisation veers towards the mechanistic or the organic-type structure. Quite apart from the rate of change, the actual nature of the technology can have a profound effect on the structure of an organisation. This was demonstrated in a study led by Joan Woodward.[11] Firms with mass production technologies were found to lend themselves to mechanistic-type systems. Firms with process-type technologies appeared to be best managed by less formal and more organic-type systems. The absence of the sheer physical effort involved in making items and co-ordinating thousands of small decisions, characteristic of large batch and mass production technology, meant that managers were left with much more time to initiate and co-operate with others. The need for specialisation was found to be reduced in the process-type industries. Their problems were further eased by their cost structure. Labour costs tended to be much lower as a percentage of total costs. This meant that they could be more generous with the quality and number of managers they employed. There was also less pressure to reduce labour costs if demand fell — reinforced by the fact that it isn't necessarily easier to run a refinery, for example, at 80 per cent capacity instead of full capacity. The organic type of structure was also found to be more appropriate with small firms which were not making standard products. It should be noted that you can have small organisations which are informal and mechanistic — the routines being so well known that there is no need to formalise them.

The importance of recognising the technological variable is further illustrated by an example given by Joan Woodward. This concerned a personnel manager who worked in a pharmaceutical company with mixed technologies. He was welcomed in the assembly department where packaging was organised on a large batch production basis. He performed a very useful 'trouble shooting' function there, particularly when new methods were introduced. Such close intervention was not welcomed in the process plant where the line managers had the time and inclination to handle most of their own personnel problems.

The personnel manager failed to recognise that the situation on the plant was basically different from that on the assembly lines. His formal training in personnel management had laid emphasis on the importance of applying personnel policy, and operating industrial relations procedures at a uniform level throughout the firm. Like the other functional specialists who had to deal with the plant managers as well as the packaging managers, he was unable to understand or accept the duality of role which was imposed upon him by having to deal with the two different technologies.[12]

Even if there is an appropriate 'fit' between technology and organisation it is necessary to consider the effect that further technological development can have on this matching. Managers in the car industry can perhaps take heart from the prospect of technological change propelling them out of their physically stressful mass production arrangements into a physically less stressful, if equally competitive, process-type industry.

Size

Another important factor is the size of an organisation. You don't need much formality if you are engaged in the small-scale production of rabbit hutches — to a large extent people can see what needs to be done for themselves. The mass production of motor cars requires much more formality because, amongst other things, people can't easily grasp what has to be done. The number of variables that has to be co-ordinated in that situation creates enormous organisational problems. It may well be that these problems increase on an exponential basis rather than a linear basis. The solution of breaking the units down into a managable size may not be an option if your technology dictates that you need a large integrated plant.

Identifying the critical function

Another factor that needs to affect the structure of an organisation is the recognition of what is the critical function at a given time. Joan Woodward attributed commercial success as, in part, stemming from the ability of those in organisations to identify the area where it was most important to get the correct decisions. If necessary, the views of the management in the critical function need to take precedence over the views of managers in less important areas. The critical function can, of course, vary over time, and one of the problems of the traditional mechanistic structure is that such movement of influence from one function to another may be inhibited. The managers in a traditionally powerful function are not likely to take kindly to having a reduced say in major decisions so that a rival function can have more say. The reluctance to make way is likely to be all the greater if the function that needs more say is seen as an upstart — as, for example, the marketing function is sometimes regarded. The managers in the traditional function may, in any case, not appreciate that the critical focus of decision-making has moved. The success of managers in solving problems can be their very undoing in this respect. If, for example, difficult design problems are overcome, this removes a constraint. The problem then can be how to increase production, or to increase advertising. The very success of design engineers can mean that for the time being they are encouraged to take a back seat. All this may be very hard to take, or even to see, but it may be crucial for the organisation that the focus of power and influence be allowed to adjust in this manner.

National culture

Organisations also need to mesh with the culture of the country in which they operate. The problems of obtaining an appropriate 'fit' obviously exist for multinational corporations and for other organisations with subsidiary overseas operations or departments. Some discretion needs to be given to the local managers to be able to adjust the organisation, as well as their managerial style, to suit local conditions. The issue of achieving an appropriate managerial style is dealt with in the next chapter. The actual structure of an organisation may however need to be modified as well. It could, for example, be counterproductive to use all the latest labour saving aids in a country where labour is much cheaper compared with labour costs in the country of the parent organisation.

The customs and values of a country also need to be taken into account. Management practices which appear to work well in a particular country may not be easily exported because the environment in which they work cannot be transplanted. This also applies to the import of practices from other countries. The import of particular management practices is often recommended without this point being grasped. At present there is often much emphasis on what other countries have to learn from the Japanese. However, Japanese success owes much to their highly developed work ethic, outstanding technical achievements and effective and sophisticated system of Government support for industry. The copying of particular management practices and customs isn't going to lead to the acquisition of these fundamental advantages. That is not to say that some Japanese practices won't work elsewhere — the point is that their success stems from more basic causes. The point also needs making that even the Japanese need to adapt their organisation's stuctures and style when they have to operate in different cultures.

THE INTERRELATIONSHIP OF ORGANISATIONAL ACTIVITY

As well as considering the nature of the organisation they are in, and how appropriate that organisation is to its environment, managers need to consider how they relate to the other functions within their organisation. Organisations may be arranged on neat departmental lines, but many of the problems that will have to be faced will not correspond conveniently with a departmental structure. Such structures, although usually necessary, are artificial. Problems may contain many different interactive dimensions. Managerial approaches to such problems will need to be integrated if they are to succeed. True, some problems may confine themselves to departmental boundaries, but this will not always be the case. Unfortunately there are often considerable barriers to lateral contact between departments. Rivalries, role conflicts, different values and differing types of expertise may all act as impediments. Staff may prefer the security of contact with like-minded people within their own department to the often more hostile contact they may encounter with other departments. A lop-sided approach to organisational problems may develop as a result. This may have a detrimental effect on the work of departments. It may also lead to problems which straddle departmental boundaries being ignored. It is all too easy for an 'ostrich'-type managerial style to develop in organisations. Managers may keep their heads down and just deal with what is clearly in their own patch. This tendency may be reinforced by their initial specialist training — as explained in Chapter 1. Managers may be much more able to identify the problems that correspond with their specialism than those outside it.

This problem can be particularly acute in the public sec
and it follows that there are many examples. The old establis
boundaries which define what is medical work and what
nursing work don't facilitate organisational change in the
Health Service. The attempt to introduce corporate management
in local government has been hampered by the 'professional'
orientation of individual departments and officers. The development of a corporate approach necessitates officers at all levels
taking a wider approach, not just those at the top tier. The legal
profession provides a particularly glaring example of where well-
established professional traditions provoke fierce opposition to
suggestions for change in work arrangements. The older established the profession, the greater seem to be the problems of
altering the occupational role and associated training in line with
changing organisational and societal needs.

Interdepartmental problems

To understand broader problems — particularly those which fall
between different departments — managers need to have some
understanding of overall activity in their organisations.
Attempts to bring departments together may be frustrated, however, because of the conflict this can generate. The objectives of
departments may not always be complementary nor will they all
operate at the same level of performance. Consequently much
time and effort can go into justifying to others the activity of a
particular department rather than developing common problem-
solving approaches. The hidden agenda at interdepartmental
meetings can be that nothing is to be proved wrong about one's
own department. However, if everyone takes that approach the
real issues to be discussed simply get lost in smokescreens. One
has only to look at the annual report of a company which has
made a loss to see the standard smokescreen that can be put out
for public, if not internal, consumption. The list of causes for
poor performance is likely to include inappropriate legislation,
international trading conditions, unfair competition, Government policy, failures by suppliers, acts of God, bad luck, trade
union activity and a deterioration in the standards of society. It
might include incompetence by previous executives but is most
unlikely to include admissions of failure that were within the
current management's control.

The magnitude of this issue is compounded by the fact that the very nature of problems can often be identified only by an interdepartmental group with complementary skills and expertise. If the current objectives of an organisation, or the major constraints impeding the achievement of those objectives, are to be defined, this may only be accomplished by a pooling of knowledge. Even when the nature of problems is identified, the causes may be far from obvious. One of the traps that people can fall into is to assume that the problems which emerge in particular departments have their causes in those same departments. In analysing manpower problems in organisations, I have often found that the causes are numerous and may involve many different departments. Productivity levels may be influenced, for example, by production control, organisation structure, investment policy and personnel management policies. It may be pointless trying to recruit more and more labour to boost production if the production process or planning is inadequate. In some cases problems, causes and solutions may all exist in the same department, but it is dangerous to assume that this is always the case.

Creating problems elsewhere

A further point of which managers need to be aware is the implications of their decisions for other departments. An example was once given to me of what was ostensibly a problem of recruiting labour by a firm making car components. People were reluctant to take well-paid jobs with the firm when it had plenty of work. It emerged that this was because of the firm's hire and fire policy. This in turn was because the firm kept its stock levels as low as possible. The firm would receive large but irregular orders from a car manufacturer for standard components. When the orders were met, people were laid off and this was well known locally. An alternative approach to the firm's 'labour problem' would have been for it to build up its stocks when orders were low and run them down when orders were high. This would have increased inventory costs but overall might have been a more effective approach than not being able to make sufficient components. As it was, the inventory costs were being maintained at a low level by the device of shunting the problem elsewhere. The basic point to be made is that managers need to take account of such effects before they make decisions and not afterwards. It may or may not have been best to keep inventory costs low — but such a decision should only have been taken if the effects had been calculated in advance. This example is meant only to illustrate the interrelationship of managerial behaviour. Such interrelationship is not confined to the personnel area: another example concerns the distribution and sales functions. One company changed its policy to accept small orders. As a result, sales went up, but so too did the transport costs because of increased problems of distribution.

The poet John Donne's observation that 'no man is an island' might equally be applied to managers. They need to see their experience as something to be shared, to help identify and deal with problems facing the whole organisation, rather than simply a means of justifying the activity of their own department. They may not be capable of resolving the problems facing their own department alone anyway. This point is explained further in Chapter 12 and illustrative examples are given from the field of industrial relations. This is a function where the root cause of problems very often lie in other areas of management activity. Unfortunately this is frequently not appreciated. Consequently attempts to improve matters can erroneously take place entirely within the industrial relations function when often the need is to remedy weaknesses elsewhere.

ROLE BEHAVIOUR

Personality versus role behaviour

When interacting with colleagues it is important for managers to be able to distinguish between personality behaviour and role behaviour. Role behaviour occurs when a person acts in accordance with the requirements of the position which he holds. Managers may meet with opposition from colleagues which can be wrongly attributed to personality factors. It would be foolish to pretend that personality factors never have an influence on people's behaviour, but it can be all too easy to miss the point that a person may feel obliged to behave in a particular way because of the demands of his job. Inspectors, for example, may harp on about the quality of work and come into conflict with production managers who may be more concerned with the quantity of work. An inspector would not be doing his job if he did not ensure that quality standards were met. The danger is, however, that the issue can be personalised. Real role conflicts can thus be exacerbated by personality conflicts. Traditions of hostility can develop and spread through whole departments. It is, unfortunately, so much easier, and often more satisfying, to blame a particular dispute on the actual personality of a protagonist. Sometimes this will even be true — a role may be clumsily or wrongly interpreted by a particular person. It can be very difficult, in the heat of the moment, to reflect that there is nothing personal in the perhaps crucial conflict in which you are involved. The basis of the conflict, however, may be entirely to do with roles and it is possible to contain the area of conflict to the role element if personalities are kept out of it. This will involve not only putting one's point of view in as acceptable a way as possible, but also recognising that the opposing points of view are not necessarily meant as personal criticisms. It is as well to remember, too, that, whilst role conflicts can be incorrectly identified as personality clashes, it is rare for the mistake to be made the other way around. The constant danger is that conflict is wrongly attributed to personalities, rather than the reverse.

Informal roles

Failure to recognise that people's behaviour stems from their roles, rather than their personality, is particularly likely when the roles are informal. An example such as that of the inspector and production manager, already given, may be fairly easy to recognise. Even the role behaviour of a shop steward can be fairly easy to identify. Often, though, people adopt positions because, for example, they have particular information to hand which is not generally available, or its significance may not be generally appreciated. This may drive them into conflict with others, even though their formal roles appear to be compatible.

Reducing conflict

The reason for distinguishing between role and personality behaviour that has been stressed so far is the need to contain the area of conflict to the minimum. It is also important to get the diagnosis right if one is attempting to resolve the conflict. If the mistake is made of assuming that a conflict is personality based, when it is in reality because of roles, the false solution may emerge of changing the personalities. Thus an 'awkward' person may be transferred or dismissed only for the same 'awkward' behaviour to re-emerge with the next job holder. The original solution, as well as having been wrong from an organisational point of view, may also constitute a grave injustice to the person who is removed. In some cases it may even be that a person is only doing his job correctly if he is being awkward. It is partially the understanding of this issue which led to the establishment of traffic wardens. The police had, and to some extent still have, the contradictory tasks of maintaining good relationships with the public and enforcing road traffic legislation. The problem is that the more that the public is in conflict with the police about their driving habits the less likely they are to co-operate with the police in other areas. The area of conflict was reduced, and the possibilities of co-operation increased, by the hiving off of the enforcement of parking regulations to traffic wardens. Traffic wardens are much less in need of co-operation from the public than the police. If there is a hostile attitude to traffic wardens there could even be advantages in that it may mean that motorists are more likely to adhere to parking regulations. (There is, of course, the further advantage that the police can be released from routine work and put on to more demanding work.) All this sophisticated reasoning seemed to go completely over the head of the mayor of one seaside town. He commented on the bad relationship between the traffic wardens in his town and the public. His recommendation was that young female traffic wardens be hired and encouraged to wear mini-skirts so that the relationships between the public and the traffic wardens be improved!

It follows from this example that, as well as working out whether behaviour is a product of the role or the person, it is important to see that people are given viable roles. If people in managerial positions are expected to issue brickbats, but no bouquets, to their employees, it is unreasonable to expect them to have an easy working relationship with the same people. There is an inevitable tendency in organisations for there to be competition for the handing out of bouquets — like wage rises, good news and perks — and a great reluctance to get embroiled in, for example, disciplinary matters. A way of making it easier for a person to handle the disciplinary aspects is to allow him also to take the credit for distributing rewards when these are available.

The task of distinguishing between role and personality behaviour can demand considerable intellectual effort and emotional discipline. However, the rewards can be considerable — starting with the more accurate diagnosis of organisational problems. This can, in many situations, lead to real instead of false solutions. The amount of personal injustice can be reduced and last, but not least, the amount of personal aggravation for oneself diminished.

MANAGEMENT AND ADMINISTRATION IN THE PRIVATE AND PUBLIC SECTORS

A factor which is likely to have a major effect on the structure of an organisation is whether it is in the private or the public sector. The differing objectives of private and public sector organisations and the differing circumstances within which they have to operate necessitate different approaches. There may be ways in which each sector can improve by adopting some of the practices of the other, but there is a sound logic to many of the differences. Public sector bodies are democratically accountable, often have to meet a wide variety of statutory requirements, tend not to have clear quantifiable aims, and are usually very large. The largest employer in western Europe is, for example, the British National Health Service. Private sector organisations are often much smaller, with clearer, usually commercial, goals and often the need to encourage delegation of authority and risk-taking in a way that would be quite inappropriate in the public sector.

The differences between management and administration

One way of viewing the differences in approach in the private and public sectors is by distinguishing between management and administration. This has been done by a British civil servant associated with the Treasury Centre for Administrative Services. These differences are shown in the chart contained as an appendix to this chapter and are likely to apply in other countries as well. The emphasis with 'management' is on results and taking calculated risks and with 'administration' on procedures, accountability and risk avoidance. The differences should not be seen as complete opposites but rather as the two ends of a continuum. There will be some organisations that operate in the middle of the continuum; with some it may even be difficult to classify them accurately as private or public sector — for example, the BBC. With the public sector there is also considerable variety. The nationalised industries were quite deliberately set up in Britain as public corporations with much more autonomy than Civil Service departments to help them operate on a commercial basis. There is, of course, great variety within the private sector. Factors such as size, product variety and risk factors will influence private sector organisations. Some private sector organisations may have more characteristics in common with some public sector organisations than they do with private sector organisations at the end of the continuum. Some companies may need to review their balance between a managerial and administrative approach just as much as public sector bodies.

Effectiveness in the public sector

The differences between private and public sector organisations are often necessary; however, there has been growing concern about the effectiveness of many public sector organisations. This has led to a considerable amount of continuing pressure for change. Whilst it is appropriate for managers in the public sector to acknowledge the parameters within which they have to work, it is also necessary for them to identify the likely changes. The Civil Service has been under scrutiny and the Conservative Governments, led by Mrs Thatcher, actually reduced its size in a drive to make it more cost-effective. There has also been a persistent attempt to make public sector organisations operate more with a managerial, as opposed to an administrative, approach. This is not an entirely new development. The Maud Report[13] in 1967 was particularly critical of local government in Britain. Amongst the many criticisms were the absence of integrated policies, the rigidity of departmental boundaries and the lack of delegation. Recommendations included the need for clarification of objectives, a greater emphasis on management, assessment of results and the creation of a management board.

These criticisms and recommendations were reinforced by the Bains Report in 1972.[14] In particular there was adverse comment about the myth of policy being a matter for elected members and administration for the officers.[15] The recommendations included the need to have much more effort at identifying and clarifying policy, with councillors in particular being more involved in this and less involved in administrative detail. This in turn necessitated a far more corporate approach, increased delegation, more financial planning, a clearer management structure and performance review.

Although these attempts to change local government have been somewhat of an uphill task, the pressures have continued. Local authorities are being continuously squeezed into trying to make more effective use of their resources by their ever increasing commitments on the one hand, and increasing government control and restriction of their spending on the other hand, including the use of rate-capping. The problems that can be created by the resulting imbalance between the demand for services and the availability of resources are explained later in this chapter. This is in the section showing the similarity between some of the problems experienced in the Health Service and local government. Other pressures include the trend towards competitive tendering, particularly in Conservative-controlled local authorities, and the requirements that direct labour organisations compete on the open market with private firms for building contracts with their own Council.[16]

The Fulton Report

As well as there being persistent pressure for change in local government, there has also been periodic pressure for change in the Civil Service. The Fulton Report[17] was very critical about the way the Civil Service was organised, saying that it had a nineteenth-century approach to the problems of the latter half of the twentieth century. Six main inadequacies were identified:

1. The senior jobs were the preserve of gifted 'amateurs'.
2. There was too little movement up the grading structure particularly into the administrative grade.
3. Specialists were given too little responsibility and were not often considered for senior appointments.

4. Too few senior civil servants were skilled managers or even saw themselves as managers.
5. There was insufficient control between the Service and the rest of the community.
6. Personnel management was poorly developed.

The response to the Report was mixed and, whilst it would be unfair to denigrate the achievements of the Civil Service, or the extent to which senior civil servants have taken on board the concept of management, relatively little progress has been made on the actual Fulton recommendations. The establishment of the Civil Service Department was intended to strengthen the personnel function, but that has since been abolished.[18] However, the pressure for change has continued. As with local government there is a steady squeeze on resources. Mrs Thatcher became increasingly involved with senior appointments and was known to favour applicants with a track record of getting results. Attempts were also made to reduce the amount of control by centralised functional departments and to give more authority to line departments. The involvement of Sir Derek Rayner from Marks and Spencer in reviewing large sections of Civil Service work was very much in line with the general policy of the Governments led by Mrs Thatcher.

Other public sector changes

Elsewhere in the public sector there has also been pressure for greater cost-effectiveness — even if private sector practices haven't always provided the answers. The Health Service was reorganised following the Griffiths Report[19] of 1983. General managers were introduced into hospitals and decision-making now rests with them, instead of the former teams, which were supposed to arrive at a consensus before taking any decisions. Additionally, the whole tier of area level administration in the Health Service was removed, and in local government the Metropolitan Councils and the Greater London Council were abolished. Organisations formerly in the public sector, such as British Telecommunications, British Airways, the gas industry, the British Airports Authority and Rolls-Royce have been sold off and the pressures on any remaining public corporations to pay their way are going to remain.

The problem Britain and other countries face is one of rising expectations and demands on the public sector combined with slow economic growth. This inevitability causes a search for cost-effectiveness regardless of the political complexion of any particular Government.[20, 21] It also creates more need for the systematic identification of priorities. This became particularly apparent in the Health Service as it became obvious that the 'open-ended commitment' to meeting the medical needs of the nation could not be sustained. Advances in medical knowledge and the 'ageing' of the population meant that there were clearly not the resources to do everything. The consensus model of decision-making, previously explained, tended to preserve the *status quo* and also lead to an uncoordinated, and at times haphazard, response to resource allocation. The Griffiths structure within the hospital service at least gives general managers the authority to take decisions about resource allocation. This structure is also operating within the context of national policies designed to identify medical priorities and redistribute resources on a geographical basis.

Similar problems are evident in local government. Some councils are committed to, or are expected to, provide more in the way of services than they have the resources to provide. If the issue of imbalance is not recognised and dealt with at a policy level by the councillors policy decisions get pushed down to the officers who have the dilemma of deciding which needs to meet and which not to. The devices that can be used in this situation, as with the Health Service, include rationing, queuing, the temporary or permanent withdrawal of selected services and reductions in quality. Considerable stress can be placed on those having to take and implement these decisions, which may be aggravated by an imperfect understanding of what has caused this stress. This pattern of imbalance between the demands placed on a service and the resources provided to meet it is likely to occur throughout the public sector. A further example, showing the imbalance and the systematic response to it, has already been given concerning the London Metropolitan Police Force in the section on role set analysis in Chapter 2.

Bureaucracy in the private sector

The attempts to increase the cost-effectiveness of organisations and to reduce any bureaucratic waste are not of course confined to the public sector. Many private sector companies find that this is a chronic issue they have to deal with. There seems to be an increasing willingness in the private sector to query the value of large head offices. An example of this was the decision taken by ICI to reduce substantially the size of its head office at Millbank in London in 1982. Successful private companies which have fairly determinedly avoided having large head offices and have opted for a decentralised structure include GEC, Plessey and the Bass Group. Decentralisation is not a panacea, but the point that is continuously emphasised by market competition is that if private companies spawn unproductive bureaucracies their future is at risk even more than public sector organisations. Underlying all this in the public and private sectors in Britain and elsewhere is the fact that limited economic growth is bound to be a continuing pressure for the more effective use of organisational resources.

CONCLUSION

The basic theme of this chapter has been that there is no one way of designing an organisation. Organisational structures are means to ends and not ends in themselves. The structure that may be ideal in one situation can be disastrous in another. The individual manager needs to examine the fit between what is appropriate in terms of organisational design and operation and what actually exists. He also needs to do what he can to make the fit as close as possible. Hopefully the organisation structure will be in line with the objectives that are being pursued and the manager can go on to the next issue which is whether his own style is appropriate. Just as with organisational structure, there is no one pattern that will always guarantee success. The topic of managerial style requires detailed consideration and it logically follows that it should be dealt with in the next chapter.

NOTES

1. F. W. Taylor, *Scientific management* (Greenwood Press, 1972); first published in 1911.
2. Henri Fayol, *General and industrial management*, translated from the French Dunod edition by Constance Storrs (Pitman, 1967);

first French edition published 1916; the Storrs translation originally published 1949.

3. F. J. Roethlisberger and W. J. Dickson, *Management and the worker* (Harvard University Press, 1939).

4. T. Burns and G. M. Stalker, *Management of innovation* (Tavistock Publications, London, 1972); originally published in 1961. For a summary of this work, see Honor Croome, *Human problems of innovation* (Ministry of Technology Pamphlet, 1970), reprint.

5. Burns and Stalker, *Management of innovation*, p. 5.

6. John Atkinson, 'Manpower strategies for flexible organisations', *Personnel Management*, August 1984, pp. 28–31.

7. Chris Brewster and Stephen Connock, *Industrial relations: cost effective strategies* (Hutchinson, 1985).

8. David Hutchins, *Quality circles handbook* (Pitman, 1985), p. 1.

9. Ron Collard and Barrie Dale, 'Quality circles: why they break down and why they hold up', *Personnel Management*, February 1985, pp. 28–32.

10. Ibid, pp. 28–32.

11. Joan Woodward, *Industrial organisation: theory and practice* (Oxford University Press, 1965). For a summary of this work, see Joan Woodward, *Management and technology* (Ministry of Technology Pamphlet, 1970), reprint.

12. Ibid, p. 232.

13. *Report of the Committee on the Management of Local Government* (HMSO, 1967).

14. *The new local authorities: management and structure* (HMSO, 1971).

15. Ibid, para. 3.16.

16. See also *Audit Commission for England and Wales. The management of London's authorities: preventing the breakdown of services*, Occasional Papers No. 2 (HMSO, January 1987).

17. *The Civil Service, Report of the Committee 1966–8, Vol. 1*, Cmnd. 3638 (HMSO, 1968).

18. For a fuller account of this subject, particularly the response to the Fulton Report, see John Garrett, *Managing the Civil Service* (Heinemann, 1980).

19. *National Health Service Inquiry Report* (the Griffiths Report), (DHSS, 1983).

20. See also Leslie Chapman, *Your disobedient servant* (Penguin, 1979); and

21. Hugo Young and Anne Sloman, *No Minister: an inquiry into the Civil Service* (BBC, 1982).

APPENDIX I: THE DIFFERENT CHARACTERISTICS OF ADMINISTRATION AND MANAGEMENT

	Administration	*Management*
Objectives	Stated in general terms and reviewed or changed infrequently.	Stated as broad strategic aims supported by more detailed short-term goals and targets reviewed.
Success criteria	Mistake-avoiding. Performance rarely measurable.	Success-seeking. Performance mostly measurable.
Resource use	Secondary task.	Primary task.
Decision-making	Has to make few decisions but affecting many and can take time over it.	Has to take many decisions affecting few and has to make them quickly.
Structure	Roles defined in terms of areas of responsibility. Long hierarchies; limited delegation.	Shorter hierarchies; maximum delegation.
Roles	Arbitration.	Protagonist.
Attitudes	Passive: workload determined outside the system. Best people used to solve problems.	Active: seeking to influence the environment. Best people used to find and exploit opportunities.
	Time-insensitive. Risk-avoiding.	Time-sensitive. Risk-accepting but minimising it.
	Emphasis on procedure. Doing things rightly. Conformity.	Emphasis on results. Doing the right things. Local experiments: need for conformity to be proved.
	Uniformity.	Independence.

	Administration	*Management*
Skills	Legal or quasi-legal.	Economic or socioeconomic.
	Literacy (reports, notes).	Numeracy (statistics, figures).

4

Managerial Style

INTRODUCTION

The basic theme of this chapter is that managers need to try to match their style to their situation. Social and other changes have tended to reduce the extent to which managers can rely on the exercise of formal authority for getting their job done. This has put a premium on the more political styles of management, with formal authority being used as a last rather than a first resort although changes in economic circumstances have sometimes caused a reversion to more authoritarian managerial styles.

There is still, however, considerable variety in the types of situation in which managers find themselves. There are many factors which can have a bearing on the style that will be appropriate in a given situation. Some of these factors are examined in this chapter, including the effect of regional differences and the problems that may be faced by managers working overseas. The concept of assertiveness and its relevance to management is also covered. Finally guidance is given on how managerial style can be evaluated, bearing in mind that ultimately it is effectiveness that matters, with style being a means to an end and not an end in itself.

THE AUTHORITY OF THE MANAGER

Managers will normally have a certain amount of formal authority. This will entitle them to issue instructions, distribute rewards and administer discipline to help them accomplish the work for which they are held accountable. Often, however, managers have to look less to their formal authority and more to other means of influencing the behaviour of their subordinates and colleagues. In some cases they may be in a powerful position with regard to the distribution of rewards and administration of discipline. In other cases managers may have little in the way of formal control over rewards and penalties. In many organisations, especially in the public sector, the individual manager may have little or no influence over a person's remuneration or promotion. He may be able to make recommendations about promotion but only subject to checks and balances such as promotion boards. The same is likely to be the case with discipline, especially given the requirement, explained in Chapter 11, that dismissal should not be effected by the immediate superior.

The autocratic styles of past periods, which may often have been appropriate then, are often less acceptable today. Despite the severe economic constraints within which managers often have to operate, they also often need to achieve a large measure of consent for their actions. The social and other pressures that subordinates can put on bosses may of course be reinforced by union organisation. Managers may also have to deal with unions amongst white-collar employees in the private sector, as well as in the more traditional areas of union organisation amongst manual workers and employees at all levels of the public sector.

All this does not mean that managers should never give orders or that they should opt out of the disciplinary side of their jobs. The point is that these are methods of a last rather than a first resort. The manager who feels that he cannot do anything unless there is total consensus will in fact be opting out of management. Conflicts are inevitable, unpalatable decisions have to be taken and, if necessary, imposed — otherwise organisations will die through paralysis. However, the continuing change in social attitudes is such that this is an area where an increasing amount of skill is required. The traditional approach of relying just on formal authority is often counterproductive. This is not just because of social change. Organisations, as well as society, have tended to become more complex. In a technologically sophisticated age the expertise necessary to cope with particular problems is often fragmented within organisations. This is reinforced by the growing, and often increasingly specialised, developments in education, training and experience. Managers are more likely to be focal points for assembling the right mix of information and personnel to deal with particular problems. If a person is mishandled he may withhold his co-operation and perhaps, more importantly, his know-how. The manager thus has to behave much more as a negotiator. It is likely that his political skills will stand him in far greater stead than his formal authority.

Sapiential authority

In piecing together the permutations of people and expertise to solve organisational problems, it should be remembered that the manager will also be contributing his own expertise. Just as he is going to be dependent on subordinates and colleagues, so they are going to be dependent on him. Much of their contact with the manager will be when he helps them to accomplish tasks which they have, or in which they are involved. This may lead to the development of a sapiential authority by the manager — i.e. leadership by virtue of his particular expertise. Such expertise will not just be technical but often, significantly, organisational. The critical skill of the manager is likely to be knowing how decisions are taken or can be taken. As much as anything he may be a facilitator. This will not just be within a department but will also involve contacts with other parts of an organisation. It is perhaps only when this facilitating, problem-solving approach breaks down that the manager need resort to his formal authority, and even then it may be inappropriate.

In some situations it may be appropriate to try to develop a sapiential-type relationship with new subordinates as soon as they start. Newcomers may, especially in professional-type jobs, be resentful of too much formal guidance about how they should do their job. If the manager gives them enough rope, so that they realise their limitations for themselves, after a little while they may then be glad enough to come to him for help. I have encountered this issue particularly with new lecturing staff. They may be very indignant if it is suggested that they need advice, especially if the formal reporting lines are blurred, and find it fairly easy to fob off suggestions about how they should do their job. The knack in establishing an effective working relationship in this type of situation seems to be to avoid souring the relationship by giving advice when the person is not ready for it. It may be necessary to make a general statement about being willing to help should it be necessary. It may then be best, provided the damage done is not too great, to let a person find things out the hard way. If he then admits to being in difficulties, that is the time to offer help, with the newcomer's face being saved by his being the one who has initiated the request for help. That may then set the pattern for a long-term effective working relationship.

Relationships with people in other departments

A manager needs political skills to negotiate, not only with subordinates but also in a more general context within the organisation. The individual manager will find that, just as his formal authority is in fact restricted by the attitudes and behaviour of subordinates, so will it of course be restricted by the behaviour of colleagues in other departments. Colleagues in other departments may have formal functional control over part of the manager's job. Even if they don't, the reality of many line and staff relationships is such that it is often very difficult for the manager to resist advice from specialist advisers. The manager may not have the knowledge to argue with the specialist on a particular topic. If he argues, there is the danger of being proved wrong in the face of advice; if he refrains from argument and things go wrong, he can rely on the protection of saying he has followed specialist advice. In any case, specialist advisers can always threaten to take an issue up the organisation to someone superior to the manager if he indicates he is going to ignore their advice. In some cases of course the manager will himself be the specialist adviser. The comments about managerial style already made may be particularly appropriate to him. He may rely on his formal relationship and perhaps emphasise this with claims to a professional level of expertise not necessarily accepted by those on whom he wishes to impose his advice.

As was explained in Chapter 3, organisation problems are often highly interactive even when organisation charts suggest that the various parts of an organisation are largely autonomous. The specialist adviser may find that he makes much more progress by trying to find out the problems that colleagues have, and then trying to help them with them, rather than by making extravagant and perhaps quite unjustified claims about his

special knowledge and right to interfere. This may have co
siderable implications for the training of specialists. It may we
be that they need training sufficient for them at least to com
prehend the nature of the various parts of the organisation they
are in. A training that is a combination of this and specialist
expertise may enable them to integrate with their colleagues far
more effectively than a training which concentrates only on their
specialist area. (This is explained further, with particular
reference to the specialism of industrial relations, in Chapter
12.) The latter approach may cause them to seek solace with
other rejected specialist advisers and, for example, to complain
that they need the backing of a professional institute with a royal
charter in order to be taken seriously.

An extension of the reasoning of the subordinates having
some control over their manager is that the manager may
similarly have some control over his manager or a significant
measure of independence in the relationship. The effect of all
this is that the individual manager is likely to be most effective if
he concentrates on the influence he can develop by political skill
and patient negotiation with those around him, rather than by
the use of formal authority. This is not to say that formal
authority should be ignored, but when it is invoked, it should be
as part of the political judgement of the manager — that is,
invoked only in such a way and at such a time that it is likely to
be effective rather than counter-productive.

TRADITIONAL AND SITUATIONAL APPROACHES TO LEADERSHIP

Having suggested that there is likely to be an increasing need for,
and emphasis on, management by negotiation, it is also necessary to state that there will always be a large variety in the nature
of managerial jobs. Factors such as the specialist expertise
required, the extent of the manager's formal authority and discretion, and the rate of change will vary from place to place and
over time. This variety is such that traditional approaches to
leadership have often not proved helpful in the selection or
guidance of managers. An exercise that demonstrates this is to
ask a person or group what characteristics are necessary for an
effective leader or effective manager. Inevitably one gets a list
which includes such attributes as honesty, intelligence,

consistency, integrity, firmness, ruthlessness, flexibility, imagination, technical excellence, charisma and so on. It can then emerge that the list could go on for ever and that the requirements be so demanding that no mortal could fulfil them. There are other problems: the attributes may overlap, be controversial and in some cases be plain contradictory. So we are left with the question of what attributes make an effective leader or manager and the answer of course is that it all depends on the situation. The attributes that may be essential in one situation may be disastrous in another. One looks at the managerial situation first and then at the person who is in that situation or who is being considered for that situation. What is important is that he possesses the key attributes relevant to that situation. This matching is similar to that explained by Joan Woodward[1] in relation to organisation structure — she maintained that it was important that the critical function or functions were able to have a significant effect on corporate policy.

The key attributes will vary over time as well. There is no guarantee that a productive matching of manager to situation will be permanently effective — situations can change as can managers. One sees this particularly in the world of politics. Great leaders can be thrown up in times of war who might otherwise have remained in obscurity — 'cometh the hour cometh the man'. They may replace leaders whose skills might have been entirely appropriate for conditions of peace. Conversely, at the end of a war, further new leaders may emerge with attributes more appropriate to peacetime again. Great revolutionary leaders may similarly prove disastrous in the period when consolidation is required — all the more so as their prestige may enable them to pursue quite the wrong policies for a while when the revolution is over. Chairman Mao Tse-tung appears to have been but one example of this, as has now been effectively admitted in China.

ALTERNATIVES IN MANAGEMENT STYLE

Just as the attributes required by a manager vary from situation to situation, so does the managerial style that is appropriate to the situation. When speed is of the essence, and critical information and expertise are vested in one person, authoritarian leadership may be appropriate and acceptable. When the conditions are reversed, a more democratic style of leadership is likely to prove more effective. It may be that a particular situation can be effectively handled in more than one way — what matters ultimately is whether or not a style is effective. However, there can be mismatches between the style and the situation. Hopefully, managers can judge what style is appropriate and operate in that way. To some extent this is done intuitively, but there are limits to the extent to which this matching is done or indeed can be done. The matching issue may not always be recognised or the wrong style may be chosen. Even when the problems are recognised there are limits to the extent to which anybody can switch from one mode of behaviour to another. It may be that people tend to gravitate to jobs and organisations that suit their natural style. Problems may occur when a situation changes, even if only temporarily, and a person needs to act in what for them is an unnatural style.

Theories X and Y

At this stage it is appropriate to consider some of the alternative styles of leadership in some detail. There are various ways of classifying leadership styles. One is to distinguish between autocratic, democratic and *laissez-faire* patterns. A particularly useful classification is that given by Douglas McGregor[2] with his distinction between Theory X managers and Theory Y managers. The implicit assumptions behind the Theory X style is that employees need, and will respond to, close direction and control. This in turn is based on the assumptions that people would prefer to avoid work if they can, do not want to accept responsibility and effectively have to be coerced if organisational objectives are to be achieved. The Theory Y approach is based on the assumption that individual and organisational goals can be integrated. This in turn is based on the assumptions that work is a natural activity, that people will respond positively to objectives to which they are committed, that emotional satisfaction can be achieved and that, employees will under the right working conditions, accept responsibility. One can use McGregor's classification to examine one's own style and underlying assumptions as well as those of colleagues. Consideration of what style is being used is necessary primarily to see if it fits the situation. People can adopt a particular style in all situations without pausing to examine when it is appropriate and when it isn't. They may also undertake tasks or jobs when they may be better left to someone with a more appropriate style for that situation.

Organisation and social developments have made Theory Y an increasingly important style in recent decades. Even in military situations the Theory X approach can fail to work — witness the increasing reluctance of the American troops to engage in combat in Vietnam. However, to suggest that Theory Y is always appropriate would be to miss the point. Styles need to match situations and the situations will vary. Theories X and Y represent different ends of a continuum rather than completely separate alternatives. There tends to be much more emotional appeal to the Theory Y approach but the reality has to be faced that the right conditions cannot always be created for it to work effectively. It may not be possible to integrate individual goals with organisational goals. In a car factory, for example, whilst work remains thoroughly boring, managements are going to be forced to adopt a more coercive style than in jobs where there is much more opportunity for self-fulfilment. It also needs to be clearly recognised that the current economic climate has precipitated a change in style in some organisations — with less emphasis being placed on Theory Y and more on Theory X. This has been because of increased divergence in the goals of employers and employees. Consequently changes such as staff reductions have often had to be imposed, Theory X style, because the opportunity for Theory Y type agreement was not possible. Thus managers need to be aware that, even if a particular style has worked well in the past, changed circumstances can necessitate an adjustment in managerial style.

ASSERTIVENESS AT WORK

One of the concepts which managers may find useful in establishing an effective managerial style is that of 'assertiveness'. Recently assertiveness training has been associated with training for women who wish to take a more active and effective part in the working environment. However, the ideas which assertiveness training promotes are equally useful for men and women and can be employed to good effect in a variety of situations. Basically the idea is that all our behaviour can be divided into three 'ideal types': aggressive, assertive and non-assertive. Behind these three types of behaviour lies an assumption about the perceived rights of the parties in the situation. If a manager behaves aggressively he may be standing up for his own rights but be behaving in such a way that the rights of others are violated. He is implying that his own needs are more important than those of others and that whilst he has something to contribute others do not. The advantage of this in the short term may be that the manager gets his own way and at the same time is able to give vent to his feelings. However, he may be creating hostility in others and also developing a situation in which tension is increased and in which his health suffers.

Non-assertiveness implies behaving in such a way that other people's needs and rights are more important than your own. If a manager behaves non-assertively there is an implication that he feels he has little or nothing to contribute. In the short term the non-assertive manager may feel pleased that he has avoided conflict and appeared as 'Mr Nice Guy' to the other party. In the long term, the non-assertive manager may lose self-esteem and become angry. These feelings may increase internal tension in the manager and eventually could lead to a deterioration in health in the same way as too much aggression could. Sometimes if a manager feels he has behaved non-assertively there may be a tendency to over-react on a future occasion, leading to aggressive behaviour in the manager's effort to compensate for his former shortcomings.

Behaving assertively involves the manager stating his rights in a way that also allows other people to express their needs, wants and opinions in a direct, honest and open way. This type of behaviour should enable both parties to feel that their rights are not being ignored. It should ensure that the manager actually increases the chances that his needs are met whilst ensuring that his subordinates behave more assertively. The manager should feel more confident, as should his staff, who will feel encouraged to take more initiatives themselves. Assertive behaviour should result in a saving of energy, both because everybody feels more at ease in the situation and because this style of behaviour leads to more effective activity.

Assertive behaviour involves behaving openly. Such statements which begin 'I think . . .', 'I would like to . . .' and 'My idea is . . .' lead to the manager speaking for himself. The skills of being assertive include distinguishing between fact and feeling, e.g. 'My experience is that . . .' and asking questions to find out the thoughts and opinions of others. A simple situation which could easily occur in the workplace serves to illustrate this. The manager wants some work doing urgently. He approaches one of his members of staff whom he knows is hard-working and who doesn't argue if he is asked to do extra work. Unbeknown to the manager this employee is feeling rather frus-trated because he has too much work to do. If the manager behaves aggressively towards the employee, the employee may simply respond non-assertively and agree to take on the extra work. In the short term this may seem the ideal solution. How-ever, in the long run the work may suffer. The manager may not realise how overloaded the employee has become and may there-fore miss the opportunity to reallocate the work in the light of the available information, thus resulting in an inefficient use of manpower. Had the manager behaved more assertively he could have asked for the extra work to be done in such a way that the employee felt able to be equally open and honest and brought the true work situation out into the open. In the face of an aggressive response from an employee who feels aggrieved about overloading, the manager could use his skills of being assertive to clarify the situation. This should enable the employee to behave in a more reasonable way without further antagonising the employee, nor making him feel that he can 'walk over' the manager. Open questions, asked in a neutral tone, would be the appropriate approach in such a situation.

In their book *Assertiveness at work*[3] Ken and Kate Back give some helpful advice on the non-verbal aspects of behaving asser-tively. These include a steady and firm voice, which is neither over-loud nor quiet, an open facial expression, eye contact which is firm but not a 'stare-down', and an upright and relaxed posture. The book provides a very useful and comprehensive account of assertiveness in general and in particular of the ways in which other awkward situations, such as giving and receiving criticism, contributing assertively to meetings and resolving conflict, can be handled.

Behaving assertively will not necessarily lead to immediate rewards, especially since colleagues may have a vested interest in the manager not being more assertive. However, the develop-ment of this approach can bring significant long-term benefits, both in terms of increased effectiveness and with regard to the personal development of the person concerned.

ENVIRONMENTAL FACTORS

A manager's style will also be influenced by the environment in which he works. Key features in the environment will be the style of senior managers, particularly the immediate boss, and regional and national culture. When managers move to other organisations they need to pay particular attention to the traditions of the organisation they have joined.

The immediate superior

The person in charge of a manager is likely to have an important say in the selection of a subordinate manager. He will also have his own style of management, which he will often see as being appropriate and perhaps a model for the subordinate manager. Even if the subordinate manager does not accept that the model is appropriate, he is likely to be wary of managing in a style which is not favoured by his boss. If the boss's style is in tune with that of other senior managers, a manager may take a somewhat pessimistic view of his promotion chances if he develops what is seen, rightly or wrongly, as a wayward style. In many cases, though, he may accept that their behaviour is the received wisdom of how managers should behave in that environment. Sometimes, however, there will be a need for the styles to be complementary rather than similar. This point was made to me by a former Air Force officer with regard to the relationship between the commanding officer of a unit and his adjutant. In his view it was necessary for the one to take a hard disciplinary line, and for the other to take a much softer line and be psychologically available so that he could find out what people really felt as well as smooth any ruffled feathers. This is, of course, somewhat reminiscent of police methods of interrogation when one policeman takes the hard line and the other the soft line. In the view expressed to me about the Air Force it was maintained that it didn't matter who took the hard line and who the soft line as long as each took one. That way effective control, based on reliable information and reasonable morale, could be exercised. If both the commanding officer and the adjutant took the same style it was argued that either there would be an excess of control and lack of reliable information or the reverse.

There is one other way in which the influence of the boss on the subordinate manager should be examined. That concerns the extent to which the boss enables the subordinate manager to develop as a manager. One of the problems of authoritarian styles is that the subordinate manager will be expected constantly to refer matters upwards and not encouraged to make his own decisions and stand on his own feet. People tend to learn by being told or by being allowed to find out for themselves. The latter approach, whilst perhaps taking more time, may lead to a greater understanding and commitment as well as to a greater amount of self-reliance by the individual concerned. In practice there has of course to be a mix, but the balance can differ radically from one situation to another. One of the harsh realities that managers may have to face is that at some stage they may find that they are working for a boss who is thoroughly incompetent or unreasonable. There can, however, be some capital in such an experience, providing the experience is not too devastating or too long-lived. This may paradoxically develop the self-reliance of the subordinate manager. He may realise quite clearly that he cannot get help from above and consequently look more to his own abilities and judgement for handling his job, even if his prime objective is to work for someone else as soon as possible.

Regional culture

As well as having to fit with the style of other managers, it is also necessary for managers to take account of the expectations and constraints of local cultures. Managers may find that they have to take account of a move from one part of Britain to another. It may even be that there are quite false expectations and prejudices about the way a manager is likely to behave because, for example, he speaks with a southern counties accent and has gone to work in Merseyside. In working with various regional companies within the Bass group, I found that there were significant variations in managerial style, particularly with regard to labour relations, which seemed to be largely connected with the regional culture. This variation was found to be particularly important when a large new brewery was constructed in Merseyside at Runcorn. Many of the managers who ran the brewery were transferred from Burton-on-Trent and soon found that a rather different style was needed *vis-à-vis* the local labour force compared with the style that was appropriate in the very different culture of Burton.

This issue of local culture and the expectations and attitudes of the manual workers in particular was also, and understandably, an issue that I found significant when working in South Wales. At one manufacturing company, where I was engaged on industrial relations research, it was apparent that the culture of the local management was overwhelmingly American. They key appointments were held by North Americans and other managers were only appointed if they conformed to that culture. Unfortunately part of the culture, emanating from the company headquarters in one of the Southern States of America, was doctrinaire anti-trade unionism. The company had no one locally in an influential position to impress on them that this was like a red rag to a bull in that particular locality. The moral of the complementary commanding officer–adjutant relationship explained above had not been learned. Consequently the firm was caught off guard by a fortnight's strike which then obliged them to recognise the Transport and General Workers' Union. Another manufacturing company in the same area had also got itself rather unwittingly into the same sort of position. They had factories throughout the country but did not have any Welsh managers in their South Wales factory. The local management were consequently seen as alien but simply had no one to point out that this was an issue of importance. Ironically the company did have Welsh managers working at other British sites — the transfer of one or two to South Wales would have improved the possibility of better rapport with the manual workers and would also have demonstrated the point that the management jobs were not all reserved for the English.

Working overseas

The problems of adjusting to local cultures can be magnified enormously when working with people of different nationalities or when working overseas. I have found on my various overseas assignments, mainly in the Far East, that the first key task is to develop some understanding of the local culture. This you ignore at your peril. On one occasion I met an engineering manager who had just started a three-year contract and had flown out from Britain on the same plane as I had. He plunged straight into the technical aspects of the job and gave no attention as to how he might adjust to the habits, beliefs and expectations of his local colleagues. Sadly, we were both on the same flight home — his contract having been terminated after only three weeks! The temptation in any strange environment, whether it be a new company or a new country, or both, is to use one's previous experience as a model. The problem is that in a different country there will be many new factors to take into account. Tradition, religion, economic and political constraints, social habits, history, the skills of the population and the very nature of the problems are all likely to be different. With the benefit of historical hindsight one realises that, whilst British colonial rule brought many advantages as well as disadvantages to her former colonies, many of the institutions that were imposed were quite inappropriate in the very different social circumstances. I have in mind particularly such institutions as large hospitals, universities and political structures. Just as institutions need to fit the local situation, so a manager must be prepared to adapt his experience. Unfortunately he may not be used to thinking in these terms and assume that his home experience represents the best practice rather than the practice that was most appropriate to the home situation. Many of the cultural differences may be all the more difficult to take into account because they are so much part of one's normal behaviour that it is difficult to comprehend that other people think or act in a different way. Consequently the expatriate manager may not even realise there is a difference and his local colleagues may not see the need to warn him about a particular convention until it is too late.

One of the critical conventions that I found it necessary to understand in the Far East was the reluctance of people to express open criticism, particularly to a visitor in a position of authority. Unfortunately this could lead to visitors assuming that their behaviour, in the absence of adverse comment, was entirely acceptable and then plough on committing blunder after blunder. In Britain hints would be dropped far more quickly but, as far as I can judge, many of the nationalities in the Far East find it far more difficult to suggest that a person is behaving inappropriately. This means, of course, that the visitor may be deprived of the necessary feedback about the effects of his behaviour which he needs all the more in a different country. This may be reinforced by the tendency of many expatriate managers to spend most of their social time in the company of other expatriates. In some cases this may degenerate into a collective condemnation of the local environment and the assertion that the home country which they voluntarily left holds no equal. The climate, too, has to be taken into account. One manager who had worked in the Far East for some years explained to me how he and his colleagues treated managers who had arrived recently from Britain. They noticed a recurrent pattern of the newcomer wanting to change things in a hurry. The local view was that, if you gave them about six weeks, the heat would get to them and make them realise the appropriate pace of work and rate of change locally.

In case the number of new factors that the recently arrived manager has to cope with seems daunting, it should be emphasised that in the process of adjustment one is likely to earn some credit for simply trying. There is also the compensation that eccentricity and mistakes can be put down to a person being new in a country — even if that isn't really the case. A particularly humorous but perceptive account of the problems of the expatriate adjusting to the local environment is given in Leslie Thomas's *The love beach* about expatriate life in the New Hebrides.[4]

Another issue which I encountered was the much greater need to save face compared with in Britain. On one occasion I was at a meeting of Indonesian managers, when one of the managers made a suggestion which soon turned out to be quite inappropriate. It seemed to take about three times as long as it would have done in Britain for the manager to retreat from his suggestion with dignity, even though he too quickly realised that his suggestion was inappropriate. However, so that his standing was not damaged for future occasions, it seemed entirely necessary in the local situation to spend so much time handling the issue.

Lest one should appear smug about adapting to local conditions, I should also relate the time I told a Canadian about the problems of adjusting to conditions in the Far East. The response I got was unexpected but fair comment — I sounded like an American explaining how to come to terms with working in Britain!

Two further points are worth mentioning about working overseas because they indicate rather different problem areas. The first is the possibility for managers, particularly on their first overseas assignment, to behave in an exaggerated fashion. This is likely to be because of their release from social constraints and conventions that would operate more in their home country. Part of the culture shock problem in working overseas is not just the new environment but the absence of the old familiar environment in which the person knows much more readily what to do in a given situation. The other problem area is what can ironically be the much more difficult problem of readjustment when the expatriate returns home. The more successfully a manager has adapted to working overseas, the greater may be the extent of the readjustment to his home country. Because this is a much less expected and less recognisable problem, it may be quite off-putting. Sadly employers often think out the arrangements for sending a person overseas much more carefully than his return home.[5] Managers working overseas may occupy positions of much greater responsibility than it is possible for them to occupy in their home country. They may return to find that the employer has not thought out how to reintegrate them and that the organisation in the home country has moved on without them, even though they have valuable experience to offer. One of the morals of this, in considering whether or not to take an overseas appointment, is to pay particular regard to the arrangements for reintegration on completion of an overseas tour.[6]

Starting in a new managerial job

Some of the problems of working overseas are similar to those experienced by a manager facing a new job. A manager can try and stamp his personality on a new job from the start or size up the situation before he tries to change it. One manager who seemed to try and impose his own personality from the start was Brian Clough, who left Derby County to manage Leeds United, following the appointment of Don Revie to the position of manager of the England football team. This backfired and Brian Clough lasted only six weeks in his new job. It could be that, in trying to follow in the shoes of a very successful and forceful manager, he felt he had no option but to try and impose his own style from the start. However, if one is to do that, and there will be occasions when to wait is to condone a pattern you want to alter, it is important for a new manager to get his decisions right in a technical and a political sense. All too often managers may feel insecure in a new job and try to impose patterns of behaviour that were appropriate in their previous and different circumstances. There is much to be said for judging the situation before making any radical changes. It does in any case often take time to diagnose what the problems really are. It is only when the diagnosis has been effectively undertaken that it is appropriate for managers to try to implement such solutions as there may be. What can be fatal is for managers to rush in with prescriptions culled from previous experience without checking whether these are appropriate in their new situation. Colleagues tend to be wary of new appointees and it may be that the first thing that a new manager has to do is to make himself acceptable. One way of doing this is to make sure that initially, in particular, he looks for improvements that have a high probability of success, so that he gradually establishes his credibility.

A convention that is sometimes adopted with the appointment of new managers, which is in keeping with practice in the armed services, is that managers are not appointed to be in charge of work groups from which they themselves have come. The reasoning behind this is that, amongst other things, the new manager will be able to impose decisions on the subordinates without being constrained by social ties. Separate catering and recreational facilities are of course provided in the services, and sometimes in industry, to prevent social contact. This may be appropriate in situations where the manager or person in charge may have to impose unpalatable decisions on the group. It is only likely to work, though, if the person in authority also has the coercive power through control of rewards and punishments to impose his will. In other organisations it may unduly restrict the choice of manager, not prove viable, or not be necessary. It has already been explained that expertise and information is often widely distributed within organisations. This and other factors may enable the work group to exercise considerable control over the manager if they want to. If the manager, however, is able to operate in an environment where by and large he does not have to impose unpalatable decisions, and where he is able to be much more of a facilitator than order-giver, the convention of not appointing a manager from the work group may be inappropriate.

EVALUATING MANAGERIAL STYLE

Now that I have established the importance of matching managerial style to the requirements of the situation, I would like to offer some guidance on how style can be evaluated. Ultimately managers should be judged by results, but to some extent this begs the question of which style is likely to give the best results in a given situation. A useful method I have found has been to take the six points that George Homans[7] has found to be relevant in suggesting who will emerge as leader in informal groups. Homans suggests that, in a wide variety of informal group situations, the behaviour of the leader tends to conform to a certain pattern. The pattern is needless to say one in which the leader's ability to adjust to particular situations is incorporated. This may well be a pattern for appropriate behaviour by many managers, as you can judge for yourself. The admittedly rough and ready method of evaluation is to see if managers who conform to this pattern are judged to be effective or not. I have repeatedly asked groups to carry out this evaluation exercise and been surprised at the high level of correlation between conformity to this pattern and judgements about managerial effectiveness. To do this for oneself it is necessary to identify one or more managers in terms of effectiveness or ineffectiveness on the following six-point scale:

1. Excellent,
2. Very good,
3. Good,
4. Meets the minimum standards,
5. Does not meet the minimum standards,
6. Should be dismissed.

It is next necessary to compare the behaviour of the manager or managers already rated against the six points identified by Homans as being characteristic of the behaviour of informal group leaders.

1. Do they represent what the group find to be most
   important in a person at that time?   Yes/No
2. Do they make decisions which turn out, by and
   large, to be correct?   Yes/No
3. Do they keep their word?   Yes/No

4. Do they settle differences between members in a way the group believes to be fair? Yes/No
5. Do they allow followers to go to them for advice and keep them informed about what is going on in the group? Yes/No
6. Do they give information to the group in the form of advice, orders, etc., and maintain two-way communication? Yes/No

When this second part of the assessment is completed one then compares the number of 'Nos' with the initial rating of managerial effectiveness. This usually correlates so that the higher the numerical rating the higher the number of 'No' responses and vice versa. Not only can this be a useful guide but it can indicate specific areas of weakness and possible improvement. If nothing else it can make one feel justified in confirming one's views about a bad manager. If one is particularly brave it may also be worth using this method to undertake some self-assessment.

The point that has been stressed with regard to managerial style is that it is a means to an end and not an end in itself. The ultimate test is how effective it is. The point about matching the style to the situation is that this is what is likely to produce results. However, it is always possible that more than one approach can work and if different individuals handle things differently, but still get results, it may not matter that they use alternative routes to the same goal. Managers also need to pay attention to their working relationships with immediate colleagues in particular as this way they are much more likely to gain their co-operation. This may help them avoid being unpopular. However, popularity, just as style, should not be an end in itself. The manager who always puts his need for popularity above organisational objectives, where the two are in conflict, can scarcely be effective from the standpoint of the organisation.

NOTES

1. Joan Woodward, *Industrial organisation: theory and practice* (Oxford University Press, 1965).

2. Douglas McGregor, *The human side of enterprise* (McGraw Hill, 1969).

3. Ken and Kate Back, *Assertiveness at work: a practical guide to handling awkward situations* (McGraw Hill, 1982).

4. Leslie Thomas, *The love beach* (Pan Books, 1970).

5. William Holmes and Fred Piker, 'Expatriate failure — prevention rather than cure', *Journal of the Institute of Personnel Management*, December 1980.

6. For a wealth of information on the practical issues concerning working overseas, see Godfrey Golzan, *The Daily Telegraph's guide to working and living overseas* (Kogan Page, 1985), 8th edition.

7. George Homans, *The human group* (Routledge & Kegan Paul, 1975, originally published 1951), Ch. 8.

5

Delegation

INTRODUCTION

Management has already been described as 'getting work done through others'. It therefore follows that delegation is a facet of every manager's job. Unfortunately, however, understanding and effective practice in this area can all too easily be taken for granted. Despite the critical importance of delegation, it tends to receive relatively little attention in management literature and training. I have repeatedly found that the competence that is assumed in this area is often not vindicated by people's conceptual understanding or behaviour in practice.

Some of the problem areas related to delegation have already been considered in previous chapters. One of the main implications of Chapter 1 was that managers may spend too much time on their historical specialism instead of delegating more in that area. In Chapter 4, on managerial style, it was explained that managers may make incorrect assumptions about the attitudes of their subordinates to their job. As a result it is quite possible for managers to fail to realise that subordinates might be only too willing to help them, if only they were allowed to do so. Good practice with regard to delegation may be difficult to achieve because of factors such as these. These problems may be compounded by misunderstandings about the very nature of delegation. Consequently the concept of delegation is explained in this chapter, followed by an examination of the need for delegation. The skills of delegation are then considered as well as the potential obstacles to effective delegation.

WHAT IS DELEGATION?

Delegation may be defined as 'a person conferring authority on a subordinate to act on his behalf'. It should not be confused with the issuing of orders or giving of instructions to subordinates. Although the manager remains accountable for the actions of the subordinate, the essence of delegation is the conferring of authority on the subordinate. Thus delegation is much more than just passing a task over to be executed.

The accountability of the person who does the delegating was illustrated in a British insurance fraud trial. The owner of a company which had been declared bankrupt was cross-examined about the contrast between his personal wealth and the state of his former company. He responded by saying that he had practised modern management techniques — including delegation — and that such questions should be addressed instead to his former financial controller. The judge understood management better than that and, when sentencing the owner to a lengthy term of imprisonment, commented that whilst authority can be delegated accountability remains.

Some further amplification of the concept of accountability is necessary. At one stage in Britain it was the practice for Government Ministers to accept responsibility and resign if there was a serious enough error by one of their subordinates — regardless of whether the Minister was personally to blame or not. This is what happened in the Crichel Down case in 1954 when it was found that land which had been compulsorily purchased by the Government for military use during the Second World War had been used later for agricultural purposes and then sold to a private buyer. This was despite an earlier assurance to offer it for sale back to the original owner. The Minister was obliged to resign even though he had not been personally involved in the decision and had had no reason to believe that his officials had acted in other than good faith. This convention of resignation, regardless of personal blame, was modified however at the time of the Aberfan disaster in 1966. This was when a slag heap slipped down a hill during a rainstorm and engulfed a school and adjacent houses. There were 147 deaths of which 116 were of children. The owner of the slag heap was the National Coal Board, and its chairman, Lord Robens, offered his resignation. This was not accepted however on the basis that the disaster was not reasonably foreseeable. This modified concept of accountability one assumes was applied during the Government crisis in Britain in 1982 when the Falkland Islands were occupied by the Argentinian army. Both the British Foreign Secretary, Lord Carrington, and the Defence Secretary, John Nott (later Sir), offered their resignations. In the event the Foreign Secretary's resignation was accepted, despite his illustrious record, but not the Defence Secretary's. Presumably this was because it was judged that the Argentinian invasion should have been anticipated and preventative action initiated.

THE NEED FOR DELEGATION

One of the main reasons for delegation is that it is a means whereby a manager can, having decided his priorities, concentrate on the work of greatest importance, leaving the work of lesser importance to be done by others. Usually the manager concerned will need to see that some jobs at least are routed direct to his subordinates rather than have every task sent to him for rerouting as appropriate.

Time constraints

The manager's time is limited and it is important for him to tackle his work in some order of priority so that the most important tasks get the appropriate attention. Thus, if at the end of the day some work has not been completed or has had to be passed on to others, this should be the work of lowest priority. Even if the work of lesser importance is not done, or is not done so well, this is appropriate behaviour for the person in charge. It would not be sensible for a manager to do his own clerical work because he thought he could do it better than his secretary or clerk. Running the risk of a slightly lower level of performance by a subordinate is a small price to pay for free time to concentrate on the more important aspects of a job. The lower the level at which a task is performed, the lower the cost of performing that task is therefore likely to be. Cost needs to be considered not just in terms of the salary of the person undertaking a particular task but also in terms of opportunity cost — i.e. the opportunity that is denied or created for the manager to do other work.

The effective use of subordinates

A further development of the case for effective delegation is that in many cases the delegated work can be performed more competently by the subordinate. It is quite posible that, given time, a subordinate would, for example, do clerical work more effectively than his manager. In some cases there would be a blatant disregard of the specialist expertise of a subordinate if the boss tried to do his job. What would be the point and the results if, for example, a managing director tried to run the accounts department if he had a finance manager?

Arising out of this is the need for managers to seek to dovetail their activity with that of their subordinates. Everybody has relative strengths and weaknesses in their work. If a subordinate has particular strengths it may be appropriate to make use of those strengths rather than compete in that area or simply ignore those strengths. What matters is the effectiveness of the team as a whole rather than the direct performance of just the manager.

Further possible advantages of delegation are that the subordinate often has more time and readier access to the appropriate information than the boss. Also, what is routine work to the boss may be challenging to the subordinate, as well as carrying prestige. The more that subordinates are developed, the more they are likely to be able to undertake in the future. This can be especially valuable in times of emergency, for example when the boss is away or when there is the sudden need for a promotion.

Finally, an advantage of effective delegation may be that a manager is setting the pattern for his subordinates to delegate in turn down the line. One adage about managerial assessment is that you judge a manager by the quality of his subordinates. Presumably Philip II of Spain would not have rated highly on this basis since it is alleged that he governed Spain in a manner which created 'apoplexy at the nucleus and paralysis at the periphery'.

THE SKILLS OF DELEGATION

The case for delegation is easy to make. Consequently people may rush into delegating without effective planning. The delegated work may then be mishandled causing the boss to withdraw the delegated authority without realising that the problem lay in the lack of planning rather than the basic idea. The factors critical to effective planning of delegation need identification and explanation.

The first critical factor is the need for clarity about just what has been delegated. A useful concept in this respect is Wilfred (later Lord) Brown's distinction between the prescribed and discretionary content of a manager's job.[1] Prescribed work is that which must be performed in a predetermined manner. The discretionary element of a manager's job is where he is expected to use his own judgement. For example, a personnel officer could be told that he has authority to determine at what point on a given salary scale a recruit to an organisation would start. The salary range to be used would be prescribed, the point along the salary range would be discretionary. Time and care need to be taken in defining a person's job in this way, particularly, for example, when a person has just started in a job. The use of discretion by subordinates must be tolerated within reasonable limits. A subordinate cannot always be expected to perform in exactly the same way as his boss. If that is the expectation, then the work concerned is prescribed content not discretionary content. If there is discretion, and it is used sensibly, it can be very demoralising for a subordinate to be told 'I wouldn't have done it quite that way'. If the discretion has been used unwisely, this may well reveal a weakness in the way the delegation was set up originally. A further critical factor is the need for a manager to set up a control procedure so that he gets feedback on the performance of the subordinate. On some occasions random or periodic feedback may be sufficient — on other occasions much closer control may be needed. The manager, being accountable, has to monitor progress.

Delegating authority to others may well be accompanied by a need to train them in the way in which that authority is to be used. It is no good delegating authority to a subordinate unless he knows what to do. All too often this stage is omitted and managers exclaim that people won't assume authority. There may be a need to start training well in advance of the delegation. Training needs to combine the substantive knowledge and skills required by the subordinate in his job with a careful definition of just what constitutes his job.

The appropriate use of discretionary powers may well involve considerable discussion between manager and subordinate. The access of the subordinate to the manager needs determining. If people are unsure of how to use their delegated powers, they may well act inappropriately or pass things back up to the manager. When items are passed up to the manager, he needs to consider whether he should do them or whether they should be passed back to the subordinate with a reminder about the subordinate's discretionary area. When an appropriate discretionary area has been established, it is up to the manager to see that the subordinate gets on with his job and does not seek to over-involve his boss. It is important to clarify what the boss does and does not need to know. Care also has to be taken with work that is routed to the manager that should be done by subordinates. In some cases colleagues will need to have it explained to them that they should go to the subordinates direct. On other occasions it will be entirely appropriate that the work should come direct to a manager so that the chain of command is not bypassed. If a manager's boss routes something to him it does not automatically follow that the manager must do the job himself. The decision as to who does it is one for the manager. The real pattern of delegation is likely to be set by the way a manager handles routing decisions such as these. The critical question to be asked, before any work is undertaken, is 'whose job is this'? Obviously authority can only be delegated to people who, in the long run, are going to be able to cope with the delegated powers. This may in turn become a criterion in selection, so that one chooses staff who will be able to integrate effectively with the work pattern of their boss.

OBSTACLES TO EFFECTIVE DELEGATION

Even when people recognise the advantages of delegation and are aware of the skills involved in planning it effectively, they still may not delegate to the extent to which they should. There are a number of barriers to effective delegation — usually these are a lot easier to recognise in others than in oneself. Also, these barriers are sometimes not so much barriers as genuine constraints — it can be very difficult to disentangle the two on occasion.

Finding the time to plan delegation

Paradoxically delegation may initially be time-consuming. It may require careful thought about just what the discretionary content of subordinates' work should be. When that has been established, time may be needed to train subordinates in the exercise of their delegated authority. Time may also be needed for the establishment of appropriate control procedures. Delegation is like a capital investment: time spent setting it up may achieve substantial dividends — but only in the future. If the manager does not carefully think through his pattern of delegation, it may backfire and discourage him from further attempts.

Factors outside the manager's control

There can, of course, be factors over which the manager may have little or no control, which prevent his delegating. He may have so little authority delegated to him that there is very little for him to pass on down the line. A manager may also just not have sufficient subordinates, or subordinates of sufficient competence, to delegate as much as he would wish. In some cases political factors, such as excessive ambition on the part of a subordinate or rivalry between subordinates, may mean that it is prudent for a manager to retain some aspects of his job that on the face of it could be delegated. These constraints may reasonably be classified as legitimate reasons for lack of effective delegation. There are however various less obvious or less legitimate reasons which need examination.

The indispensable employee

One particularly interesting case history was brought to my attention by a postgraduate student whom I was supervising on a study of redundancy at an electronics company. A whole division had been closed and it transpired that this particular division had been managed by no less than seven different divisional heads in the seven years prior to its closure. Before that it had been managed very competently by the same person for 27 years. The problem which emerged was that the one person had managed the division so well that no-one could follow in his footsteps.

Ironically, had that divisional head been less capable, he might have left behind a management structure which would have been more able to cope with his retirement. It was his very competence that had prevented the necessary delegation!

A variation of the above theme was encountered by my brother when he was a councillor in South Wales. This case concerned a borough engineer who deliberately set out to make himself indispensable, as opposed to the electronics division head who seemed accidentally to achieve this effect. Some of the maps of the local underground drainage system had been destroyed and the borough engineer was the only person who knew the exact locations of the drains in the relevant areas. He consistently refused to commit his knowledge to paper on the basis that as long as only he knew the complete layout the council would not dismiss him. When it was put to him that if he suddenly fell ill or died the lack of any record of the complete drainage system would cause obvious problems, he responded by saying that they wouldn't be his problems.

The desire to feel indispensable can, of course, represent a psychological need as well as an attempt to improve job security. This was apparently the case in a further case history concerning a college principal who had all the college mail addressed to him personally. He would open the envelopes and when rerouting mail to subordinate staff instruct them on what action to take. This enabled him to complain that no-one else in the college worked as hard as he did or was prepared to assume responsibility. The fact was, of course, that he would not permit anyone else to take responsibility. One of the psychological pay-offs in his game was that, if one starts with the assumption that one's subordinates are no good, this can then become a self-fulfilling prophecy — as good staff will be driven away. There was, I am told, some progress in this particular case. Eventually the principal's secretary was allowed to open the envelopes before the principal himself took out the enclosures! Lest this case seems too fanciful I should add that the last time that I related it on a course for managers one of the course members confessed to me afterwards that he really would have to get his secretary to open his mail for him!

The connection between delegation and promotion

There are, of course, disadvantages for managers, as well as their employers, if they refrain from effective and necessary delegation. This is illustrated by the final case that I shall quote, which I was able to examine when conducting a research investigation into the management structure of a group of hospitals. Two small hospital groups had been merged, partly because of the ineffective management style of the chief administrative officer of one of the groups. He had operated on the classic Theory X assumptions about his subordinates explained in the previous chapter. The chief administrative officer of the other group now had to administer both groups. He was much more prepared to delegate and interestingly had attracted around him a much more capable group of administrative officers than had his retired colleague, despite a common salary structure. Initially he tried to cope with his own increased workload by increasing the delegated authority of the senior administrators in the group which he had taken over. I was able to observe the effect of this on one of the officers in particular. He tried to cope by doing all the extra work as well as the work he had traditionally undertaken. The total workload was too much for him and sadly the work which he left undone was most of the extra work which had been delegated to him. He was quite unable to identify his new priorities and to delegate down the line, as his new boss had delegated to him. Consequently the chief administrative officer had to take back most of the delegated authority recognising that this particular person had apparently reached his limit as far as his capacity to assume responsibility was concerned. Ironically he was then able to delegate even more authority to the senior officers in the other part of the group as they were used to coping with increased work. The administrator who had been relieved of part of his authority had imposed his own limit. By demonstrating his inability to cope with increased authority he had not only restricted his own job but ruled himself out of consideration for future promotion. In ways such as this people can set limits on their career without necessarily realising it.

It may seem that promotion decisions are taken by the manager responsible for making the appointments. In reality, though, it may be much more the case that it is the managers being considered for promotion who decide for themselves whether or not they get it. Managers responsible for appointments do not make decisions in a vacuum. The existing pattern of behaviour of a manager is likely to influence any decision about his promotion. If a manager has got his pattern of delegation right, and because of that gets promotion, the onus may then be upon him to establish a new pattern so that he prepares himself for even further promotion. The same reasoning can apply to people running small businesses. The expansion or non-expansion of a small business may depend less on external factors than is often imagined. Much may depend on the ability of the person running a small business to identify and concentrate on the key tasks, leaving the less critical, even if more enjoyable, tasks to others.[2]

NOTES

1. Wilfred Brown, *Exploration in management* (Pelican, 1965), p. 123.
2. For a fuller account of this topic, read Herbert M. Engel, *How to delegate: a guide to getting things done* (Gulf, Texas, 1983).

6

Motivation

INTRODUCTION

In this chapter we examine the variety of reasons why people work. It is important to consider the range of reasons because it is all too easy for incorrect assumptions to be made about why people do or do not work. If the diagnosis is incorrect, corrective action may be entirely inappropriate. We then turn to behavioural theories concerning motivation, and the practical use that can be made of them. Consideration is given to the ways in which job content and the individual's abilities can be matched. The ways in which jobs can get distorted, particularly because of the impact of high levels of unemployment, are examined. The dangers of over-involvement in the job and managerial stress are also covered.

WORK PERFORMANCE

An appropriate starting point for this chapter is to suggest that, if people are not working effectively, or in some cases not working at all, it is the match between job and person that needs examining and not just the person. It may be that some people will never work effectively under any circumstances; it may also be the case that some jobs will always pose motivational problems — whoever is supposed to be doing them. However, it is also likely that there are circumstances in which most people will work effectively, just as there are circumstances under which the same people will not work effectively. Similarly with most or many jobs there are likely to be many people who will perform them effectively and other people who will perform them ineffectively. If there is a problem of ineffective work performance, the basic question is whether it is the fault of the person, the job, or the matching of the two. Remedial action will depend on the diagnosis. In some cases it may be that in the short term neither can be changed, in which case attention needs to be paid to either the type of person selected in the future, or the job structure, or both, according to the diagnosis of the reasons for poor work performance.

Diagnosis of reasons for poor performance

I have stressed the need for accurate diagnosis because it is all too easy for the diagnosis of reasons for poor work performance to be wrong. It is at best a subjective area. The very criteria for judging effective work performance may be difficult to establish, as the section on the definition of objectives in Chapter 2 demonstrated. The essence of good diagnosis in this area is to analyse the situation in role terms and not personality terms. Here the explanation of role behaviour given at the end of Chapter 3 is pertinent. One of the problems of analysing work performance in role terms is that the conclusions may be uncomfortable for the person carrying out the analysis. If the blame is put on the person working ineffectively, that absolves the boss, who may then fail to see the connection when the next person in the job also performs ineffectively. In some cases of course the fault will be with the person in the job; the point to realise is that this will not automatically be the case. When the fault is not with the person in the job, then uncomfortable implications for the boss may emerge. The onus may then be on him to examine the structure of the job, or the support given to the person in the job. It may be that he needs to change his behaviour rather than the job holder. It may require considerable insight and intellectual honesty to explore these implications. Such a line of thought may or may not run counter to the implicit assumptions that the manager has about why people work.

Assumptions about why people work

Alternative sets of assumptions that managers may have about

92

why people work were identified in Chapter 4 in the explanation of Douglas McGregor's Theory X and Theory Y approaches. The fact that one has implicit assumptions does not mean that they are necessarily correct. It may be that they need careful examination in the light of particular situations.

One of the dangers of assumptions is of course that one is guessing about people's motivation. In assessing one's own reasons for working one has self-knowledge to go on, and this is likely to lead to a more charitable set of assumptions than those always made in respect of other people. An exercise which demonstrates this, that colleagues and I have frequently used with managerial groups, is to ask groups to complete the following questionnaire: managers are asked to rank the factors listed below in order of importance in so far as they affect the manager's motivation in his current job. The managers are then asked to repeat the ranking in respect of their current subordinates.

Reasons for working

Chance to use initiative at work
Good working conditions
Good working companions
Good boss
Steady, safe employment
Money
Good hours
Interest in the work itself
Opportunity for advancement
Getting credit and recognition

Invariably a comparison of the rankings shows that the managers see themselves as giving more importance to factors such as 'interest in the work itself' and 'chance to use initiative at work'. Conversely the subordinates are invariably seen as paying more attention to factors such as 'money' and 'steady, safe employment' than their bosses. It may be that the difference in rankings achieved is, as far as anyone can judge, justified. It may also be that managers are too ready to assume the worst as far as their subordinates' motivation is concerned. This makes the results of a survey commissioned by the Royal Commission on Trade Unions and Employers' Associations[1] a little worrying. Five hundred foremen and 300 works managers were asked whether their subordinate workers 'could reasonably be expected to put more effort into their job than they did'. Forty-three per cent replied in the affirmative and, when asked why more effort was not forthcoming, gave as the three principal reasons 'a lack of financial incentive, laziness and lack of interest'. The exact pattern of responses might differ if this 1968 survey were repeated today but one wonders if the tendency to jump to too hasty conclusions about the motivation of one's subordinates has changed.

Other variables

The motivation of subordinates is, of course, just one variable affecting work performance. Factors such as capital equipment and work programming have their effect as well. In one study commissioned by the National Economic Development Office[2] it was established that at some large construction sites workers could spend more time idle than working because of factors such as shortages of materials and late design changes. It would not be much use in situations like that trying to increase output by 'getting the whip out'. Factors such as technology also have to be considered — if the pace of production is determined by an automatic process, rather than by human effort, then it may be more rewarding to spend one's money on efficient maintenance of the process rather than production bonuses for employees for a process over which they may have relatively little control.

JOB DESIGN

If one accepts that it is the match between person and job that needs examination, it follows that this should be considered before people are selected for a job. It may be quite disastrous to design a job and then assume that people will be available to fill the vacancies. One horror story given to me to illustrate this point concerned a factory which was built in North Australia. Unfortunately no-one would work there because it was too hot in the factory and consequently it was unused. There are, though, examples of this lack of anticipation rather closer to home. Many jobs in engineering factories involve the repetition of a cycle of operations that may be measured in seconds rather than minutes. People may be expected to repeat the same cycle of operations hundreds of times during the same working day. In the current climate of unemployment it may be easier to recruit people to do such jobs than was the case in periods of high employment, but the motivational problems for those doing these jobs may be immense. The point that needs emphasising is that engineers, when designing such jobs, need to take the motivational implications into account to see if a better match between person and job is possible.

This is admittedly easier said than done but can at least be tried. Too often the procrustean approach is taken to job design. Procrustes was a legendary figure in Greek mythology who had a special bed. He was obsessive about guests fitting his bed exactly. If they were too long for the bed he cut off their feet, whilst if they were too small then he stretched them on a rack until they fitted. The moral is, of course, that jobs can be designed with little or no thought to the matching with the individual — the assumption being that people can always be found who can be made to fit the job. In some cases this can have an almost literal procrustean meaning — some capstan lathes have been designed that would be best operated by a man 4 foot 6 inches high but with the arm span of a gorilla.

Few companies would seek to make products unless they had checked whether there was a market for those products. The same approach needs to be taken in job design. It is appropriate for employers to check whether there is a supply of labour for the jobs they have designed. Their analysis needs to take account of the optimum match between person and job, not simply seeing if they can notionally fill every vacancy. As well as the individual tasks being examined, jobs need to be looked at as a whole to see if they constitute a sensible collection of tasks or not. One danger is that the span of tasks in terms of the level of skill required may be too great. The two apparently quite different jobs of craft worker and general practitioner both tend to suffer from this problem. The tendency is for both of these jobs to contain a relatively small amount of work requiring considerable skill and knowledge and a large amount of work that is relatively routine and undemanding in terms of skill and knowledge requirements. The structure of both jobs is shown in Figure 6.1.

The problem about filling such jobs as these is that the person who is particularly capable may be bored and under-utilised

Figure 6.1: The skill pyramid

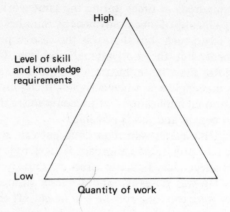

with the more routine aspects of the work. People with that conflict may tend to over-concentrate on the work they find interesting at the expense of the work they find boring. They may even try to build up the most interesting part of their job, even though it may be more appropriate for them to refer that work to others. The problem may be compounded by the fact that, particularly for example with general practitioners, there may be no obvious opportunity for promotion. The problem at the other end of the scale may be that the person who copes well with the routine aspects of the job may not have the skill and knowledge to cope with the more complicated aspects of the work. Unless the work can be restructured the problem may be like that of a man with a small blanket — either the feet or the shoulders are cold. The answer, of course, is to restructure the job — but that is easier said than done. Some progress has, however, been made in having auxiliary staff such as social workers and nurses assist doctors in general practice. There has also been some progress in reducing the length of time of apprenticeships for skilled trades and sometimes in increasing the range of skills that are taught. The problems in these jobs are far from being completely overcome, but the examples serve to illustrate a general problem.

It is all too easy to arrange jobs so that the requirements are incompatible. I was regularly asked to recruit engineers by one manager who insisted that candidates had 20 years' varied experience yet were aged between 25 and 30. Another trap can be to create dead-end jobs with no prospects of progression to anything else. This can't always be avoided, but the time to consider the possibility is when the job is first established. The problems of role contradictions in jobs have already been explained in the section on role behaviour in Chapter 3.

Individual motivation

In seeking to match individuals to jobs it is, of course, also necessary to examine the motivation of the individual. The motivation of individuals will vary. Different factors will affect different people in different ways. Additionally the motivation of any one individual is likely to vary in accordance with their personal circumstances and the situation they are in. One useful framework for examining the motivation of the individual is that provided by A. H. Maslow.[3] He argued that man's behaviour is centred on a series of needs arranged in a hierarchy. Satisfaction of needs at one level leads to attempts to satisfy needs at the next level up the hierarchy as shown in Figure 6.2.

The hierarchy is like a ladder — people need to start at the bottom rung and satisfy their basic needs, such as hunger, before moving up to the next rung to achieve safety. The third rung consists of social needs such as friendship, followed by status needs, and finally at the top of the pyramid the opportunity for self-development. The theory is that people proceed up the ladder rather like a donkey with a carrot in front of it. What is likely to motivate a person at a given time is the factor that is just within reach. If lower level needs are threatened, people would redirect themselves to securing those needs before resuming any pursuit of higher level needs. There are in practice overlaps between the levels — the precise pattern would vary from one individual to another. Some people would be more prepared to trade off satisfaction at one level for satisfaction at another — for example, security for self-development. Others may have greater status needs than others. People would, of course, find themselves at different points along the hierarchy at different times. For example, a person with a large young family would be more concerned with meeting their basic needs than with the self-development he or she might seek when the children were independent. There would of course be class, cultural, regional and national differences. Not only will values vary from one part of the world to another but so will the level of attainable

Figure 6.2: Maslow's hierarchy of human needs

needs. Self-development may be a meaningless concept for much of the population of South America, but a potent motivating factor for professional-level employees in the developed Western countries.

If one accepts Maslow's line of argument, the next question is what is the practical value of his model of human needs? The answer to this is that it may help in the recurring problem of matching people to situations. One can examine what motivational factors exist in a particular job, or the factors that can be built into it, and then consider what sort of person should be selected for the job. This may mean in Western society that one should strive to see that there are opportunities for self-development in work situations. However, that will not help if a person is more concerned with lower level needs. A practical example of how an understanding of Maslow's theory may help concerns the recruitment of women, or for that matter men, with considerable domestic commitments. It may be that, whilst they have these domestic commitments, they prefer not to be too stretched in their jobs and that their needs at work may be more orientated around financial considerations and the desire for social contact. When the domestic commitments cease, they may then, of course, wish to proceed up the 'ladder' and seek opportunities for self-development. The extent to which individuals wish to self-actualise may depend on their 'need to achieve' according to McClelland.[4] He suggests that this can be a very powerful motivating force which appears to be derived from social conditioning during childhood.

Job motivators and job dissatisfiers

Further research which complements the work of Maslow is that undertaken by Frederick Herzberg.[5] He conducted an investigation into the reasons given by engineers and accountants in America for what satisfied them and what dissatisfied them in their jobs. What emerged was that the survey group identified two different sets of factors — one which could cause positive feelings about the job and one which could cause negative feelings. Care obviously needs to be taken not to over-generalise from the subjective responses of a group of professional workers in America, but Herzberg's work does throw up some very useful concepts concerning the practical application of motivational theory. One of these concepts is the distinction between job context and job content. The American survey group, when identifying factors which had caused them to feel dissatisfied about their jobs, mainly referred to matters that were external to the basic job structure. The main items in this set of 'dissatisfiers' were: company policy and administration, supervision, interpersonal relations, status, salary, security and the impact of the job on personal life. The absence of dissatisfaction on these counts was not enough to cause positive feelings about the job. Consequently Herzberg referred to the set of factors likely to cause dissatisfaction in jobs as 'hygiene factors'. They operate in rather the same way as having the wrong room temperature. If it is very hot or very cold in a room that can cause profound dissatisfaction. If the temperature is ideal that does not particularly induce positive feelings about anything. For that to happen in a job people need to find an outlet for their creative energies and, in Herzberg's terminology, to be able to achieve 'self-actualisation'. Six main motivating factors were identified: achievement, recognition of achievement, responsibility, advancement, interesting work and the possibility of growth. Thus positive feelings about the job could only be accomplished if the job content was appropriate for the individual concerned.

The people in the survey group appeared to prefer to be a little 'stretched' in their work and through being 'stretched' found that they developed as individuals. The hygiene factors needed to be right so that people were not distracted from getting on with the job. If people had insufficient salary that could expose a need that was not being met lower down Maslow's hierarchy. A low salary could prevent a person from taking or staying in a job but appeared to do relatively little in the way of creating long-term positive feelings about a job. Similarly company policies needed to be such as to facilitate people getting on with the job and not to frustrate them from doing so. The issue of 'fairness' also emerged amongst the set of dissatisfiers. Employees could have strong feelings of injustice if they felt, for example, that company policy was 'unfair'. Equitable treatment did not, however, cause strong positive feelings about the job.

The practical implications of Herzberg's work are considerable. The basic message is: don't ignore the hygiene factors but don't stop there. People may want considerable involvement in their jobs for their own self-development. Employers may find that this is a considerable source of energy that is available. The ignoring of this source of energy may lead to trouble. Frustrated workers may not only be poor workers but may engage in destructive activity. Examples I have been given of 'the devil finding work for idle hands' include public corporation employees in Britain ringing up the next room via Hong Kong — to see if it can be done — and airline pilots allegedly competing to see who could land nearest to the *far* end of the runway. I have often taken the opportunity to check out Herzberg's basic approach with managerial groups in Britain and Indonesia. The use of a crude survey using his basic approach has, I have found, invariably produced similar responses. For example, the Indonesian captain of an oil tanker said that his most positive feelings about his job were after he had successfully, and very skilfully, navigated his ship through a typhoon off Hong Kong in which many ships had sunk. His most negative feelings about the job occurred shortly afterwards when the ship's agent carefully checked all the damage to the ship and neglected to inquire or comment about the risks that had been experienced by the captain and crew! This particular example illustrates that the dividing line between situations which can lead to strong negative and strong positive feelings about the job can in some cases be very fine. If a person has a job that they can just accomplish that may be fine — but if it is just that little bit too hard for the individual concerned, he may experience failure and the feelings or consequences that go with it. Also credit and recognition need to be based on real achievement. Positive feelings are likely to stem from the reality of achievement, with the credit of achievement being rather like the icing on a cake. The withholding of credit can, of course, lead to negative feelings and the giving of credit and recognition where there has been no real achievement can be rather meaningless.

Perhaps more care has to be taken in generalising from one social group to another than in applying Herzberg's research to professional groups in different countries. There has also been some criticism of Herzberg's research because of his heavy reliance on the 'critical incident technique'. Nevertheless, one can see that the most important thing for a manager to do with his subordinates may be to set up their work, if he can, so that it provides a challenge and then help to see that the challenge is met. Excessive help may be quite counterproductive. The human relations skills of the manager may be relatively unimportant compared with the challenge of a job — at least as far as positive motivation is concerned. Perhaps the main pay-off with human relations skills is the avoidance of upsetting employees rather than the achievement of positive motivation. The control of the manager over job content will vary, but that is an area that obviously merits the closest attention as far as the motivation of subordinates is concerned. In some cases it will be one of the few areas that the manager can actually control. He may find that many of the 'hygiene factors' such as salary level, working conditions and company policy are not within his control. To some extent, however, his pattern of delegation will be. There are obviously selection implications — it is possible to engage a person who is too good for a job, just as it is possible to choose a person who does not have the necessary capability. This mistake is often made, for example, by organisations who recruit over-qualified people for status reasons. Another way in which this type of mistake can be made is to pay high wages as a means of attracting and retaining people in boring jobs. The problem is that the higher the wage the greater may be the ability of the person who is attracted to a job and consequently the greater his frustration if the work is boring. One of the problems for the prospective employee is that it is often much easier to judge the job context — for example the salary, fringe benefits and working conditions — than the often more elusive factors such as independence within the job. Consequently the prospective employee may only find out after he has started in a job that it lacks positive motivational features.

Work structuring

A further implication of the work of Frederick Herzberg is that jobs need to be consciously structured so that they take account of the motivational needs of employees. Ideally the employee and job are matched so that the individual meets his own motivational needs in achieving the requirements of the employer. This matching may be done before people are engaged, or through the alteration of existing jobs, or both. Terms that are used in this context are job enlargement, job enrichment and job rotation. Job enlargement is a generic term used to indicate a widening of the job, either by increasing the range of activities, or the level of responsibility, or both. Job enrichment is a more specific term indicating that the responsibility level of a job has been increased, either by altering the balance of responsibility within the job, or by adding a new level of responsibility, or both. Job rotation occurs when just the range of activities is increased, which may give the individuals concerned the opportunity to have increased work variety but without any increase in the level of responsibility. Work structuring or restructuring may require a considerable amount of sophisticated design effort, or it may, to some extent, be within the control of the immediate supervisor or manager. Thus in the engineering industry much of the structure of a job may be dictated by the capital equipment and plant layout. However, it may be within the control of a supervisor whether a person be allowed to set up the machines that he also has to operate. Progress has been slow in the car industry with attempts to enrich manual jobs — despite some noble attempts at Saab and Volvo in Sweden. The technological environment in electronics appears to offer a more promising opportunity for the enrichment of manual jobs, as Philips Industries and Texas Instruments in particular have demonstrated.

The implication for the individual manager is that he needs to ensure that the work of subordinates is structured, as far as possible, to take into account and capitalise on their motivational needs. The manager may need to consider the validity of his own assumptions about his subordinates, so that he neither overestimates nor underestimates their appetite for work and responsibility. The manager will also need to examine the extent to which the structure of his subordinates' jobs is within his control. One relatively easy way of getting advice about this is to ask the subordinates themselves. Often jobs cannot be changed but alterations that would be beneficial to all concerned are simply not realised. One approach which can be helpful is the practice adopted in the nursing profession of staff 'acting-up', so that subordinates assume the responsibilities of their immediate superior when the superior is away. If the subordinate staff can cope, this means that they at least get a measure of job enrichment when the boss is away. The reverse would happen if a policy of 'acting-down' was used. But extra responsibility does not always have to be at the expense of another job. Often there are tasks which could be undertaken or opportunities which could be exploited that would enrich a number of jobs simultaneously.

Matching individual needs and job demands

Consideration of the motivational match between individual and job is obviously something that needs to be carefully considered because of the potential gains to both individual and employer if the matching is optimised. However, just as it is important that this area be investigated, so it is necessary to recognise that, in some cases anyway, there will be constraints or problem areas. The technological constraints in engineering have already been discussed. In jobs such as that of an airline pilot, the required safety standards may dictate that you employ people whose capabilities are far in excess of what they will require for their normal duties. In other situations managers may assume that the ego-satisfactions that they get in their job are also experienced by their employees. This can easily happen in small businesses where the proprietor may almost completely identify himself with his business and assume that his employees do, or should do, the same. The point that he may miss is that, whilst he may be prepared to make many sacrifices for the business, he is the one who will reap most of the financial and psychological rewards if the business prospers.

The amount of involvement corresponding with the position in an organisation's hierarchy is not confined to working in small businesses that are managed by the proprietor. A documentary film about the financial problems of *The Observer* newspaper shown by the BBC revealed useful insights into the motivation of the journalists and print workers employed by the newspaper.[6] The journalists were much more co-operative with the employer about key issues than were the print workers. The journalists often seemed prepared to work for relatively low salaries, despite the financial hardship that this often gave their families, because of the psychological satisfaction they obtained from working for the paper. This co-operation with the employer extended to agreeing to a voluntary redundancy to help keep the paper going. A much more instrumental attitude was displayed by the various groups of manual workers, particularly about manning levels and redundancy. Manpower reductions were only achieved when the paper was on the brink of bankruptcy; later, when the paper was taken over by the American oil corporation, Atlantic Richfield (prior to the Lonrho take-over), there was strong pressure to restore the old manning levels. The point I wish to make is simply that, given the reduced opportunity for psychological satisfaction by the manual workers, who in the main were doing jobs that had become technologically de-skilled, it was hardly surprising that their involvement and co-operation were at a much lower level than was the case with journalists.

Another issue that needs to be faced is that the objectives of employer and employee do not always coincide. People may see many opportunities for self-development at work, but the employer is hardly going to welcome them if they do not coincide with his objectives. To complicate matters there may be important differences of perception about what is for the good of the organisation as a whole. It can be very tempting to assume that work which you find particularly interesting and developmental is bound to be of benefit to the employer. In some cases, though, employees may even find that the organisation of activities that are quite obviously against the employer's interests provide both psychological and material rewards. The adrenalin can run for a person perpetrating a fraud just as it can for the honest employee who develops himself in his employer's interests instead of by outwitting him.

It is also necessary to take into account the views of the expectancy school of motivational theorists. They emphasise that people are likely to respond positively to motivational stimuli only if they perceive that there is a realistic chance of obtaining a significant reward if they perform in a particular way. It follows that it is necessary to check to see that the reward system in an organisation actually works in the way that is intended. It is no good, for example, expecting to motivate people by offering incremental salary increases or promotion for meritorious performance, if the reality is that such rewards are based on seniority. Even if reward is based significantly on merit it is necessary to convince people of this as motivation is likely to depend on what people perceive happens, which isn't always the same as what actually happens. It is also necessary to review how equitably rewards are distributed as, even if people are inclined to respond to a particular incentive, they may be discouraged from doing so by perceived unfairness in the way in which rewards are allocated. The gap between intended and actual reward systems can be alarmingly high in the case of incentive payment schemes. As is explained in the section on these schemes in the next chapter, some can degenerate into arrangements where output is carefully restricted.

Job distortion

A further and increasing complication is that brought about by the high levels of unemployment. Employees may be increasingly frustrated in their jobs because of lack of promotion opportunities, lack of jobs elsewhere and 'over-selection'. This can lead to employees building their jobs up, both as a relief from boredom and as a means of obtaining an upgrading. If you take the case of a graduate recruited to do a routine clerical job, the graduate, although perhaps glad to have got employment, may rapidly get bored because of the lack of intellectual stimulation. Consequently the most interesting parts of the job may be expanded and as much as possible of the routine aspects ignored. This can lead to 'job distortion' as shown in Figure 6.3. The continuous lines represent the boundaries of the job that the organisation requires to be performed, whilst the broken lines represent the boundaries of the job as it actually is performed.

The problems that such distortion can create for the organisation were vividly illustrated to me by the behaviour of an office junior working in the post room of a local authority. Although the young man in the job had been doing it for five years, and

Figure 6.3: Job distortion

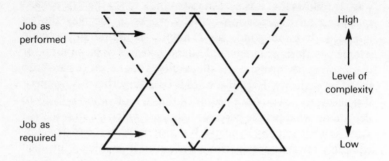

although there was not a significant increase in the volume of mail, the post kept on being distributed later and later in the day. As the officers in the directorate had meetings to attend and visits to make it became an increasingly common occurrence for them to have to wait a full day before being able to read their mail. An investigation revealed that the cause of the problem was the boredom of the office junior. As a counter to this, and the fact that he didn't have enough to do anyway, he had taken to actually reading the mail before distributing it. This coupled with excessively long refreshment breaks and much social chatter was a way of him spinning out the day — even though the effect on the directorate was to create a certain amount of chaos. An obvious solution was to move him into a more demanding job but unfortunately his reputation had become such that no-one else in the directorate wanted him. However, it was clear that it was quite wrong to let the job holder rot in a dead-end job and that somehow he had to be moved to another job. It was also clear that the job should be filled in future by a person for whom there was planned progression or by a person who would be content with such routine work — and even then thought had to be given as to what to do about the long periods of inactivity.

Other pressures which can lead to job distortion may arise because of the frustrated desire of job holders to obtain jobs they consider to be in line with their ability. This can clearly arise in the previously quoted example of the graduate doing routine clerical work. It can also happen with people who have 'outgrown' their existing job and find that they cannot easily progress. This can all too easily happen in the current economic climate as opportunities elsewhere may be limited and the person or people above a particular job holder may be similarly blocked from moving on. The solution for the individual caught in this trap may be to build the job up and, particularly if there is a formal job evaluation scheme, claim an upgrading. My own experience, as an arbitrator who often has to judge such grading issues, and that of colleagues — especially in the public sector — indicates that many job evaluation schemes are coming under severe pressure by claims for such upgradings. It is only sensible for employers to exploit any opportunities for job enrichment — especially if job holders are frustrated by the limitations of their current job. However, there is also the danger that poor supervisory control may lead to subordinates undertaking a wrong balance of work in order to engineer an upgrading that is not in line with organisational requirements.

OVER-INVOLVEMENT AND MANAGERIAL STRESS

It is also necessary to recognise that people have lives outside work and that this will, and indeed should, affect their aspirations at work. We have already noted that people with domestic commitments, such as single parents with young children, may want to restrict their job involvement until such time as those commitments are reduced. Such people may be particularly in need of social contact at work, so attempts at job enrichment and job rotation may be counterproductive. Job rotation may increase the work variety, changing one boring job for another, but it may break up the very social contact that an employee may value.

The achievement of an appropriate balance between work and other activities is an issue that needs to be considered by all employees, including managers, and not just single parents with small children. The total immersion of a person in his job may not be best for him or his employer. This is not to suggest that it is a bad thing for people to be involved in their work, far from it; rather that, as in most things, the problem is finding the appropriate balance. The dangers to the employer of having a 'workaholic' are that he may be difficult to replace when the time comes, he may damage his health, and he may lose the sense of perspective and good judgement that comes from having other interests as a counterbalance. The workaholic needs to ask just what risks he is running and just why he is so involved in his work. The risks include just what he does when he retires or if he is made redundant. In an age when unemployment is sadly likely to remain at a chronically high level, people are often going to be forced to seek their developmental needs outside work — either because they cannot get a job, or because they cannot get one that is sufficiently demanding.

Increasing attention is now being given to the dangers of managerial stress. Stress may be caused by the problems inherent in a particular job, or the mismatch between the abilities of an individual and the requirements of a job, or a combination of the two. The consequent work style may generate an excessive flow of adrenalin within the body, dependence on physical stimulants such as nicotine and alcohol, and thus prevent an individual from having an appropriate diet and sufficient physical exercise and rest. A sobering and relevant statistic is that established by McClelland in a 20-year follow-up study of Harvard graduates who had scored high on the need for power; 58 per cent were found to have high blood pressure or have died from heart failure.[7] Individuals can hardly be expected to change their personalities so that their basic responses to situations are altered, but they can at least try and move out of or change a situation if that is the source of unacceptable levels of stress. If the stress is self-induced it is perhaps just as well to face up to the medical implications in case there is any scope for personal adjustment. It is also hoped that the content of this book will give useful ideas to readers on how situations may be changed or handled more effectively so that stress is reduced.

Having sounded a cautionary note about the dangers of over-involvement in the job — a point rarely made in connection with motivational theory — it is necessary to restate that the main problem is that of under-involvement. It is as well, too, to remember that people tend to live up to, or down to, the expectations that are made of them. In matching people to jobs, managers need also to bear in mind that both sides of this equation can and do change. People can, for example, develop, so that the work that stretched them historically has now become boring. Jobs too can change, for example because of technological change. The attempt to match people and jobs is a continuous process that needs to be linked to appropriate remuneration. Sometimes remuneration can be used as a direct financial incentive as well as a means of attracting people into jobs. The use of financial incentives to increase performance may be used as well as, or instead of, the more psychological approaches that have been explained so far. Financial incentive schemes can be an appropriate way of motivating people, a regrettable necessity or a downright menace, and it is to a consideration of these issues that we will now turn in the next chapter.

NOTES

1. W. E. J. McCarthy and S. R. Parker, 'Shop stewards and work-shop relations', Royal Commission Research Paper No. 10 (1968), paras 175–8.
2. National Economic Development Office, *Large industrial sites* (HMSO, 1970), p. 13, table 1, para 73; and p. 23.
3. A. H. Maslow, *Motivation and personality* (Harper & Row, 1970), second edition.
4. D. C. McClelland, *The achieving society* (Van Nostrand, 1961).
5. F. Herzberg, B. Mausner and B. Synderman, *The motivation to work* (Wiley, New York, 1960).
6. Film, *Crisis at* The Observer, BBC Film Enterprises (1975).
7. D. C. McClelland, *Power: the inner experience* (Irvington, New York, 1975).

7

Payment Systems

INTRODUCTION

Having considered the relevance of various behavioural theories to motivation it is now necessary to look more explicitly at the role of money as a motivator. The advantages and disadvantages of financial incentive schemes are therefore considered in this chapter. The issue of internal relativities is also examined and the way in which job evaluation may assist in establishing and maintaining a rational pay structure. The various types of scheme are explained and the ways in which schemes need to be chosen, operated and maintained if they are to be effective. Finally consideration is given to the considerable impact that the equal value regulations may have on pay structures.

FINANCIAL INCENTIVES

Probably the ideal arrangement for most jobs is that people have an interesting job, good supervision and an appropriate basic wage or salary. If the theories of Maslow and Herzberg mean anything at all, that arrangement should lead to effective work performance and satisfied employees. However, the achievement of such a happy state of affairs is, needless to say, not always possible. It is particularly when this cannot be achieved that financial incentives may be appropriate, but it is most important for managers to ensure that their diagnosis is correct before they try to improve work performance by the use of financial incentives.

Diagnosis of need

As has previously been explained, problems of work performance may be due to factors outside the control of the worker.
Even when it would seem that employees could increase output
by reasonable increases in effort, it is necessary to ask why the
effort is not forthcoming. The structure of jobs and the matching of individuals to jobs should be examined. If poor performance is because of poor supervision, it may be that it is the
supervision that should be changed and not the arrangements
for payment. It is particularly necessary to check this, as the
long-term effect of incentive schemes can be to diminish the role
of the supervisor. Employees operating under incentive schemes
may see themselves as akin to independent subcontractors with
the supervisor as an external figure who is likely to come into
conflict with them over a host of issues concerning the operation
of the incentive scheme. This can lead to the exclusion of the
supervisor from the work group, because of attempts by him to
monitor schemes in the interest of the employer rather than of
the employee. Alternatively the supervisor may be 'captured' by
the work group so that he does not, for example, report on
manipulations to the incentive scheme, or show excessive concern about safety and quality standards. Unfortunately either of
these developments can lead to the continued erosion of the
supervisor — perhaps to the extent that happened in the docks in
Britain where the 'ganger' came to be seen as the representative
of the dockers rather than of the employer.

Appropriate conditions

However, there are jobs in which the 'ideal arrangements'
previously identified will simply not always be attainable. There
will, for example, be situations when the structure of jobs is such
that they are inherently boring and that, in the short term at
least, output will be best achieved by the use of financial
incentive schemes. When I was employed at a factory making
diesel engines, I had to recognise that in the large machine shop
the withdrawal of the incentive scheme would have had a catastrophic effect on production, despite all the problems that it
created. The circumstances under which Payment by Results
schemes might be appropriate are identified in a checklist drawn

111

up by the National Board for Prices and Incomes as part of one of their investigations.[1] The four necessary conditions for the introduction of Payment by Results were stated to be where:

1. The work can be measured and directly attributed to the individual or group; in practice this generally means highly repetitive manual work — as found in mass production manufacturing.
2. The pace of work is substantially controlled by the worker rather than by the machine or process he is tending.
3. Management is capable of maintaining a steady flow of work.
4. The tasks are not subjected to frequent changes in method, materials or equipment.

Even under these conditions and with proper monitoring the NBPI commented on the inevitable slackening that occurs in schemes because of factors such as technological change. They found that, even under ideal conditions, there is likely to be an unavoidable wholly unproductive wage drift of at least one per cent a year.[2] It is to be regretted that there are so few independent studies of the effects of incentive schemes to warn employers of the ways in which they can be counterproductive. Much of the literature is either in textbooks explaining how schemes are supposed to operate or in literature provided by consultants who make their money in selling and installing incentive packages.

Long-term effects

Proposals for introducing incentive schemes and their short-term benefits can seem very convincing. However, managers need carefully to review their diagnosis of the real reasons for poor performance and the possible long-term effects of incentive schemes before committing themselves to this route to higher output. Figure 7.1 shows what can happen in the short and long term if, for example, a Payment by Results Scheme is introduced.

Output may well increase by about a third after the introduction of a scheme, with earnings going up in relation to output. However, as time goes on, even in relatively static production situations, there are likely to be improvements in work methods

Figure 7.1: The long-term pattern of incentive schemes

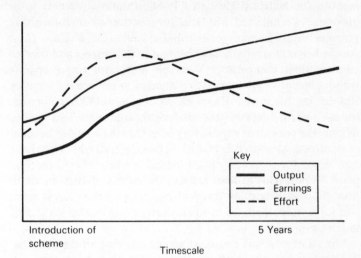

Key

———— Output
———— Earnings
– – – Effort

Introduction of
scheme

5 Years

Timescale

that are not entirely clawed back by the employer in terms of consequential reductions in time allowances. There may also be errors in initial time allowances and employees can be remarkably ingenious in manipulating schemes to their advantage. The most sophisticated manipulations involve 'capturing' the supervisor and other potential 'enemies' so that the higher levels of management are not aware that ultimately effort may decline whilst output and earnings increase. Schemes can degenerate to such an extent that they actually become arrangements for restricting production — for fear that, if normal effort is resumed, the output achieved would give the whole game away. The erosion of the position of the supervisor that may accompany these developments may facilitate, or be because of, the rise of shop steward influence.

The connection between these developments may not be seen, but I would suggest that this was one of the reasons for the ferocity of much of the industrial action in the British Winter of Discontent in 1978–9. In the 1960s, when labour was in short supply, financial incentive schemes were widely introduced for manual workers employed in the hospital service and by local authorities. The use of the schemes, for example for hospital porters and local authority transport maintenance workers, hardly seems to comply with the situations in the previously

113

quoted NBPI checklist. The strength of the shop steward movement in the National Union of Public Employees seems to be inextricably connected with the introduction of such incentive schemes. Management at British Leyland's car division (now Austin Rover) eventually saw the light in this respect and tried to emulate their competitors Vauxhall and Ford's and operate without incentive schemes. Their attempt to replace Payment by Results by Measured Daywork in the late 1970s collapsed, though, partly because the piecework traditions had helped destroy the control at supervisory level that they needed in order to operate a Measured Daywork Scheme effectively. They have now opted for a plant by plant incentive scheme based on total plant output. This at least reduces the points of friction about time allowances and job comparisons between the shop steward and supervisor which led to so much strife and uneven wage drift in the past.

The point that it is necessary to stress is that all the potential disadvantages of incentive schemes need to be taken into account before they are adopted. The trouble is that the short-term tangible benefits may be much more obvious than many of the long-term intangible, but nevertheless important, consequences. A policy of choosing 'horses for courses' is appropriate rather than any dogmatic assertion that one should always use incentive schemes or never use them. Despite the masterly exposition of the disadvantages of piecework given in Wilfred (later Lord) Brown's book *Piecework abandoned*,[3] piecework was subsequently reintroduced at the Glacier Metal Company. The matching of pay arrangements to situations can, however, be ill-conceived. One example concerns the failure to take account of the change in technology when the continuous steel strip mill at Port Talbot came into full production in the 1950s. Many small steel works were closed down where group incentive schemes were traditional and very appropriate. The conditions specified in the NBPI checklist were met and the group nature of much of the production work meant that group incentive schemes were appropriate rather than individual schemes. Group bonuses under those conditions were one thing, but the introduction of a tonnage bonus for production workers, based on total mill output, at Port Talbot was different.

Production was no longer controlled directly by the men and the group now consisted of all the production workers. Ironically they often had to work harder when the process was not working satisfactorily than when it was running smoothly. To complicate matters further the forecasts of production were too low and the production workers therefore received very high wages which infuriated the maintenance men who felt that it was their skills which now made the critical contribution to production. Once the incentive scheme was installed, however, it was not easy to withdraw and the discontent that it created rumbled on for years.

Group schemes

Apart from making the point that payment schemes need to fit with the technology, the steel example also brings out the point that the size of the work group also needs to be considered. Group schemes seem to work best when the group is no bigger than eight and the task is inherently a group rather than an individual task. If a plant-wide scheme is used, the relationship between individual effort and reward may be too small for there to be any significant causal relationship between the effort of the individual and overall output. Individual earnings may move in parallel with total output but that does not prove that people are working harder because of a group incentive scheme. Employees may perceive that their earnings will be very much the same, however hard or however little they work. They may also perceive that many factors other than their effort, or even the effort of them and their fellow workers, may affect total output, for example workflow and technological change. Much the same comments can be made about cost-reduction production programmes or profit-sharing arrangements. A fallacy about profit-sharing is that it is often assumed that, once an employee has a shareholder role, he will forget about his far more important wage-earner role and simply behave in the best interests of the shareholders. It is when 'weights' are attached to these two roles that it becomes apparent that any link between group performance and group profits may not actually be caused by a profit-sharing incentive. Employees may behave in such a way that they protect their wage-earner role and subordinate any shareholder interests to this much greater primary role. Variations in profits may in fact have little to do with the supposed motivating effect of a profit-sharing scheme.

The importance of careful thought about the appropriate

arrangements for paying employees is not confined to groups of manual workers. It has recently come to be appreciated that the method of paying dentists in Britain — based on physical services provided — may have discouraged attention being given to advice about dental hygiene. This has led to financial incentives now being offered for dentists to employ dental hygienists. The ramifications of incentive schemes are such that considerable thought has to be given, not only as to whether they should be used or not, but also as to how they should be managed if they are used. A former colleague found that at power station construction sites incentive schemes were sadly often seen as a soft option to enable the engineers to get back to their 'real job' of engineering. The fact is that, if incentive schemes are used, they may require just as much, or even more, managerial effort, to see that they are effective, compared with the managerial effort involved when people are paid just a basic wage or salary.

JOB EVALUATION

Another aspect of remuneration that needs careful consideration is that of internal relativities. Even if employees are paid well in comparison with similar work in other organisations there can often be acute discontent about perceived internal inequities. Every organisation needs to have some sort of policy with regard to its own wage and salary structure. One way of establishing a pay structure is by use of the techniques of job evaluation. This is very often the way in which the salaries for white-collar employees are established. Pay for manual employees is more usually determined by traditional methods of negotiation, as explained in Chapter 12. An outline is given in this section of the different types of job evaluation schemes and of their advantages and disadvantages. Particular attention is given to some of the practical snags that are often overlooked in expositions of how such schemes are supposed to work as opposed to the way they may work in practice.

Objectives

The overall objective of job evaluation schemes can be described as assisting in providing a cost-effective pay structure. Sometimes pay structures seem to have a life and direction all of their own but they should be synchronised with other organisational processes such as manpower planning and budgetary control. Such integration is necessary if overall organisational objectives are to be achieved. Few people would argue that the process of job evaluation is scientific — it is essentially a systematic way of making a series of judgements about pay. The elimination of all discontent about pay being an impossible target, the value of job evaluation is that it may enable pay relativities to be established in such a way that discontent is less than if job evaluation was not used. Job evaluation should also provide a basis for comparing an organisation's pay structure with the external labour market.

Types of schemes

A basic distinction between the various types of schemes is between the analytical and the non-analytical ones. Examples of the latter are the Job Classification, Job Ranking and Paired Comparisons. With Job Classification, jobs are looked at as a whole and then grouped into families to which a grade is allocated (as in the Civil Service). Definitions are sometimes given of the basic characteristics of a classification or grade to judge where particular jobs should go. With Job Ranking, jobs are arranged in a hierarchy and the vertical rank order can be split up into various job grades. The technique of Paired Comparisons is a more sophisticated way of arriving at a rank order. It involves comparing each job with every other job to identify the correct rank order. The basic feature of all three of these non-analytical approaches is that the ultimate grading is achieved by comparison with other jobs rather than by systematically identifying the component elements in each job.

The main analytical schemes are Points Rating and many of the proprietary schemes offered by consultancy organisations. Points Rating involves identifying the common factors in jobs and then allocating points to these factors according to the specific demands in each job. The points allocation, or weight, for each factor is established after systematic internal discussion about the relative importance of the factor to the organisation. Each factor in a job is then assessed and a total points score for

117

the job obtained. The total points score indicates what job grade is appropriate. The proprietary schemes are often sophisticated versions of this points rating approach.

Choice of scheme

The dilemma for the individual employers is what, if any, scheme to adopt. No one scheme, or approach, is superior to all others, it is basically a question of choosing 'horses for courses' and then operating whatever scheme is chosen in a sensible manner. However refined and sophisticated schemes may appear to be it must always be remembered that any statistical calculation is erected on a basis of subjective judgements of, for example, what factors should be chosen and what weights they should be given. Consequently one should beware of spurious accuracy and of claims that everything is near perfect because ratings are very consistent. Ratings may be consistent in applying a scheme but as schemes rest on subjective judgements this can lead to consistent error. One ingenious personnel officer, bewildered by the rival claims of competing consultants, found the easiest way of finding out the weaknesses of proprietary schemes was to invite comment from rival consultants!

The costs of installing and maintaining a scheme also need to be considered. The more sophisticated the scheme the greater such costs are likely to be. Another critical cost is the uplift in pay that usually results from the introduction of a scheme. Job evaluation is unlikely to leave the existing pay structure undisturbed and the holders of jobs that are downgraded normally have their own salary protected. Consequently an immediate effect of job evaluation is that as no-one has less pay and some will get more pay the total wage and salary bill will increase. A rule of thumb for major restructuring exercises is that such an uplift will be in the order of three per cent of the total pay bill.

Another factor is the size of the organisation or sector of it that is to be studied. The investment in a costly scheme for a small group of employees may simply be too expensive. The ranking and paired comparison methods however may prove difficult to apply in large organisations because the number of jobs that need ordering and comparing is simply too great.

A factor that should not be, but often is, ignored is the expected rate of change in an organisation. A cautionary tale in this respect was given to me by a personnel officer who had been at an engineering company where a scheme had been installed at great expense only to become obsolete within four months because of the rapidity of technical and organisational change. Job evaluation schemes are usually introduced on the assumption that the organisational arrangements are fixed. However, the pace of change is such now that one has to ask the question of all schemes how well they would cope with projected change. There is not much point in having an expensive sophisticated scheme that is soon going to be out of date. This question also needs asking in a slightly modified form of existing schemes. It may be that existing schemes, which may historically have been sound, have fallen into decay through not being adjusted, or not being capable of adjustment, in line with organisational change.

Implementation and operation

Basic issues which need consideration involve whether a scheme should cover the whole of an organisation or just part of it and trade union involvement. Whilst it may seem convenient and fair to have one scheme for the whole of an organisation this is not always practicable. There can be so little in common between, for example, manual, technical and managerial grades that one may have to develop different schemes so that the jobs being compared and evaluated have a reasonable amount in common. There is not much point in having an overall scheme that seeks to assess a managing director's job in terms of factors such as physical strength and monotony and boredom! However, a counter-argument that has emerged in favour of schemes covering all employees is that it may help in defending cases brought under the equal value regulations where comparisons are made between different parts of an employer's pay structure (the regulations are explained later in this chapter).

Trade unions are likely to take more than a passing interest in job evaluation and their involvement in schemes has to be considered. They are likely to see job evaluation as a framework for bargaining. In any case, regardless of whether there is a trade union or not, one needs to consider the issue of employee involvement. If schemes are supposed to incorporate internal views about equity and fairness there needs to be some mechanism for taking employees' views into account with regard to the design and operation of schemes. Also if anyone ever did design a perfect system representatives would still feel obliged to bargain about the matter, as what trade union could countenance being told it had no bargaining role? The state of the art though is such that unions rightly query the basis on which schemes are based and the results they give. Unions may have to distance themselves a little from schemes however as otherwise they may be seen as implementing managerial pay policies. Once a scheme has been established they tend to acknowledge it and to retain and use the right to represent any individual who feels that he has a case for upgrading. Irrespective of whether or not there is union involvement in a scheme, or even union recognition, some sort of appeals mechanism is necessary. Appeals criteria need to be specified, such as a change in duties, and appeals bodies established. These may be managerial panels, joint management-union panels or involve the use of an outside arbitrator — either sitting alone or chairing a joint panel.

There is a range of other operational issues that need careful attention. One of the basic issues is to remember that it is the job that is being evaluated and not the person. If a job holder has 'outgrown' a job the real answer is for him to be encouraged to seek promotion rather than to distort the pay structure by giving an upgrading that temporarily meets his needs but not the organisation's. One must also beware of the danger, explained in the previous chapter, that employees may distort a job to justify an upgrading. In contrast, if a person is not up to a job, it can sometimes be that this is because the job is not graded highly enough to attract people of the right calibre.

Factors have to be chosen carefully so that they don't overlap. Otherwise a job holder can benefit twice under such factors such as 'job complexity' and 'education required', which may be different ways of measuring the same requirement. Another complication can arise from the establishment of 'weights' for factors. Apart from the judgemental problems of doing this anyway, there is the statistical problem that the real 'weights' depend not just on, for example, the points allocated for a particular factor, but also on the extent to which those making judgements use the full extent of the scale. There was once an attempt to introduce a new scheme for nursing officers in the Health Service. It rapidly became apparent that for some jobs the only factors on which the scores differed were those related to the size of the unit in which a person was employed. The reality was that in practice the scheme for some jobs was based on a single factor — the one that was easiest to measure! A further explanation of these statistical problems is given in the section on recording and rating in Chapter 10.

There can be misconceptions about the extent to which employees can be expected to change their duties without receiving any extra remuneration. Changes in the range of work at a given level do not normally constitute a case for upgrading. Work at a higher level of responsibility may provide a valid basis for upgrading, but even in this case it has to be remembered that job grades normally embrace a range of jobs and a person's increase in, for example, responsibility level may not be sufficient to lift him into the next grade. There is a common law requirement for employees to accept reasonable changes in job content and the prudent employer will reinforce this by the use of generic job titles and a flexibility clause in any job description.

Claims for upgrading can also be made on what may turn out to be basic job requirements rather than additional demands. Schemes need to be operated on the basis that there are minimum performance requirements which justify retention in a given job as opposed to justifying an upgrading. However, one cannot but admire the ingenuity with which some cases are argued. One fork-lift truck driver applied for an upgrading at an oil refinery. His case rested on his responsibility for expensive plant and equipment as evidenced by the fact that he had recently fractured a fuel line and caused a fire causing over a million pounds worth of damage! Another such case involved a telephonist/receptionist who was asked to elaborate on the decision-making elements in her job — which consisted mainly of routing telephone calls and visitors. She beamed and said she had to decide whether to come in each day or not! The argument advanced was that she had to decide if she was fit enough for work or not as if she wasn't it would be bad for the external image of the firm.

A crucial issue in establishing the grading of any job is its effect on the overall equilibrium of the pay structure. Serious inequities obviously should be corrected but not unsubstantial cases for locating jobs in a higher grade. The key issue is not the extra direct costs this would involve but the 'knock-on' effect. The danger is that by solving one person's perceived (but

121

imagined) grievance you can create a host of repercussive claims. Another key issue concerns the relationship of pay to the external job market. It is no good having a scheme that is out of line with the market. However, markets don't always operate so clearly and systematically that you can dispense with job evaluation. In making comparisons with pay in other organisations care has to be taken to ensure that you are comparing like with like. The use of job titles alone may be dangerous as a term such as 'fitter' can cover an enormous range of different jobs in terms of actual duties and responsibility level. Sometimes there can be a marked conflict between internal relativities and the market rate for particular groups, such as computer staff, for whom there is a strong demand. The realistic answer in cases like this is not to have a spurious re-evaluation of the staff concerned but to openly recognise and deal with the problem. It may be necessary to pay a market supplement for such staff or even take them out of the evaluation scheme altogether. This way at least the rest of the pay structure can remain consistent.

A further issue concerns the transferability of evaluation schemes to different organisations, countries and cultures. It can be tempting to do this as it may seem a short cut to copy someone else's scheme or use one's own in an overseas subsidiary. The usual rationale for job evaluation schemes is that they reflect the attitudes within an organisation as to what is a fair set of relativities. However, the attitudes towards what is fair may be quite different in an organisation or country in which there is a different set of values. Consequently such transfer of schemes may be an extremely 'hit and miss' affair.

Equal pay for work of equal value

As if the complexity above were not enough, there has been one recent development in the UK which may turn out to be a potential time bomb beneath many pay structures — whether or not they are established by job evaluation. This concerns the legal right of employees not to be discriminated against in terms of pay and conditions on grounds of sex if their work is of equal value with someone of the opposite sex in the same organisation. This is a consequence of the UK Government being obliged to comply with the requirements of the Treaty of Rome. Previously, under the Equal Pay Act of 1970 there was a limited right to equal pay but just for equal work or broadly similar work, or for work rated as equivalent under a job evaluation scheme. This was not enough to prevent the European Commission successfully bringing an action against the UK Government in 1982, requiring it to comply with the relevant requirements of the Treaty of Rome and in particular with the Equal Pay Directive of 1975. Consequently the Equal Pay Act of 1970 has been amended to enable claims for work of equal value to be made, with effect from 1st January 1984. The Industrial Tribunal regulations have also been amended to establish a special procedure for processing these claims.

The new statutory right provides a right to equal pay where the job demands are the same in categories such as 'effort, skill and decision-making'. This implies a need for some sort of analytical job evaluation if the employer is to try and defend his position. Unless the tribunal decides that there are no reasonable grounds for the claim, and if the parties fail to reach an agreement, an independent expert will then be called in. The expert will report on whether or not the jobs that the claimant claims are of equal value are so. The tribunal subsequently decides in the light of the expert's report. All this may sound rather convoluted and specialised but the crunch comes when an individual claim succeeds. This may reveal that there is the basis for further claims and if any of these succeed the process may continue. The 'knock-on' effect can lead to the undermining of the whole of an existing pay structure.[4] It remains to be seen how narrowly or widely this law will be interpreted and the extent to which 'genuine material factor' defences — particularly market forces — will be allowed but it is necessary to emphasise again how subjective schemes inevitably are. They all involve making judgements about how dissimilar factors or whole jobs should relate to one another. People sometimes think that the use of sophisticated statistical techniques enables objective decisions to be made. However, what such techniques do is to provide elaborate means of establishing *opinions* about job relationships. Consequently an independent expert may well have a different view about job relationships from those who established a particular pay structure. This is particularly likely if the existing pay structure reflects, for example, traditional attitudes by a male majority about the value of jobs usually performed by women.[5, 6]

General issues concerning job evaluation

Job evaluation can be a complex business because the whole issue of pay structures can itself be complicated as well as being sensitive and of key importance. The issues won't go away if ignored and job evaluation can be a framework within which these issues are tackled. One of the advantages is that even if individuals don't always agree with the results they can at least see that the employer has tried to resolve pay issues in a fair and systematic way. As all schemes are inherently subjective there may be a premium on having schemes as simple as possible, particularly bearing in mind the pace of change and appeal load that schemes can generate.[7] The equal value requirements are a pressure for some sort of analytical scheme where there may be discrimination in the pay structure. The existence of an analytical scheme won't however automatically protect employers from claims of sex discrimination. The evidence is that allegations of sex discrimination are also increasingly featuring in pay negotiations, so it is not just an issue left to legal processes.[8] A particularly important example of this was the national agreement concerning the pay of local authority manual workers, concluded in 1987. This pay agreement involved the systematic evaluation of jobs, covering one million employees, and the restructuring of the previous arrangements in an attempt to eliminate discrimination. One also has to consider the whole question of motivation in terms of the acceptability of internal relativities. There is no way in which discontent about pay can be eliminated, but job evaluation may provide a framework for minimising discontent and integrating the pay structure with general organisational objectives.

CONCLUSION

Just as in other areas of managerial activity, the effective motivation of employees is likely to depend on patient intellectual effort on the part of the manager. It can be very tempting to pretend that poor performance is all the fault of employees. Saying that doesn't automatically make it true. The use of financial incentive schemes may help in motivating employees, but that also requires patient diagnostic work. Incentive schemes are not always appropriate and, even when they are, the right

124

one has to be chosen. Schemes also have to be monitored very carefully if they are to remain effective. Issues of remuneration have to be looked at collectively as well as individually. Even if employees are well paid in relation to the external market they may bitterly resent perceived internal injustices. Job evaluation can help reduce the level of discontent — but schemes have to be carefully chosen, operated and monitored. The basis of schemes is inherently subjective, which is one reason why the new legal right to claim equal pay for work of equal value may cause significant and continuing change in pay structures.

NOTES

1. National Board for Prices and Incomes, *Payment by results systems*, Report No. 65, Cmnd. 3627 (HMSO, 1968), p. 11 of pamphlet summarising the above report.
2. Statistical supplement to *Payment by results* report (above), p. 50, para 22.
3. Wilfred Brown, *Piecework abandoned: the effect of wage incentive systems on managerial authority* (Heinemann, 1962).
4. For a further account of the implications for pay structures, see David Wainright, 'Equal value in action: the lessons from Laird's', *Personnel Management* (January 1985), pp. 18–21.
5. For a further account of the new regulations and their likely impact, see Deirdre Gill and Bernard Ungerson, *Equal pay: the challenge of equal value* (Institute of Personnel Management, 1984).
6. See also *Equal opportunities: job evaluation schemes free of sex bias* (revised edition, 1985), and *Equal pay for work of equal value* (1984), both published by the Equal Opportunities Commission.
7. For an excellent account of the strengths and weaknesses of the various job evaluation schemes, which may help with the development of rational pay structures, see *Job evaluation review* (Incomes Data Services, Top Pay Unit, 2nd edn, 1986).
8. David Turner, 'Equal value as a bargaining lever', *Personnel Management* (June 1986), pp. 38–41.

8

Communication

INTRODUCTION

This chapter is probably the most important in the whole book. It starts with an explanation of why communication is such an important topic. The barriers to communication are examined. This is followed by a detailed consideration of the skills that the manager requires, particularly that of effective listening. The emphasis in the earlier part of the chapter is on oral communication, but attention is given later to the need for, and skills involved in, effective written communication. There is also a section on the problems involved in evaluating information and views presented by television. As well as standing in its own right, the chapter also serves as a foundation for much of the material in the remainder of the book.

THE IMPORTANCE OF COMMUNICATION

Managers are likely to spend most of their time engaged directly in some form of communication process. Even when they are working alone — for example, studying or preparing reports — they are relying on other people's attempts to communicate with them or they are preparing to communicate with others. Accuracy in decision-making depends, in particular, on effective communication. If the communication process is faulty then everything else can be affected.

Experiments, research and sheer personal observation show that most people are far too optimistic about the accuracy of the communication process. This applies not just to communication processes within employing organisations but to life in general. Even when errors are identified this may be too late, or the inherent faults in the process that will lead to further errors may not be recognised. The barriers to effective communication are far greater than most people realise. The effective communication of factual information can be difficult enough, but often attitudes and feelings need to be communicated and that can be far more complicated. The number and nature of the barriers are such that there is a strong case for communication skills training being given as part of the standard school curriculum. This is not yet the case and in this chapter the attempt is made to give managers practical guidance on how to identify the communication processes in their organisations with a view first of all to evaluating their effectiveness. This evaluation can then provide the basis for the development of the manager's own practical skills of communication.

In Rosemary Stewart's previously quoted study of how managers spend their time,[1] it was established that on average the 160 managers in her sample spent two-thirds of their time working with other peole. The rest of their time was mainly engaged in preparing reports. It seems reasonable to assume that most managers spend the bulk of their working day in some type of communication activity. Even the 33 managers in the sample in 'backroom'-type jobs spent about half of their time working with other people. This may be through attendance at meetings, the giving and receiving of instructions, discussions with colleagues and contact with customers or suppliers. Such contact may be face to face or over the telephone or a combination of both. Much of the remainder of the time is likely to be concerned with the assimilation or preparation of written information. If managers are to make the correct substantive decisions in their jobs, it follows that they need to be able to handle the communication process effectively.

My own experience, and I would suggest that of most people, is that managers differ markedly in their ability to communicate effectively. It follows that the need to develop skills of effective communication may be a critical priority for many managers. Regrettably this need is often not perceived and managers may neglect the importance of, and the opportunity for, development in this critical area. Communication skills tend to be taken for granted and lack of skill far more easily recognised in others than in oneself. The process of communication is often far more complex than people realise and this is a further reason why skills development in this area tends to be neglected. It is only when people realise the subtleties concerning effective communication that they may become communication conscious and start to develop their own skills. The complexities are such that even the person who is good at communication is likely to become even better if he systematically evaluates and considers his own effectiveness in this area.

THE CAUSES OF INEFFECTIVE COMMUNICATION

Having stressed the importance of the communication process, it is appropriate to develop further the hypothesis that communication in organisations is a great deal worse than most people realise. This will be done by explaining the nature of communication processes, and the potential for breakdown. Case examples are given to illustrate some of the major points.

Listening problems

It is appropriate to explain one major misconception about communication at this stage. This point is not only important in its own right but develops the argument that the approach of many managers to communication may not be sufficiently sophisticated. Communication is usually seen as the need to brief other people. The reality is that most of a manager's time needs to be concerned with the receiving rather than the imparting of information and views. The reason for this is simple — in any conversation between two people there is a need to alternate between talking and listening. There is not much point in anyone talking if the intended recipient is not prepared to listen. If the two people involved in a discussion take equal turns talking and listening, they will obviously spend half of their time in the listening role. As much of the communication in organisations involves face-to-face discussion between more than two people, it follows as a mathematical fact that most managers will need to spend more time listening than talking. There will, of course, be exceptions to this, but the very existence of exceptions reduces the time available for others to do the talking. Admittedly managers may often need to take the lead in explaining things to their subordinates, but a statistically unequal share of talk in this direction may easily be counterbalanced by the time they have to spend in discussions and meetings involving a number of people when they talk only for a minority of the time. The basic point of this argument is that managers may fail to see that they will normally need to spend more time listening than talking.

Effective listening does not come naturally to all managers, particularly if they do not recognise the importance of it. The mistake of assuming that 'good communication' is synonymous with the imparting of information and views is often made by people who set out to improve the quality of communication in organisations. House magazines, letters from the chief executive, briefing meetings and training in public speaking are based mainly on the assumption that the problem is in disseminating information. The reality may be that it is more important to unblock the obstructions to information and views flowing in to the decision-makers. The problem may be though that, until such time as communication is effective, managers may not realise that the obstructions are there. In any case if everyone concentrates on imparting information and views, just who will be left to receive all these messages?

One case which illustrates this point concerns a nursing officer who attended a review meeting three months after he had attended a middle management training course. When asked what had happened as a result of his training, he explained that the area on which he had been able to concentrate was the development of his communication skills. He had worked on his listening skills and had put a chair by the side of his desk, on which people were invited to sit when they came into his office. He explained that he was amazed at the extra amount of information that he obtained this way compared with his previous pattern of letting people stand up or sit on a chair the other side of the desk. He then realised the limited nature of the information he had been obtaining before and on which basis he had been taking decisions. Before, being unaware of the information that was available, he had not tried to get it. It was only after he had discovered his 'blind spot' that he realised that it existed.

Lack of feedback

The problem of effective communication is unfortunately greater than just the recognition of its scale and importance and the comprehension that one needs to receive information as well as disseminate it. It is all too easy for people to assume that they have effectively communicated and be blissfully unaware that their attempts at communication have only been partially successful or, in some cases, totally unsuccessful. I have often used a simple exercise to demonstrate the undue optimism concerning the effectiveness of communication with groups of managers on training courses. This particular exercise involves asking one of the group to tell the rest, without any questions by them, how to draw a diagram consisting of six rectangles. The manager is asked to sit facing the wall and convert a diagram such as that shown in Figure 8.1 into words so that the group can reproduce the diagram from his oral instruction. This exercise is described in detail in Leavitt's *Managerial psychology*.[2] In practice one would not try to explain how to reproduce a diagram by oral instruction, but there are advantages in using this artificial example. It is easy to check the accuracy with which it is reproduced and it is no more complicated than some of the instructions that people do try to explain orally.

Figure 8.1: Communication exercise

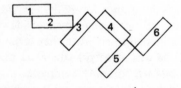

All the rectangles are of equal size and the angles either of 45° or 90°. The rectangles touch one another either at the corner or the mid-point. Invariably there is considerable error in the attempts of the groups to convert the oral instructions back into the original diagram. Sometimes the results are devastating. On one occasion a zero score was achieved by a group of 16 managers because their instructor had unwittingly described the rectangles as triangles. But invariably the instructor significantly underestimates the amount of error made by the group.

After the results of the attempt to explain the diagram using one-way communication have been recorded, the same manager is asked to repeat the exercise but the second time facing the group and with unlimited opportunity for questioning. A similar type of diagram is converted into words and back into a diagram again by the rest of the group. There is a standard pattern to this second stage of the experiment. It takes longer, the accuracy is usually much higher, it is rare for there to be no error, and again the instructor overestimates the level of accuracy. The assumption is usually made that, if people have queries, they will raise them. The reality is though that, even in the relatively placid context of a training course, people may have inhibitions about asking questions. They may feel embarrassed about their inability to draw the diagram, be confused by the instruction, have wrongly thought that their reconstruction was correct, have failed to catch the eye of the instructor at the right time, or lost interest. The instructor may fail to appreciate that there can be this variety of reasons for people not raising queries and make the common error of assuming that silence means that everyone has accurately reproduced the diagram.

Bogus feedback

One of the crucial points that emerges from the rectangles exercise is that people responsible for initiating communication need to consider both what the evidence is for them assuming that communication has been effective and the consequences of communication being defective. You can be very aware of situations when you are on the receiving end of an instruction that you do not understand. It can be very tempting, for the sorts of reason outlined above, to create the impression by silence that you have understood something when you in fact know that you have not. The problem is that the initiator may be left with quite a false impression of his effectiveness. If a message is particularly important it is up to him to search for more positive corroboration than mere silence that communication has been effective. He will need to consider other forms of feedback and to distinguish between accurate and bogus feedback.

Silence is not the only way in which people give false impressions about having understood explanations. There are occasions when people actually say they have understood when they have not. A common situation when this arises is when you ask the way and are so baffled by the instructions on how to get to a particular place that you may meekly say that you have understood when you have not. This type of breakdown can happen within organisations and for a variety of reasons. These reasons may be the same as those given for people remaining silent when they have the opportunity to ask necessary questions during the rectangles exercise. Another reason can be the fear of admitting ignorance, to authority figures in particular.

In discussing this issue with nursing groups I have been deluged with examples of when this has happened. One example concerned the student nurse who was asked to give a patient an air ring. She apparently wasn't quite sure what to do but guessed that the appropriate interpretation was to move the patient's bed on to the verandah and remove the bedclothes. She had in fact been expected to get an air ring so that the patient could sit on it and receive a blanket bath. Another student nurse was given the same instruction but with slightly different phraseology — she was told to go and get an air ring. Allegedly she returned three-quarters of an hour later saying how much she had enjoyed her walk! Pride of place of the many examples I have been given goes to the case of the student nurse who was expected to give a patient a warm drink of potassium citrate. As is so often the case, an abbreviation was used and she was asked to give the patient a 'hot pot cit'. Unfortunately her interpretation of this instruction led to the patient being sat upon a bedpan of boiling water! In these cases the students' guesswork fortunately just led to comic results. That will of course not always be the case and such errors in the communication process may be picked up too late or not at all. The errors in the previous examples may be seen as stupidity or feebleness on the part of the student nurses, but such an interpretation is to miss the point. The fault really lies with the person who gave the instruction not ensuring that he had made himself properly understood. Either he needed to make a positive check that the instruction was understood or have a working relationship with the student nurse such that queries would be raised if necessary. The objective with communication needs to be to see that it is effective rather than being able to lay the blame at someone else's door if things go wrong.

Nursing examples have been given to illustrate the need to get accurate feedback. This is not to suggest that nursing is more prone to this type of problem than other occupations; it is simply that examples come easily to mind from my experience with nursing groups. The culpability of the authority figure can be even worse than I have so far suggested. Some people may contrive to go through the motions of obtaining feedback when in fact what they want is simply the pretence and alibi that people have had a fair opportunity to raise queries. Rhetorical questions may be used such as 'is that clear?' which do not really invite responses. At one company at which I worked there was amazement when a person sought to take up the managing director's written offer, issued in a standard letter to all new employees, to have an appointment with him concerning a grievance. The technique can be observed with lecturers, or after-dinner speakers, who leave the opportunity for questions until an impossibly late stage in the proceedings. I also recollect it being used in the services, when orderly officers had to go through the routine of asking if there were complaints about the food. Some mastered the technique of asking if there were any queries in such a way that servicemen would deserve a medal if they actually did make a complaint. This of course enabled the orderly officer to maintain the fiction that people had been given an opportunity to complain about the food if they were dis-satisfied. Should subordinates nevertheless voice criticisms in situations like this they may have the blame put back on them, however unjustly, to discourage further criticism.

Resistance to criticism

There may be occasions when feedback is sought but resisted if it turns out to be unfavourable. I vividly remember one occasion when I explained to a subordinate personnel officer that I would always welcome suggestions if she thought there were ways in which the running of the department could be improved. She took me at my word and one day somewhat hesitantly started to explain how a change I was planning was, in her view, ill-judged. My immediate response was one of irritation, but fortunately I was just able to hide this and found to my chagrin that she was right and I was wrong. I was relatively new in the job and realised in retrospect that in the moments when I as seeking to control my irritation the future working relationship was being determined. I was able to show, at least with this person, that I would not bite her head off if she expressed views that were contrary to mine. After this incident the personnel officer concerned came to me when she thought that there was a likelihood of my committing other errors. This meant the occasional swallowing of pride when she picked up points that I had missed. There is a strong temptation in situations like this to block off criticism for fear of losing respect amongst subordinates. The conclusion I came to was that one was likely to lose much more respect if one simply hid from criticism. The route I chose did at least enable me to get advice before decisions were finalised. There is a much greater danger of losing respect if one cannot accept critical but helpful advice, especially if that is then compounded by decisions that are incorrect.

The importance of these points is sadly illustrated by the problems that the advisers to the late President Lyndon Johnson had in explaining to him that the war in Vietnam was not progressing as favourably as he imagined. President Johnson was not renowned for his sensitive handling of people, particularly those who voiced criticism. Consequently he was more psychologically available to those who reported favourably on the progress of the war, and who suggested that a military solution was possible, than to those who suggested the reverse. It was apparently not until the spectacular Tet offensive by the Viet Cong in 1968 that President Johnson realised that all was not as well as he had imagined. The organisational point to be made is that there is an understandable temptation to encourage processes which bring good news and a reluctance, if only subconscious, which can still be just as critical, to discourage processes which bring bad news.

It is important to recognise that any manager is going to prefer to hear good news than bad news and the temptation for colleagues and subordinates is to tell people what they want to hear. In the long term this can of course be disastrous, and managers and political leaders alike need consciously to recognise the distortion that can occur in channels of communication and beware of succumbing to it. This can be checked if the danger is consciously recognised and if the ancient Greek tradition of slaying the messenger who brings news of defeat in battle is avoided. It may also be necessary to take independent checks to evaluate the information that is received. It was comprehension of this point which led some generals, at the time of the First World War, to say that 'if you want to know what's going on you have to go to the trenches'. Having said this, it is necessary also to make the point that there are few people, if any, who can cope with the whole truth all the time. Total exposure could be destructive to the individual concerned. What is needed is a realisation that the information fed to one in organisations needs careful evaluation and that other information may be needed but not be passed on. Managers may need to seek out the bad news to the extent that it is necessary and to the extent that they can cope with it. An adage concerning delegation is that 'managers get the subordinates they deserve'. The same adage can be used with regard to communication, that 'managers get the communication they deserve'.

Selective perception and bias

In considering barriers to communication, it is also necessary to deal specifically with the problems caused by selective perception and bias. The sheer volume of data that is available means that one has to have some basis for deciding what to look for and what to react to. However, careful judgement is needed in making these decisions.

A totally open mind can simply mean that a person is swamped with data but a closed mind can mean that a person doesn't respond to what is under his nose. Particular dangers are seeing only what you want to see, making the 'facts' fit what has already been decided, and suppressing unpleasant facts. Norman Dixon, a former Army psychiatrist, explains a number of Western military disasters in terms of such selective perception on the part of the military leaders concerned, in his book *On the psychology of military incompetence*.[3] Three of the many examples he documents concern the Japanese attack on Pearl Harbor, the fall of Singapore and the failure of the Arnhem offensive in Holland. The pattern according to Dixon is clear and recurrent — the warning signs were there but, because they did not fit into the established thinking, they were ignored until too late.

The extent to which people can be misled or even coerced into believing things which are untrue can be alarming. In one experiment conducted with American students it was found that a quarter could be coerced into stating that straight lines were of identical length when one was 25 per cent shorter than the other.[4] This effect was achieved by priming the seven other students in the experimental group to say that the lines were identical in length. One must be careful not to over-generalise about the amount of social coercion possible from the results of a series of experiments in America with a particular group and at a particular time. However, if social pressure can have this effect on such obvious matters of fact, what is the scope for social pressure on matters that are more subjective or where people's self-interest is involved?

As well as having to cope with one's own subjectivity, it must also be recognised that many of the data which are available within organisations are subjective or actually misleading. In Chapter 3 some of the reasons were given as to why department managers might be more concerned with protecting their reputations than with supplying objective data about their performance. Most people working in organisations are likely to be concerned with the pursuit of truth, but people in organisations, as in life generally, are under a variety of pressures to highlight some things and not others. There are also pressures to view events in a particular way. This means that a manager, as well as being aware of the pressures on him to see things in a particular way, and to report selectively, needs to evaluate carefully the information that is being fed to him. One of the themes of the TV comedy series *Yes Minister* is that information is fed to the Cabinet Minister by his Permanent Secretary in such a way that the Minister thinks that he is taking the decisions himself. One stratagem is that the options are put so that the Minister is bound to choose the one preferred by his Permanent Secretary. This is why politicians at both national and local government level often have political advisers and support staff to provide them with alternative viewpoints and other information. It is also necessary to be careful to evaluate the information that is fed down the line. For example, I have found that if I examine carefully the policy decisions that are actually taken by my own Local Education Authority, they sometimes bear little relationship to many of the interpretations that work their way down the structure to individual College departments.

Selective reporting and misunderstanding are not phenomena confined to upward reporting. Corroboration of the existence and nature of these problems is given by a former civil servant, John Carswell, in a *Sunday Times* article.[5] He explained that, when he was working on the administration of retirement pensions, an experienced superior said to him that there were three National Insurance schemes, not one: 'The scheme we put in the instructions, the scheme the Permanent Secretary talks to the Minister about, and the scheme they administer in the local offices.'

THE SKILLS OF EFFECTIVE COMMUNICATION

Much of the skill in effective communication lies in recognising the problem areas I have just identified. Effective communication is achieved as much as anything by avoiding these traps. Positive approaches are, however, also necessary. One positive approach is that of coaxing information out of people.

Coaxing information

It may be necessary for managers to work hard at this, particularly if people feel inhibited about discussing a particular issue. The lament 'why didn't someone tell me' can be as much a condemnation of a manager's lack of skill in developing effective channels of communication as a condemnation of others for keeping him in the dark. It can be very hard for those in authority roles to realise the difficulty that others may have in communicating with them. The authority figure may feel totally relaxed and uninhibited and not appreciate that perhaps the very factors which create his security create difficulties for others. The proprietor of a business may feel totally self-confident and secure and be amazed to find out, if he ever does, that people who are very dependent on him are reluctant to tell him anything unpleasant. The same problem can be encountered by parents with their children. They may forget what it was like to be a child and be blissfully unaware of many of the thoughts and anxieties that their own children have and see any suggestion to the contrary as quite preposterous.

Listening effectively

Adopting a listening role can be harder than taking the lead

137

by talking. The problem with this can be that, the more the authority figure talks, the less the other person may be inclined to talk. There can be a critical moment when people in the subordinate role might just start saying what they really feel, if only the authority figure stays quiet long enough. Once the 'subordinate' has started talking, things may come out with a rush and to the amazement of the authority figure. I have often found that such a critical moment can occur when I am leading classroom discussions. One useful technique in any such situation can be to count silently to five before breaking the silence after a particularly important question has been asked. Time after time I have found that such a delay has resulted in someone making a contribution that I had not thought possible. Once a person has started to talk it can be relatively easy to get him to continue and for any others to join in. The problem is likely to be how to get them started. The authority figure needs to be aware of letting his ignorance, impatience or even his own nervousness prevent such a process starting. Care has to be taken with the timing of invitations for people to open up — it is not only the time and the place that can be important but also the stage in a discussion. It may be necessary to build up rapport gently before the invitation is given. Thought also needs to be given to the way in which questions are put. They can be 'leading' in nature, giving the impression that all that is required is confirmation of the questioner's obvious views such as 'don't you think this is a good idea?' Alternatively they can be probing and phrased in such a way as to encourage the respondents to state their own views.

The choice of time and place

The choice of time and place to invite people to talk can be critical. Just as one knows oneself that there are times when one is prepared to open up and times when one is not, so this can obviously be the case with other people. One of the skills of communication is picking up the cues as to whether a person is or is not prepared about a sensitive matter. Even if the place cannot always be chosen, sometimes the geography of a room can be arranged to encourage, or for that matter to discourage, a person from talking. The more status symbols surrounding the authority figure, the less likely a subordinate is to feel free to talk. I remember one personnel officer, who was over six feet tall, always made a point of seeing that he and an able but peppery works superintendent who was short were both seated if anything of consequence was to be discussed. The personnel officer had learned from experience that the superintendent was self-conscious about his lack of height and so he did his best not to emphasise it.

Choice of language

Language difficulties can obviously hamper communication between people who have different national languages. Regional dialects can also, and predictably, complicate matters. However, there can be many other and more subtle language problems even between people who are from the same country, region and class. Technical language may be used in discussion which is beyond the comprehension of some of the participants. In any organisation there are likely to be abbreviations, words with special connotations, and 'in-terms' whose meaning is taken for granted by those inside the organisation. A colleague of mine recently gave an example of two nurses trying to communicate about sterilisation policies in their respective parts of the Health Service. One was a midwife and the other a community nurse. It took a quarter of an hour before they realised that one was talking about sterilisation as a means of birth control and the other about sterilisation as a means of protecting babies from infection! Problems of language invariably get exposed in the rectangles drawing exercise previously explained. The diagram may be explained by the use of geometric language, points of the compass, the hands of a clock or the use of symbols such as 'L shaped' and 'an inverted V'. The language chosen by the instructor is likely to be more convenient to some people than others and a person's ability to understand the instructor will in part depend on whether the instructor chooses a language convenient to him or not.

The recurring problem with language in communication is that the person who is trying to explain something may understandably use the language that is most convenient to himself without perhaps realising that there is a choice of language. The person receiving the explanation may also, understandably, be reluctant to admit that he cannot understand the language that is used. The skill is in recognising that, even when ordinary English is used, there may be problems of comprehension. The initiator of any communication needs to get positive confirmation that the 'language' he is using is one that can be understood.

In identifying the appropriate 'language' for communication, attention needs to be given to the possibility of ambiguity. The more important the consequences of error, the more attention needs to be devoted to avoiding ambiguity. If stress is needed on this point, it can be provided by the ambiguous use of words which contributed to the world's worst air disaster at Tenerife in the Canary Islands in 1977. The pilot of a KLM Jumbo Jet, who was ironically also the head of their Flight Training Department, was preparing to take off at Tenerife. He explained that he was ready to the air traffic controllers and in response was told 'Okay. (pause) Stand by for take-off. I will call you.'[6] In the pause after the word 'Okay' there was radio interference because of a radio query by the Captain of a Pan-Am Jumbo about the intentions of the KLM captain. It seems likely that this caused the KLM captain to assume that the word 'Okay' was the complete message. In any event the KLM captain then took off and collided with the Pan-Am Jumbo killing a total of 573 people. The investigators commissioned by the American Airline Pilots Association concluded that this was the most likely explanation of events. They also commented on the ambiguous use of the term 'take-off'. Their comments on the use of the term 'Okay' were as follows:

> The word (or letters) 'OK' can be ambiguous also: to the controller it was either a word of acknowledgement or a delaying term to allow a moment to think. It can also mean a host of other things, such as a state of well being, a check-off of a task accomplished, or a statement of approval. It could have have had the latter meaning for the KLM crew.

Recognising cultural barriers

Cultural differences can obviously present barriers to effective communication as well. Some of the cultural barriers — such as language — are obvious but there may be more hidden obstacles. A recent example given to me which illustrates this point concerned the communication between the male Asian

140

workers and the female canteen workers in a London factory. There was a certain amount of friction when food was being served, part of which was said by the canteen workers to be because of the surly response by the Asians when they received their food. In particular it was commented that the Asians never smiled. Their response to this was initially one of bewilderment as, in their culture, it was seen as being altogether too familiar for a man to smile at a woman he didn't know. Far from trying to create offence they had been trying to avoid it by their impassive expression. When this incident was recounted to the receptionist at the college where I work, she said that she could now understand why she received so few smiles from Asian callers compared with the broad smiles of other people.

Another example was offered by an Arab colleague who maintained that a problem of communicating in Britain was the British tendency for understatement. In his experience this was aggravated by a tendency in Middle Eastern cultures to overstate the case. Evidence about such issues is perhaps inevitably anecdotal and one must be very careful about making generalisations. However, one should at least be aware of such potential obstacles to effective communication and take them into account.

Body language

The expressions, gestures and other body language that people may use, without necessarily realising it, can be important cues as to what they really think. Communication is not just imparting information; it often involves, or needs to involve, understanding people's attitudes and feelings which are not always clearly expressed in words. In some cases people may even feel obliged to say the opposite of what they really think. It is not uncommon, for example, for people to say 'how interesting' but in a tone of voice which indicates that they are in fact bored. An adage which makes the point that people sometimes accidentally misrepresent themselves is 'listen to what I mean not what I say'. As words can be an inadequate, or even a misleading, guide as to what people really think, it can be important to look for other cues as to people's thoughts. A catalogue could be prepared of what particular physical cues could mean — fidgeting, that a person has other things on his mind; a glazed expression, that a

141

person doesn't understand, and so on. Given that such a list could be very long and only a guide anyway, the point that needs stressing is simply to watch for physical cues as to a person's real thoughts, especially when it is likely that a person is not able to be, or does not want to be, frank about a particular topic. It can be very tempting to rely just on the words that a person uses, particularly if he gives the answer that one wants to hear. To rely on words alone can be quite insufficient.

Interesting examples of how people can unwittingly reveal their true intentions are given by the American agent Mark McCormack who negotiates on behalf of many international, particularly sports, celebrities. In his book he explains how:

> When I am meeting at someone else's office I have often noticed that people will sort of 'lean in' to the situation when they are ready to get serious, even unconsciously using their hands to push everything on their desk a couple of inches forward. Yet almost as often I have seen people at this same point lean back in their chairs and feign a totally relaxed position.[7]

McCormack also explained in a British radio interview how one negotiator would unwittingly reveal his intentions by moving his chair back before making his final offer. The advantage of recognising such a cue is obviously to keep asking for more until the person moves his chair back!

Another, and even more intriguing example, concerns an allegation about Nikita Khrushchev's behaviour during the famous United Nations debate when he interrupted proceedings by banging on the table with his shoe. This was part of his protest about American reconnaissance flights over the USSR in their U2 spy planes, which came to light when the American pilot Gary Powers was captured. This occurred during President Eisenhower's second administration. The allegation is that TV cameras revealed that Khrushchev had shoes on both feet and that the one he banged on the table must have been brought into the conference chamber expressly for that purpose. If the allegation is true it reveals that the demonstration was a calculated piece of histrionics and not a spontaneous burst of anger.

WRITTEN COMMUNICATION

The emphasis in the chapter so far has been on oral and visual communication. But much communication is written, and some consideration of the special features of written communication is necessary. The main point that needs stressing is that written communication is one-way and the recipient or recipients have, for the time being at least, to rely on the writer's accuracy of expression. The rectangles experiment, described earlier in the chapter, indicated some of the problems with one-way communication. The type of language chosen may not be convenient to the reader, and errors, ambiguities and complicated explanations cannot be questioned until later, if at all. This means that the writer needs to give considerable thought as to how best to express himself. An explanation that seems clear to him may be far from clear to a reader. A person once explained to a friend that he was sorry that he had written him a long letter. This was because he had not had time to write a short one! The point is that it may require considerable effort and concentration to write in a clear and simple manner. It also involves the writer being prepared to state what he really means instead of concealing his real thoughts, or lack of real thoughts, behind a smoke-screen of words. Unfortunately people can easily be taken in by verbose or complex explanations, believing that their failure to understand is because of their own limitations rather than those of the writer. It may often be a more appropriate and accurate assumption that, if a person hasn't explained something clearly, the fault is with their thinking rather than with the reader's comprehension.

Sometimes matters have to be expressed in a precise technical way and the use of a particular language is unavoidable. This can be the case with legal documents where the only way of achieving the necessary clarity is to use precise legal expressions. However, even when technical language is used, there are differences between good and bad expression. Whether technical language is used or not, there would seem to be no virtue in explaining matters in a more complicated way than is necessary. All too often, however, sophisticated terms can be dragged in unnecessarily because of a desire to impress or because of clumsy expression or lack of clarity in the actual thinking. The use of many sociological terms in particular can be for these reasons. One of the ironies concerning many Government forms is that those who have to complete them may need a graduate level ability to do so. Person with that level of ability, though, would not often be applying for many of the services in question. Much of the underclaiming of social security benefit may be because of the difficulty people have in understanding the benefit application forms.

This is illustrated by the following example published in the 'Diary' column of the *Guardian* newspaper. It quotes the reply sent by the Department of Health and Social Security to a mentally ill 19-year-old living on invalidity benefit who managed to get a job for two days, washing dishes at Olympia:

> The claimant is disqualified for (sic) receiving non-contributory invalidity benefit for 17.5.82 because he failed without good cause to observe the rule that he should do no work other than work which he had good cause for doing and from which his earnings were ordinarily not more than £16.50 a week. S. S. (Unemployment Sickness and Invalidity Benefit) Regulations reg 12(i) (a) (iii).
>
> As a result, an overpayment of non-contributory invalidity benefit has been made amounting to £2.95 as detailed below. Repayment of this sum is required because it has not been shown that the claimant has throughout used due care and diligence in the obtaining and receipt of benefit to avoid overpayment (Social Security Act 1975 sec 119(1) and (2)).
> *£17.75 ÷ 6 = £2.95.

The *Guardian* diarist went on to add that the reply could, of course, have been worded: 'Please pay back one day's benefit because you worked.'

TELEVISION AS A SOURCE OF INFORMATION AND ITS EVALUATION

The need to evaluate carefully the accuracy and quality of information is not confined to data that is generated within an organisation. All organisations collect much of their information from external sources which are also subject to distortion. Television is an increasingly important source of information for managers and it is appropriate to comment about the problems of distortion which are now becoming apparent in this area. I have become particularly aware of this in teaching industrial relations, and refer to some of the problems of reporting in this area in order to make the general point about the need to evaluate television carefully as an information source.

Industrial relations is an area that has been seized upon by the media generally, and television in particular, for extensive coverage. People's views and knowledge about the subject can be as much influenced by media sources as anything else. This presents difficulties, as increasingly evidence is emerging to suggest that the profile of industrial relations presented by television in particular is not very representative. The obstacles to balanced reporting are considerable and to a large extent stem from the conflict between the obligation of television producers to present fair programmes and the pressures on them to catch the attention of audiences and attain high viewing figures. This can lead to sensationalised reporting, emphasis on the unusual rather than the usual, and 'camera bias' because of the visual impact of anything dramatic. Other problems can include confusion between the symptoms and causes of industrial disputes, the juxtaposition of industrial relations reports with other news items, the limited understanding and work experience of television journalists, and the subconscious judgements and values of those responsible for making programmes. The problem is exacerbated by the simplistic reaction of many television producers and jounalists who believe that, because there is no conscious bias, nothing is wrong.

I find that my first task in teaching industrial relations has now become to make people aware of the need to evaluate carefully the information presented on the media rather than simply to accept the pattern of events which is presented. The problems of effective reporting of news and current affairs have led John Birt and Peter Jay to comment on the 'bias against understanding' inherent in television reporting. This observation was based on their own experience as producers for Independent Television and led to them trying in their own productions to strive for balanced reporting, explanation and analysis of the information they presented. The Glasgow University Media Study Group in their monitoring of news bulletins has been particularly critical of news reporting.[8] In their analysis of news bulletins in January 1975 they found that the five industrial disputes in vehicle building, accounting for 21 per cent of the days lost through strikes in the month, received 125 out of a total of 130 news reports of strikes in the UK.[9] They also established that in 22 news reports of the Glasgow dustcart drivers' unofficial strike in the same year, the unofficial strikers were not represented in any of the 21 interviews shown on the national news during the 13 weeks of the dispute.[10] One may or may not have had sympathy for the unofficial strikers, but viewers were not likely to be able to make that judgement for themselves if one side of the case was not presented.

The criticisms of television coverage of news and current affairs reporting received some endorsement in the Annan report on the future of broadcasting published in 1977.[11] Comment was made about the variability of current affairs presentation and for the need for improvement in news bulletins. This included the observation that 'Both BBC Television News and ITN, but particularly the former, could be improved. News is presented in too stereotyped a fashion; there is too little variety, too little punch and there are too few attempts to give brief explanatory comments.'[12] Whilst the Annan report did not endorse all the criticisms made of television reporting, they did point out a large number of other weaknesses in some areas. These included the lack of understanding of industrial life by some producers, the preference by others for presenting current affairs in the style of a boxing promoter, the dangers of social insularity of television producers, and camera bias.[13] These problems are not so pronounced with radio because of the absence of visual images which can have a dominating effect on television programmes. In fairness it should be said that the problems of providing balanced and sensitive TV coverage are immense. The awareness of this and of British achievements in this area has led the TV critic Milton Shulman to describe British TV as 'the least worst in the world'. Readers can judge for themselves the extent to which the media have taken note of the criticisms made in the Annan report in particular. The topic has been stressed because of the increasing importance of television as a medium for communication, particularly in view of the increasing availability of video cassettes. The point that needs stressing above all others is that one needs actively to evaluate the information with which one is presented when the easiest course of action may be passively to accept it.

CONCLUSION

The obstacles to, and skills involved in, effective communication are formidable. The main aim in this chapter has been to make the reader aware of some of the major pitfalls. It is probably most constructive for readers to assess their level of skill in communication rather than aspire always to be an effective communicator. The volume of communication and problems involved means that one can only hope to develop one's level of skill rather than overcome all the problems. Effort in communication needs time, and time is invariably at a premium. However, it is important that people recognise that accuracy in communication is usually much lower than is assumed.

Decisions need to be based on realistic assessments of what has been effectively communicated rather than on naively optimistic assessments. There also needs to be recognition of the matters that it is critical to communicate accurately. Not just managers but everyone needs to have a range of communication skills that they can use when appropriate. The lack of attention in schools and organisations in this critical area means that people generally need sensitising to the problems and skills involved. The sad fact is that often feedback is not obtained when it is required and that, even when it is obtained, it is not evaluated. People tend also to see the main need in this area as communicating with others rather than the, quantitatively at least, more important task of letting others communicate with them. The volume and problems are such that experiment in this area is likely to lead to the relatively easy development of one's existing skills which may in turn encourage more experiment and a further development in skill. The bonus for this can be reflected in a more accurate basis for decision-making for oneself and for those one has to deal with, not just within organisations, but in other aspects of life as well.

NOTES

1. Rosemary Stewart, *Managers and their jobs* (Pan Piper, 1970), p. 68.
2. Harold J. Leavitt, *Managerial psychology* (University of Chicago Press, 1978), revised edn, pp. 117–26.
3. Norman F. Dixon, *On the psychology of military incompetence* (Cape, 1976).

4. For a summary of S. E. Asch's experiments see P. F. Secord and C. W. Backman, *Social psychology* (McGraw-Hill Kogakusha Ltd, 1964) International Student Edition, pp. 304–7.

5. John Carswell, 'The slave of the lamp', *The Sunday Times*, 29 March 1981, p. 39.

6. Air Line Pilots Association (American) *Aircraft accident report: engineering and air safety — human factors report on the Tenerife accident* (1978), pp. 22–4.

7. Mark H. McCormack, *What they don't teach you at Harvard Business School* (Collins, 1984), pp. 23–4.

8. Glasgow University Media Study Group, *Bad news* (Routledge and Kegan Paul, 1976). See also *More bad news* by the same authors and publishers (1982); and *Really bad news*, by the same authors, (Writers and Readers Publishing Co-operative, 1982).

9. The Department of Sociology (SSRC Media Project), Glasgow University, *Evidence presented to the Committee on the Future of Broadcasting* (June 1975), p. 23.

10. Ibid, p. 32.

11. *Report of the Committee on the Future of Broadcasting* (the Annan Report) (HMSO, 1977).

12. Ibid, p. 286, para 17.53.

13. Ibid, pp. 279–80, para 17.35.

9

Selection

INTRODUCTION

One of the most critical decisions that managers may have to make is the appointment of subordinate staff. Managers may also be involved in the appointment of subordinate staff for other managers — for example, by membership of interview boards. New staff may be appointed from within the organisation or by external recruitment. It is easier to exercise discretion at the appointment stage than later — it is much more difficult to remove staff once they have joined you. Considerable effort may be needed to train and develop staff, especially if they have inappropriate experience, aptitude or qualifications. The ability of subordinate staff can have a critical effect on the performance of the manager concerned. Even though managers may only be involved in appointment decisions relatively infrequently, it is important that they make the right ones. It is for this reason that a chapter has been devoted to selection. Many managers may have the advantage of a specialist personnel service but, even if that is the case, they need to know the nature of that service and how to make best use of it. Managers also need to be able to recognise when specialist advice in this area is inadequate and, if appropriate, to press for a better level of service.

The first topic covered in the chapter is the need to identify carefully the nature of a job that has to be filled. The long-term nature of the job has to be considered as well as the immediate requirements. The next step is the drawing up of a person specification. The ways in which information can be collected about candidates is explained. So too are the actual skills involved in selection interviewing, including the skills that may be required at board interviews. Consideration is also given to the dangers of discrimination in selection and the relevant law relating to sex and race discrimination. The final section deals very practically with the rather different skills that may be required if one is the person being interviewed for a job. A self-assessment form is included as an appendix to help readers see how they might develop their selection interviewing skills.

DEFINING THE JOB

Whether a job is new or old, considerable care needs to be taken in defining its exact objective and scope. The material in Chapter 2 concerning the identification of objectives and key tasks may be relevant in this context. Even when jobs are well established it is important to remember that the requirements may have changed. The actual tasks that have historically been performed may not be appropriate in changed circumstances. A manager may be unaware of some of the adjustments that have taken place in a job since he perhaps occupied that position. A starting point for identifying the requirements of a job may be to get the existing incumbent to prepare an updated job description. Other information may, however, also be necessary. A job may have been tailored to take account of an individual's strengths and weaknesses. It may be necessary, therefore, to consider the extent to which such 'tailoring' should remain if a new person is being appointed. An account given by a person of his job may not be accurate, or may reflect what is done rather than what needs doing. The manager concerned may need to consider what changes he and others think are necessary in a particular job. It may even be that the job does not need filling — either because there is no longer any purpose to it or because the individual tasks can more effectively be redistributed amongst other staff. Peter Drucker gives such an example in his book *The practice of management*:

> For 20 years a large shipping company had difficulty filling one of its top jobs. It never had anyone really qualified for the position. And whoever filled it soon found himself in trouble and conflict. But for 20 years the job was filled whenever it

became vacant. In the twenty-first year a new president asked: 'What would happen if we did not fill it?' The answer was: 'Nothing.' It then turned out that the position had been created to perform a job that had long since become unnecessary.[1]

I have witnessed more than one case where the clear identification of the purpose and content of a job was only completed after the candidates were interviewed. The original reasoning about the job in question was inadequate and the questions asked during the selection interviews led to a more accurate assessment of what was really required. On one occasion this led to a redefined job being advertised and the whole process of selection being started again. On another occasion it was decided, as in Drucker's example, that no appointment was necessary. The consolation in these examples was that at least the initial error of inadequate assessment of the real job requirements was not compounded by an appointment based on inadequate job definition.

SHORT-TERM AND LONG-TERM NEEDS

A further problem area, which is often overlooked, is the distinction between the short-term and long-term needs in a job. A person may be recruited to fill a pressing but temporary need. The problem that may then arise is what to do with him when the need has passed. The pace of technological change, in particular, means that this is likely to be an increasing problem. Traditionally jobs have often been seen as positions which will remain substantially the same during the working life of the job holders. The problems that this approach to selection can create have been demonstrated particularly in the shipbuilding industry. Skilled shipbuilding workers have understandably shown resistance to the introduction of new technology, or new work arrangements, when these have threatened to reduce even further the demand for the specialised trade which they had expected to be able to practise for the whole of their working lives.

Once people join an organisation they become part of the political power structure. They are likely to take a lively interest in the prospects for security and promotion for people with their particular range of skills. This concern is by no means confined to skilled manual workers. I have found that academic staff can take a ferocious interest in seeing that college departments run courses that provide the maximum prospects for advancing their particular specialism. This does not necessarily lead to a conflict of interests between what is good for the individual and what is good for the organisation and its prospective clients, but this certainly can happen. This means that it is necessary to anticipate the pressures that potential employees will put on the organisation to develop in a particular way or remain in a particular mould.

This problem has to some extent been tackled with skilled workers in the engineering industry. The length of apprenticeships has been gradually reduced and opportunities for apprentices and skilled workers to increase their range of skills improved. The concept of the multi-craft worker is also making some headway. The advantages that these developments can bring include the possibility of reduced resistance to technological and organisational change because the employees are more able to adapt to changed circumstances. To spend five years training a riveter and then to tell him that his trade is obsolete is asking for trouble. The same type of problem should be anticipated with professional-level employees. I found that there was a clear recognition of this problem with one large petrochemical firm with which I was once involved on a consultancy assignment. They recognised the dilemma of acquiring people with specialist skills for immediate problems and of nevertheless needing people who would be prepared to adapt to the rapidly changing circumstances of their industry. The solution adopted was to recruit some graduate chemical engineers with specialised training to cope with immediate specialist needs. Other graduate chemical engineers were also recruited with a more general training who were given either technical or managerial jobs. They were recruited with a view to being moved around the organisation so that they developed a range of technical and/or managerial skills. The reasoning was that, as the organisation needed to adapt, so this latter group would be able to fill the emergent new jobs. Had only narrowly trained specialists been recruited it seemed much less likely that the organisation would have been able to adapt to the rapidly changing circumstances of the petrochemical industry.

The distinction between short-term and long-term needs has

to be considered whenever appointments are made. The pace of technological change in particular is such that one has to ask whether a person will be prepared and able to adapt to the radical changes in job content that are increasingly likely. Admittedly in some cases one may say that the short-term problems are those that have to take priority and that if necessary future inability to cope may have to be dealt with by redundancy. It seems prudent, however, at least to consider taking on a person with a temperament and range of skills that would make adjustment an easier process compared with applicants who may be over-specialised.

PERSON SPECIFICATION

Having defined a job and balanced the short- and long-term needs, the next stage is to specify the attributes required for a person to undertake the job effectively. One way of creating a specification is to use the seven-point plan described by the late Professor Alec Rodger in a pamphlet published under the auspices of the former National Institute of Industry Psychology.[2] The headings which need specification are:

1. Physique, manner and bearing
2. Attainments
   (a) educational
   (b) experience
3. General intelligence
4. Special aptitudes
5. Interests
6. Disposition
7. Circumstances

One may consider adding an eighth factor — the motivation to do a particular job. Care obviously needs to be taken in itemising the various requirements. Even though a job may have been carefully defined, the specification can be completed so that it gives a spurious impression of accuracy and certainty. If possible, it may be appropriate to consider the extent to which people satisfactorily performing the same or a similar job fit the specification that has been established. Care also needs to be taken in looking at the totality of a job and of an applicant so

153

that one sees the applicant as a whole person and does not get lost in the detail. Consideration also has to be given as to what constitutes a good 'match' between a person and a job, as explained in Chapter 6. A person with high intelligence may make a poor 'match' for a routine job. The likelihood of problems arising because of people being appointed who are too good for a job is sadly increasing because of the continuing high levels of unemployment. An intelligent person who gets bored with a job may perform less well than a less intelligent person who does not get bored with a routine job. The performance of people selected in accordance with a person specification will provide some indication as to whether the specification is appropriate or not.

Particular care has to be paid in identifying the differences between a person's previous work experience and the job for which he is applying. A person who has performed admirably in one job will not necessarily perform well in a different job, particularly if that different job necessitates work at a higher level of responsibility. There is more than a grain of truth in Northcote Parkinson's concept of people passing through their threshold of incompetence.[3] His theory is that people are promoted on the basis of having done their last job well until they find themselves in a job which they cannot do, which is when the basis for promotion ceases. This particular danger was observed by David Lloyd George when he had to establish the Ministry of Munitions in 1915. In his memoirs of the First World War he commented:

> I cannot claim that my first choices were always the best. They were, I think, the best available at the time. I found that some were admirable workers provided they were under the control and direction of others, but not equal to the responsibility of a supreme position. It was then that I realised thoroughly for the first time that men ought to be marked like army lorries with their carrying capacity: 'Not to carry more than three tons.' The three-tonners are perfect so long as you do not overload them with burdens for which they are not constructed by Providence. I have seen that happen in Law and Politics. The barrister who acquired a great practice as a junior and failed completely when he took silk; the politician who showed great promise as an Under-Secretary and achieved nothing when promoted to the headship of a department. As I went along I discovered that one or two first-rate men were

better suited for duties inside the department other than those for which I had originally chosen them.[4]

THE COLLECTION OF INFORMATION ABOUT CANDIDATES

Information about candidates can be collected from a variety of sources. The identification of a realistic person specification can be of great value in determining what information is relevant to selection decisions. Scrutiny of job advertisements indicates which employers have worked out the sort of person they want and the information they require, and which employers have not. A well-designed application form can present the relevant information to an employer in a way that he will find easy to follow. Examples of a person's work may help, as may references and testimonials from current or previous employers.

There is often confusion between the terms reference and testimonial. A testimonial is an open letter given from an employer to an employee to show to future prospective employers. As it is given to the person who is the subject of the testimonial, the writer may be reluctant to say anything detrimental about the person concerned. On the other hand, the fact that a person is prepared to praise a former employee in an open letter may be because the person deserves it. References are communications direct with a prospective employer which are given in confidence and not normally revealed to the person who is the subject of the reference. This means that the current or past employer may be more prepared to be frank about the person concerned. But care has to be taken in the interpretation of written references. A person writing a reference may feel reluctant to state the shortcomings of a person and mention just his good points. It is often the omissions that are the most important feature of a reference. Oral references may be the most accurate, but it is important to beware of the employer who praises an employee in order to get him off his hands. It may be appropriate to approach an employer that a candidate has worked for previously, rather than a current employer, so that the candidate's relationship with his existing employer is not compromised. In evaluating a reference, whether it be good or bad, it needs to be remembered that the information received is about a person's performance in a job which may be significantly different from the job for which he has applied. The past

155

record, although often useful, should only be seen as a guide in making selection decisions.

If a candidate is applying for a transfer or promotion from within an organisation, there may be a wealth of information available about him. Care needs to be taken in evaluating the information, but the quantity and quality of the information may mean that any interview is much less important than may be the case with external appointments. This distinction is often insufficiently stressed. It is one thing using the interview as a prime method of obtaining information and making judgements about a person about whom little is otherwise known. It can be unjust and incompetent to rely extensively on the interview when a person has been with an organisation for a number of years. There may be little further that an internal applicant is able to add at an interview and any suggestion that what matters is the candidate's performance on the day may do scant justice to his previous record with an organisation. The main purpose in interviewing internal applicants may be to probe for relevant information not otherwise available to the people responsible for selection. The other relevant information needs to be taken into account and may be much more important than that which is established at an interview.

THE SELECTION INTERVIEW

Various studies have shown that the selection interview can be much more subjective and unreliable than people realise.[5] However, it is often the only practical way of arranging for decisions to be taken. Even if an employer were to dispense with the interview, he would need to consider how he was going to provide the candidates with information and answer their queries so that they could make their decisions as to whether or not they should apply for, or accept, a job. The existence of a clear person specification does enable an interview to be conducted systematically with the interviewer at least knowing what he is looking for. All too often the information collected at interviews is relatively worthless because the interviewer has not identified clearly enough what he wanted to know. Even when this has been done, a significant amount of skill may be needed to obtain the relevant information. The interviewer may have identified what he wants to know, but a candidate may quite understandably be concerned with emphasising his strong points and with concealing his weaknesses. There is a considerable amount of technique in obtaining information from a candidate.[6] Readers are likely to have noticed the variation in skill demonstrated by people who have interviewed them for jobs.

Planning

The first stage in the interview is fairly obviously the prior preparation. Interviewers need not only to have established the person specification but also to have studied any relevant information before the interview starts. They also need to consider what information should be given to a candidate before the interview. The location of an interview needs to be considered so that it takes place in surroundings that are as congenial as possible for interviewer and candidate. Interviewers should have a good idea of what they want to find out during an interview. They may also want to identify the basic information that they will need to convey to a candidate. Check-lists of information to be obtained and imparted can be very useful. It is also prudent to bear in mind that candidates are often understandably nervous and may not absorb what they are told. It is necessary to consider the structure and sequence of an interview so that the dialogue can be as effective as possible. If candidates are nervous it may be best to get them speaking as early as possible. It may be only when they have settled down that they are capable of absorbing important information.

One way of providing a clear and useful structure is to undertake a biographical interview. This involves the candidate being asked to explain what qualifications be obtained in school and what his employment history has been subsequently. Having done this in a demonstration at the invitation of John Munro Fraser,[7] I can testify that it immediately sets the agenda for the candidate in a way that puts him at his ease and enables him to explain his record in a systematic way. The interviewer can then concentrate on asking the supplementary questions that are needed to fill in any gaps. Even if the biographical approach is not used, thought needs to be given to the structure of an interview and the agenda explained to the candidate. All too often interviews can be conducted in a grasshopper style with questions being asked at random with little if any thought being given as to how to lead up to sensitive issues. This can be caused, not just by lack of skill on the part of the interviewer, but also by his nervousness. Careful preparation and consideration of the techniques of interviewing can have the bonus of giving the interviewer sufficient confidence to conduct an interview in a relaxed and effective manner.

Interviewing skills

Two of the critical and related skills in selection interviewing are questioning and listening techniques. The interviewer will want to find out if there are any reasons why he should not appoint a particular person. He may need to ask his questions in such a way that he does not reveal what he is after. To do this he will need to frame his questions in a neutral manner. He may also want to ask indirect questions as the use of direct questions may be pointless. Even if one were to convert a leading question such as 'do you work hard?' into a neutral question, it would be fairly obvious what the interviewer was after. It may be more appropriate to ask what were the tasks in a previous job that most interested a candidate and which were the ones which least interested him, and why. It may also be appropriate to ask questions in an open-ended way so that the candidate may open up and talk freely. The more a candidate talks, the more the interviewer is likely to learn. The role of the interviewer may be to guide the interview gently, to look for leads that need following up, to watch out for under-lying feelings and attitudes and to be on the watch for inconsistencies in the candidate's answers. The nervousness or lack of skill of the interviewer may prevent this. One of the most common errors in interviews is for the interviewer to do most of the talking. This reduces the information that can be obtained from the candidate on which the decision needs to be based. A useful rule of thumb is for the interviewer to spend no more than a quarter of the time talking, and to allow in any such estimate for the tendency to underestimate the amount of time that one speaks oneself. Listening carefully can require much more self-discipline and concentration than talking. If answers are unclear to the interviewer, it may be important to clarify just what an interviewee has meant. It may require considerable tact and patience to establish whether one has properly understood the point that a candidate is trying to make.

A hidden agenda in interviews may be that the interviewer, in particular, may be frightened of losing control and suffering one of the greatest punishments of all in the British culture — embarrassment. This may be a reason why interviews are often played far too cautiously with important issues remaining unexplored. The acquisition of the techniques of interviewing can be the most effective way of overcoming this obstacle. This may particularly affect the close of the interview and the explanation to the candidate of just what the position is with regard to his application.

Many selection decisions turn out to be fairly straightforward. This is most likely to be the case with people who are clearly unsuitable. Much more time may be needed to eliminate the possibility of weaknesses with a candidate who turns out to be suitable. The greatest time, particularly interviewing time, usually needs to be taken with those candidates who are genuinely marginal and where extra relevant information may justifiably tilt the balance one way or the other.

The development of one's interviewing technique may not just depend on practice but on getting feedback on one's performance and adjusting future performance in the light of such feedback. It may be possible for readers to do this themselves and for this reason a questionnaire which can be used for interviewing self-assessment is included as an appendix to this chapter. Readers can complete the questionnaire and identify any weaknesses with a view to seeing if these have been eliminated or reduced when they do their next interview.

Problems to recognise

One of the major problems in selection interviews is that both the interviewer and the candidate may 'freeze' into a set pattern of question and answer, with the candidate feeling fairly restricted about the information that he can volunteer. I used to find, when interviewing in the engineering industry, that candidates could relax considerably when invited to come and see around the plant. A dialogue could then develop under much more relaxed circumstances. I have also noticed that, when managers are being taught how to interview, they can relax and talk far more casually and usefully to candidates when the interview is apparently over. I have often contrived to let managers and people playing the part of candidates stay together when a practice interview is apparently over. I have repeatedly been amazed at the way in which the exchange of information, which should have taken place but didn't, can then occur.

There are further pitfalls that need to be avoided. One is the danger of over-reacting to a particular selection failure. A current or former employee may have a particular failing which blinds those responsible for choosing a successor to the other ways in which a person can fail in a job. There is also the danger of choosing in one's own image. There is almost an argument for not choosing in one's own image so that one employs people with a range of views. One of the frequently voiced criticisms of civil service selection is that administrative grade entrants have the same relatively narrow background as those selecting them.

Ironically it may well be that the higher up an organisation that selection decisions are taken, the less appropriate they may be. The peer group may often be in the best position to judge what is really required in a candidate because of their close knowledge of the demands of the job. The observations of the peer group about internal candidates should not be lightly ignored — though they often are. Factors such as seniority and length of experience tend to weigh heavily with interview boards in particular. This may be because they do not have the detailed knowledge of candidates and jobs that those closer to the situation have. Consequently their decisions may be based on very superficial reasoning. One is reminded in this context of the tart observation that one particular candidate did not have 20 years' experience in a job but rather one year's experience 20 times. It may be that senior managers see requirements in a job that are not perceived by the peer group. It is also possible, though, that they do not have as much understanding of the job's demands as they think they have. They may also be unduly influenced by seniority and may not have to suffer the direct consequences of a wrong appointment.

Care also has to be taken to avoid the 'halo' effect, where a particular strength in a candidate leads to over-generous assessments of his other attributes. A reverse 'halo' can also develop where a particular weakness leads to a candidate being unnecessarily marked down in other areas. Obviously employers also need to be aware of their own subjective views and biases and to allow for such factors in making decisions.

INTERVIEW BOARDS

Selection interviewing has so far been considered on the assumption that interviews are between a single interviewer and candidate. Often, however, selection interviews will be conducted by interview boards which may consist of several people. This may be necessary because of the various interests that need to be represented at the selection stage. One of the historical reasons for the establishment of interview boards in the public sector was the need to see that jobs were not allocated on the basis of patronage. Even when there is no formal requirement for interview boards, there may be a preference by the representatives of an employer to see a candidate together rather than separately. Thus a line manager and personnel officer may conduct a joint interview.

Problems of board interviewing

Whatever the organisational reasons for conducting board interviews, it needs to be recognised that interviewing can be a process requiring considerable skill on the part of the employer and many extra problems can be created by the establishment of a board. It may be very easy for the board members to take it in turn to ask questions, but the formality may be very off-putting for the candidate. The quality of the information that the board needs, in order to make its decision, may suffer accordingly. Sometimes it is argued that part of the requirement for a job is an ability to cope with board-type situations. In some cases it may be that a critical aspect of the job is dealing with situations similar to interview boards. However, this is not often the case and this argument may be used as a rationalisation for a selection procedure which has been adopted for quite different reasons.

The art of coaxing information out of a candidate that is relevant to a job application, and which in some cases is to the detriment of the candidate, can be difficult enough in a one-to-one interview and can be much more difficult in a board interview. The amount of time that each board member can have needs to be rationed. Lines of enquiry that are opened up may be unwittingly terminated by board members who are unsophisticated in the techniques of interviewing. The fact that boards often come to unanimous decisions about selection choices does not necessarily validate the selection. It could be that a board has gleaned very little useful information about a candidate and finds a decision easy because of the limited information obtained. Selection decisions are vindicated, or not, by the actual performance of the person chosen.

It is necessary to explain the extra problems created by board interviews, so that managers, where they have the choice, can consider whether they opt for board or single interviewing. Where there is no choice and boards are part of the established selection procedures, then the interviewers should realise the pitfalls.

How to improve board interviews

Something may be done to improve the chances of effective decision-making at boards by careful chairing. Board members may need training in interviewing techniques. If this is not possible, the person chairing may be gently able to coach board members in the skills of interviewing and selection — bearing in mind that often the worse interviewers are, the less they are likely to recognise their deficiencies. Where the information obtained by board interviews is of little value, at least it is best to recognise that, and use what other information is available as a basis for decision-making.

In some cases, the option of sequential interviewing may be open to managers. Instead of, say, four people on a board spending an hour with each of four candidates, the board members might each spend an hour alone with each candidate. The board could then take its selection decision in the light of the information obtained at the separate interviews. In theory this need take no more time; there could even be a saving by reducing the time for the single interviews to below an hour. The candidates would have to spend more time being interviewed, but might not mind this if they felt it was a more effective method of selection. However, even where it is possible to do this, objections might come from the board members, who would be far more exposed in a single interview compared with a board situation where they need not say anything if they do not want to. The extra information that can be generated by sequential interviewing might lead to much more argument about who gets a job because the interviewing had been more intensive. However, my own preference has always been for sequential interviewing where this is possible, on the basis that it is normally much easier to coax information out of a person when you are seeing him alone.

DISCRIMINATION

It is also necessary to bear in mind the legislative rights that prospective employees, and those applying for promotion, have to protect them against discriminatory employment practices. These rights are embodied in the Sex Discrimination Act 1975 and the Race Relations Act 1976. Applicants who feel they have been the victims of discrimination can pursue their case at an Industrial Tribunal claiming damages. Anti-discrimination orders about future selection practices by the organisation concerned can be issued by the relevant agencies and enforced in the courts. The relevant agencies are the Equal Opportunities Commission and the Commission for Racial Equality. The Commissions may also assist applicants in pursuing claims at a tribunal. The protection under the Sex Discrimination Act also covers the right not to be discriminated against on the basis of marital status.

The Equal Opportunities Commission and the Commission for Racial Equality have both published Codes of Practice advising employers on how to avoid discriminatory practices.[8, 9] A key method of doing this is by monitoring the composition of the work force. It is perhaps easier for employers to fall into the trap of indirect discrimination than direct discrimination. Indirect discrimination occurs when an unnecessary selection criterion is used which has an adverse effect on applicants from a particular sex or ethnic group. One such established example was the use of an upper age limit of 28 for people applying for positions as executive officers with the Civil Service. This was held to be discriminatory against women — because of the likelihood that family commitments would disproportionately reduce women's chances of applying for such positions.[10] Another example, this time concerning racial equality, was the requirement that unnecessary standards of English were demanded of applicants for manual work. The Commission for Racial Equality helped seven Bangladeshis pursue such a case against the British Steel Corporation. The seven were deemed to have failed a language test when they reapplied for work after an extended holiday in Bangladesh. The Corporation argued that the tests, for production workers, were necessary for safety reasons. The applicants argued that 'the test had an adverse impact on ethnic minorities whose language was not English and was not justifiable having regard to the job in question'. Under the terms of the agreed settlement the Bangladeshis were compensated and re-engaged, and the Corporation also agreed to obtain professional help in reviewing its test procedures.[11]

A related phenomenon which can occur is that of subconscious bias. Those responsible for making selection decisions may genuinely believe that they do not practise discrimination but may do so by, for example, their preference for the candidate who has, as far as they are concerned, a conventional background.

It is appropriate to bear in mind that these legislative provisions are not only to ensure social justice but also should be of positive assistance to the employer in ensuring that job applicants are not unnecessarily excluded from consideration for jobs which they may be quite adequate to undertake. Some employers, particularly in the local authority area, have developed their own comprehensive equal opportunities policies which cover other groups as well. Obviously if one is employed in such an organisation it is necessary to know the details of such policies.

BEING INTERVIEWED

This chapter has been written from the perspective of the employer selecting candidates for a job. People applying for jobs may find some of the information relevant, as it helps to see what the process should be from the point of view of those making the selection decision. However, the skills of interviewing are not the same as those which may help a candidate sell himself at an interview. It is particularly important for job candidates to work out before any interview just what information they need to extract from an employer, and to work out what information they need to get over to that employer, either during an interview, or in some other way. It may also be useful to remember that it is usually possible to ask for time to make up your mind whether or not to accept an offer, if it is made. This is the time when the negotiating position of a candidate is likely to be at its strongest and when vital questions can still be asked before a job is accepted. If a candidate is unsuccessful it may be appropriate to reflect that this is often simply because one does not meet a particular specification. There are likely to be other, perhaps more appropriate, jobs where one proves to be a better match with the employer's specification which with luck will be filled to the mutual advantage of both employer and candidate.

CONCLUSION

To some extent the evaluation of selection procedures will always be speculative. Whatever follow-up investigations may reveal about the level of performance of people who join an organisation, one cannot really make judgements about how the people would have performed who were not selected. However, it would seem prudent to review selection procedures in the light of the performance of the people who are chosen. Even then, care has to be taken in coming to conclusions. A person whose performance is poor may still have been the best of a bad bunch. There can also be other explanations for poor performance such as ineffective work arrangements. There is also the problem of whether you judge people by their contribution to short-term needs or by their long-term contribution to an organisation.

If selection procedures are lengthy, they may lead to the best candidates taking jobs elsewhere. Consideration also needs to be given to the public relations aspects involved. Quite apart from considerations of natural justice, it would seem sensible for employers to leave unsuccessful candidates at least with the impression that their application has been considered fairly. It is also necessary to bear in mind the legislation concerning sex and race discrimination.

The systematic review of selection methods, whilst not leading to any magic answers, may reveal weaknesses which can be corrected in the future. One of the advantages of exit interviews is that personnel officers, in particular, can consider whether the pattern of people leaving indicates weaknesses in the selection procedure.

NOTES

1. Peter F. Drucker, *The practice of management* (Heinemann, 1955), p. 320.

2. Alec Rodger, *The seven point plan* (National Institute of Industrial Psychology, London, 1970), third edition.

3. C. Northcote Parkinson, *Parkinson's Law, or the pursuit of progress* (J. Murray, 1961).

4. *War memoirs of David Lloyd George* (Odhams Press, 1938), Vol. 1, p. 149.

5. P. E. Vernon, *Personality tests and assessments* (Methuen, 1953). See also H. J. Eysenck, *Uses and abuses of psychology*, Ch. 5, 'From each according to his ability' (Pelican, 1953).

6. Harold F. Lock, *Interviewing for selection*, Paper No. 3 (National Institute of Industrial Psychology, London, 1970), third edition.

7. John Munro Fraser, *Employment interviewing* (Macdonald and Evans, 1978), fifth edition, completely rewritten.

8. Equal Opportunities Commission, *Code of practice for the elimination of discrimination on the grounds of sex and marriage and the promotion of equality of opportunity in employment* (HMSO, 1985).

9. Commission for Racial Equality, *Code of practice for the elimination of racial discrimination and the promotion of equality in employment* (HMSO, 1984).

10. *Price* vs *the Civil Service Commission*, Industrial Relations Law Reports (Industrial Relations Services, 1977), p. 291.

11. Industrial Relations Legal Information Bulletin No. 131, 21.2, 1979 (Industrial Relations Services), p. 12.

APPENDIX I: INTERVIEW ASSESSMENT FORM

When making your judgements try to relate these to specific acts or omissions on the interviewer's part. Be sure *why* you rate each item as you do.

+ +   Very good
+   Largely satisfactory
0   Not so bad, could have been better
—   Not so good

	+ +	+	0	—
1. *Preparation.* Was the interviewer well prepared? Did he know the brief? Did he have a plan?				

	+ +	+	0	–
2. *The opening.* How successful was the interviewer in opening the interview?				
3. *Putting the subject at ease.* Was the subject very nervous? Could he talk freely?				
4. *Facts.* Did the interviewer collect all the facts needed? Did he find out why and how as well as what?				
5. *Attitudes/feelings.* Did he manage to discover these as well as the facts?				
6. *Questions.* Did he ask open-ended questions, probe where necessary? Did he ask leading questions or answer his own questions?				
7. *Listening.* Did he listen enough? Did he talk too much?				
8. *Giving information.* Did he give all the information the subject needed in a way that the subject could understand?				
9. *Manner.* Was the interviewer courteous, factual, tactful? Was he tense, abrupt, argumentative? Was he given to making value judgements?				
10. *Closing.* In what frame of mind did the interviewee leave?				

10

Appraisal, Training and Counselling

INTRODUCTION

In this chapter attention is paid to three interrelated areas —
appraisal, training and counselling. The various objectives of
appraisal are identified, and the point made that this is an area
that can be fraught with difficulties. One of the difficulties is
that if schemes are not thought out properly they may contain
conflicting objectives. Particular attention is paid to performance appraisal but also to the skills that are required in
appraisal situations generally. The ways of identifying training
needs are covered as is the manager's responsibility for training.
This involves accepting responsibility for acting as coach as well
as working out how to make good use of an organisation's
training department.

The need for the manager to have counselling skills is also
explained and the nature of these skills is analysed. These skills
may be needed in appraisal, training and a variety of other situations. The techniques of counselling won't solve all the problems
in these areas, but a mastery of the techniques can lead to the
avoidance or resolution of a great deal of aggravation with the
bonus that often potentially destructive situations can, with
proper handling, have thoroughly constructive outcomes. A
complication is that there is often very little advance warning of
when counselling is required, so that managers need to have the
skills at their fingertips.

APPRAISAL, TRAINING AND COUNSELLING

Objectives

There are a variety of reasons why managers may need to appraise their subordinates. The main reasons are likely to be:

1. Performance assessment
2. Identification of training needs
3. Merit payment
4. Upgrading
5. Promotion
6. Probationary review
7. Review of duties

The distinction between upgrading and promotion is that upgrading normally means that a person is paid more because it is recognised that most of his work is, or will be, at the higher levels of responsibility within the existing job. Promotion on the other hand normally involves transfer to a *different* job that is at a higher level of responsibility.

In many organisations managers are required to undertake appraisal of their subordinates as part of a formal scheme. Formal appraisal may, however, need to be supplemented by informal assessment, and the absence of a formal appraisal scheme does not remove the need for the manager to consider systematically, for example, the performance, training, payment or suitability for promotion of subordinates. Inevitably appraisal involves a dialogue between the manager and subordinate. This is not just to ensure that the assessment is accurate, but to enable any action to be discussed and hopefully agreed between the two parties. For this to be productive a manager needs to have clear ideas of what he is trying to assess and why, especially as this is an area where managerial thinking is often very muddled.

The first point that needs stressing about appraisal is that the objective or objectives needs to be clearly defined. There is little point in appraising just for the sake of it. This may not only be a waste of time but may actually be counterproductive. If judgements are made and communicated for no apparent purpose, the people who are judged may rightly feel resentful. Unfortunately there is a great temptation for people in organisations, as in life

169

in general, to make judgements about other people simply because they like doing it. This may be compounded by superficiality in the judgements and tactlessness in the way any views are communicated.

The compatibility of appraising with different but simultaneous objectives also needs to be considered. Often this point is overlooked and organisations adopt multi-purpose appraisal schemes not realising that some of the objectives may be contradictory. Some employers even carry this to the extreme of formally including the maintenance of discipline as one of the objectives of a multi-purpose scheme. If a person being appraised sees his level of pay or future promotion as being influenced by the outcome of the exercise, he may be eager to demonstrate how good he is and to play down any shortcomings in his performance or training requirements. If the objectives of appraisal conflict in this way, it is much better to pursue the various objectives at different times rather than have the subordinate push in a single interview to achieve the objective he has singled out as being the most important.

General problems with appraisal schemes

Lack of thought about the objectives of appraisal, or of the managerial skills required for it to be successful, means that many of the formal schemes adopted by organisations are of little use and may actually do more harm than good. Explanations in textbooks about appraisal tend to suggest by implication that formal schemes can be relatively easily implemented. What is lacking in the literature is an appraisal of appraisal schemes. I have had the opportunity to see a number of investigations by mature personnel management students into the appraisal scheme in their own organisations. The overwhelming pattern in practice that has been presented to me is that the formal schemes are badly thought out and badly implemented. I don't pretend that this evidence is totally representative, but I have found corroboration when discussing the actual effectiveness of such schemes with a wider audience of personnel specialists and personnel management students, who have not actually conducted investigations into their appraisal schemes but who have been in a position to comment about the schemes they have experienced. This is also the experience of the author of an article about appraisal schemes which appeared in the journal *Personnel Management*. He reported:

> One thing that is common to most [appraisal schemes] is a marked lack of evidence that they work, or have any clear impact on the day-to-day management of the company. Increased productivity, improved profit, a more effective organisation, still elude precise links to any appraisal process.[1]

There may be some schemes that operate in the recommended textbook manner, but on the evidence that I have been able to accumulate they must be rather atypical. It is necessary to show the potential problems of formal appraisal schemes, to caution people against over-optimism about such schemes, and to explain how to try to make a formal appraisal scheme work, or at least minimise the possible damage if one has to operate such a scheme. Regardless of whether there is a formal scheme or not, appraisal may need to be handled informally either to supplement a formal scheme or to provide an alternative. The skills of effective appraisal can be explained in part by identifying the potential difficulties.

The rest of this section on appraisal is meant to show how schemes might be made to work effectively. The subsequent sections on training and counselling are also relevant. Effective training necessitates accurate diagnosis of training needs and appraisal may play a critical part in the identification of these needs. Whatever purpose appraisal is used for and whether it be formal or informal, or both, counselling skills are required by the managers handling the process. Consequently the section on counselling is an integral part of this chapter.

The need for clear and compatible objectives for appraisal schemes has already been stressed. What also needs stressing is that it is not enough to select one objective and to assume that the logic of having a scheme geared around that is self-evident. Care has to be taken to ensure that the objective is realistically attainable and that the actual scheme devised will facilitate the achievement of that objective. It will be no good, for example, deciding to have a performance appraisal scheme that is based on unreliable, inconsistent and irrelevant judgements. Whatever the scheme, a considerable amount of intellectual effort is likely to be needed in identifying its precise objectives and the operational detail that is required if the objectives are to be accomplished. Because precise objectives, and the circumstances in which schemes have to operate are likely to vary widely from one organisation to another, it is unlikely that one can simply buy an 'off the shelf' scheme or copy someone else's. This may not stop people doing just that, which is no doubt one of the reasons why evidence of schemes actually working is so scarce. If schemes are to have a chance of success, much patient effort is needed in developing appropriate 'in house' arrangements. The stages in the process include identifying and agreeing objectives with appropriate managers, the preparation of appropriate forms and briefing notes, and pilot runs to test the system. It is only then that the next essential step of training line managers in how to operate a system can be undertaken.

Appraisal interview preparation

One of the critical contributions that line managers need to make in operating an appraisal scheme is spending an adequate amount of time in both preparing for and conducting interviews. Their 'homework' needs to include thoroughly understanding a scheme and also being clear what it is they want to get out of an interview. This commitment is required by all the managers involved and it is necessary to point out that often more than one manager is involved in appraising the same employee. A common practice is for both the immediate boss and the boss's boss (the organisational 'grandparent') to assess a subordinate. This practice, amongst other things, helps to reduce the extent of biased judgements.

Preparation prior to an interview is likely to involve rather more than understanding the paperwork associated with a scheme. Whatever data are relevant and available should be assembled prior to an interview. There is no point in making judgements about, for example, levels of output or attendance patterns if objective data are available which give exact details. Judgement may be appropriate about the reason for a particular level of output or attendance pattern — but not to establish what the figures actually are. Care will be needed in deciding what judgements are relevant. Criteria also need to be established to ensure that the judgements are made systematically. The ways in which judgements may be rated and recorded are explained in a later section. Other relevant documentation that will need to be assembled includes details of any previous relevant appraisals — and particularly of any follow-up action that was planned. The job description and person specification are also likely to be needed.

Both the manager conducting an appraisal and the employee who is being appraised need time to prepare for the interview. The process should be seen as a two-way discussion and both parties need to think beforehand about how the interview can be constructively handled. It is hardly satisfactory if the interviewee is not given notice, or, perhaps worse still, is told he has an interview but not told what it is to be about! A certain amount of tension and anxiety should also be anticipated which may affect both interviewer and interviewee. Appraisal interviews may reveal conflicts between the parties. This may well happen in performance appraisal interviews — as is explained later — but can happen in any type of appraisal situation. One implication of this is that the interviewer may need to consider what adjustments he needs to make, either in his own behaviour, or in organisational support, to help the interviewee accomplish his legitimate objectives. It is all too easy to see appraisal interviews as situations where adjustment just has to be made by the subordinate but such a view is profoundly misconceived. A further way of endeavouring to secure a constructive outcome is to ensure that recent achievements by the interviewee are clearly acknowledged. All this means that a manager should not try and conduct too many appraisal interviews in one day. The interviews, as well as being likely to be time-consuming, may also be emotionally demanding. Time also has to be allowed for writing up and planning any appropriate action.

Performance appraisal

One of the most common reasons for appraising the work of subordinates is to review their level of performance with a view to improving it. If that is the objective, it then follows that what needs to be assessed is the performance of subordinates and not their personalities. There is no point in making judgements about the people themselves unless such judgements are a necessary part of the assessment of performance. Considerable thought and care may be needed to identify just what the appropriate criteria are for assessing peformance. A way of establishing appropriate criteria has already been suggested in Chapter 2 when 'management by objectives' was considered. It is also necessary for managers to think carefully about what they plan to discuss with subordinates. This is another area where there is much muddled thinking. The objectives of the communication involved need to be thought out, just as the overall objectives of appraisal need to be identified. Discussion about a person's performance only seems to be appropriate if that discussion is likely to have some constructive effect. There is little or no merit in discussing performance with a subordinate just for the sake of it, or if such discussion is likely simply to result in recriminations. If a person is performing perfectly adequately, it may simply be appropriate to give him that level of encouragement to help him maintain his level of performance. Conversely, if a person doesn't perform adequately, but can't do much about it, there seems to be little merit in discussion unless the level of performance necessitates disciplinary action. There is little point in telling an employee, for example, that you know he is slow but there is no need to worry because you also know he can't do anything about it and you are not going to sack him. An extremely dangerous fallacy is that employees always want to know exactly where they stand and will always welcome feedback about their performance. The reality is that most people make a sharp distinction between receiving praise and receiving adverse criticism. Praise is invariably acceptable but the extent to which people are prepared to accept adverse criticism is severely limited. One principal nursing officer I know of failed to make this distinction and conducted a frank appraisal interview with a senior nursing officer since when they have apparently not spoken to one another!

As well as recognising that people don't automatically warm to those who criticise their job performance, it is necessary to recognise that there can be considerable conflict built into an appraisal situation, particularly performance appraisal. A subordinate will not automatically accept that the criteria by which he is being judged are appropriate, or that the judgements made about his level of performance are accurate. This may be because of misperception by the subordinate of what is appropriate or because, in some cases, the subordinate has the best appreciation of what is required. The deployment of people in organisations cannot reach that level of perfection where the manager is always more competent than the subordinate. There

174

is the additional problem that the subordinate may appreciate what is required, as far as the organisation is concerned, but recognise that this is not necessarily in his own best interests. This was a point that was raised in Chapter 2, when considering 'management by objectives', and is sufficiently important to need reinforcing here. Organisational and personal objectives do not always neatly coincide. This can mean that at an appraisal interview a person finds himself under pressure to do what he doesn't want to do. This could involve developing the job in a way he finds inappropriate, or making cost savings that could affect his status, promotion prospects or even job security. The delicacy of these and the other issues that have been identified, which can arise during appraisal, is such that the manager may require considerable skill and sensitivity to handle the situation. The danger of formal appraisal schemes is that managers may be precipitated into confrontations with their subordinates that they cannot handle. The 'pat' answer to this is to train the managers in appraisal interviewing, but the reality is that many managers, however good they may be in other aspects of their job, will never have the sophistication to handle delicate appraisal interviews effectively. Many, perhaps wisely, just pay lip-service to formal appraisal and simply complete any necessary forms with as little embarrassment as possible. Others may simply upset their subordinates, often without realising it. Silence by the subordinate may be taken to mean agreement when the reality may be that the subordinate may just be managing to avoid losing his temper. A recognition of these problems does at least give the manager a chance of handling performance appraisal constructively, or of seeing when it is best to leave the issue alone.

Self-appraisal

If one is to embark on the performance appraisal of subordinates, whether formally or informally, it is likely that the best results will be achieved by encouraging the subordinate, as far as possible, to engage in self-appraisal. This can be done by asking the subordinate to identify the appropriate criteria, the extent to which criteria have been met, and areas of possible improvement. Employees may welcome the involvement this offers and may be more prepared to criticise themselves than have it done by others. People often tend to be their own harshest critics. Subordinates may also tend to over-criticise themselves for fear of seeming immodest. If this approach is taken, the manager may ironically find that he is in the position of telling the subordinates that they are being too harsh on themselves and explaining that his assessment is more favourable. There may of course be aspects of a subordinate's performance where the subordinate does not appreciate the need to improve. The manager is in a far stronger position, psychologically, to try to draw such aspects tactfully to the attention of the subordinate if he has previously been building him up, than if he had made such observations 'cold'. Careful judgement has to be made, however, as to the extent to which a subordinate is able to benefit from criticism. If a person is simply going to reject it, there may be little point in pursuing discussion. Often, however, a person may be able to take a certain amount of adverse comment and the skill is in recognising how much a person can take. If a person has volunteered three ways in which he will try to improve his job performance, and is able to accept directive comment about one out of three other areas in which he needs to improve, it may be best simply to forget about the other two areas. If his attention is drawn to these other areas, he may become so defensive and demoralised tht he refuses to accept the case for any improvement whatsoever.

Informal guidance

This general philosophy can be used in giving people informal guidance about how to improve their performance. It may be best to help people see for themselves how they can improve, but only to do this when it seems likely that the person will be able to benefit from such 'steering'. The timing of discussion can be critical as well, with the manager needing to distinguish between when the time is ripe to help people improve and when such advice will be resisted. Often this will be best handled as problems actually occur. One of the further dangers of formal schemes is that they may be seen as a mechanism for raking up old scores which are best forgotten. When problems do arise, a counselling technique may still be appropriate. If a subordinate has a problem, it may be best to start by asking how he thinks it should be handled. This may not only give the required result, but may develop in the subordinate the capacity to work things out for himself.

Handling other appraisal situations

Many of the points already made concerning appraisal generally and performance appraisal in particular are relevant to other appraisal situations. Material relevant to these other situations is also included elsewhere in the book: the appraisal of training needs is covered later in this chapter, merit payment is referred to in Chapter 6 and promotion in Chapter 9. Comment is appropriate here about the process of handling upgradings. A particular issue that will need careful thought in this respect is the choice of the criteria by which upgradings are given or withheld. These need to fit with organisational objectives and to enable consistent and defensible decisions to be made. Upgrading arrangements should also motivate employees to acquire any extra knowledge and skills that are needed so that they can cope with their new pattern of work. However, care also has to be taken to ensure that there is an appropriate balance of employees at the higher and lower grades, otherwise there may be a mismatch between people in a grade and the work available at that level. It would be somewhat counterproductive, for example, to upgrade everyone in a section leaving no-one to do the routine work.

A particular point that needs making about probation appraisal is that arrangements for handling this often seem to be 'more honoured in the breach than the observance'. Employees are frequently left to infer that their probation has been completed successfully by the absence of any comment whatsoever. It may even be that their performance has not been satisfactory but the manager concerned has indicated otherwise by default — i.e. by not saying anything at the end of the stipulated period. Apart from anything else this may create difficulties in terminating the employment of an unsatisfactory employee. Even if a person does not have sufficient service to take an action for unfair dismissal to an industrial tribunal, organisational procedures for dismissal are usually much more comprehensive for the person who has completed his probation. One useful device that can be used in the case of marginal performers is to extend their probationary period. This can give the probationer more time to improve whilst retaining the relative freedom of the employer to terminate if the required improvement does not materialise.

The other appraisal situation that requires specific comment at this stage is where the duties of an employee are reviewed. This may be as a consequence of another type of appraisal or because the primary objective of an appraisal is to review the duties of an employee. Regular reviews of job content may be needed for a variety of reasons. Misunderstandings can easily arise about what actually is required. Additionally job demands change and the capacity of employees to undertake particular tasks can also change. The motivational needs of employees also need to be considered, as was explained in Chapter 6, as is the danger of employees wanting to do, or actually doing, work that is not in the best interests of the organisation. It is necessary to remember the propensity of people to neglect managerial work in favour of specialist activity, as explained in Chapter 1 and the pressures for job distortion, as explained in Chapter 6.

Rating and recording

The final area concerning appraisal that needs explaining is the way in which ratings are made and these and other material recorded. An example of an appraisal form showing one way of rating and recording the managers' comments is shown in Appendix 1 of this chapter. The first step at this stage is to ensure that the criteria that are used to judge the employees are the appropriate ones. Ratings also need to meet the following criteria:

1. Validity: ratings must relate to observable behaviour.
2. Reliability: ratings made by different raters should be comparable (i.e. produce closely similar results), as should ratings made by the same individual at different times.
3. Relevance: the behaviour or qualities rated should be important to success in the particular job concerned.
4. Discrimination: the ratings should genuinely discriminate between above average, average and below average individuals.
5. Comprehensiveness: ratings should cover all aspects of behaviour relevant to the purpose of the scheme.
6. Assessability: loyalty, sense of humour and such mean different things to different people.

Particular care is needed to ensure that ratings really are reliable. The dangers of inconsistency are considerable and can easily bring a scheme into disrepute. The hazards include the 'halo' effect where there is a spin-off from one desirable quality in an employee which causes over-generous ratings on other factors. The 'reverse halo' effect occurs when an undesirable quality causes other factors to be marked too harshly. Another phenomenon can be the 'blue-eyed boy' (or girl) syndrome. This occurs when people are favoured for characteristics or behaviour unrelated to the job. It is concern over issues such as these that can arouse considerable union hostility to appraisal schemes. Another problem that can arise concerns the need to reconcile the ratings of managers who rate the employees either consistently highly or consistently badly. Other managers may create another problem — that of rating nearly everyone as 'average'. Care has to be taken to ensure that any weighting of the various factors has the effect that the designers of a system intended. One illuminating example where this proved not to be the case concerned a merit-rating scheme in which the most important factor was 'punctuality'.[2] This was not the intention of the designers of the scheme but was a consequence of the way the raters operated. It was much easier to assess punctuality than other more important but less tangible factors. As the dispersion of ratings for punctuality was therefore much wider than was the case with the other factors the result in practice was that the differences in the total scores for individuals were accounted for more by the 'punctuality' rating than by any other single rating.

Various methods of recording ratings and other relevant information can be used — some of which are aimed at producing statistical reliability and consistency. The methods include:

1. Comparison with established standards
2. Rating on a graded scale
3. Comparative rating of employees
4. Paired comparisons of employees
5. Forced choice questions
6. Forced distribution of marks or grades
7. Critical incident recording
8. Written reports

Combinations of the above methods are likely to be used, the exact choice depending on the specific appraisal scheme. Another issue that has to be resolved is whether or not appraisal reports are shown to the employees who have been appraised. One consequence of having 'open' systems is that, not surprisingly, they are likely to lead to only mild criticisms being made by the manager. If any information is kept in a computer system the subject will have the right to see it. This is as a consequence of the Data Protection Act, 1984, and the Subject Access provisions, operative from September 1987.[3,4]

TRAINING

Identification of training needs

It is appropriate to consider next the appraisal of training needs. This, in practice, may overlap with performance appraisal. Shortfalls between required and actual performance may indicate a training need. In identifying the training needs of subordinates, managers need to consider any impending changes in the job which could necessitate training, even though a person may currently be performing perfectly adequately. Changes in organisational policies, structure or activities invariably have training implications. The impact of changing technology, particularly in the area of electronic data processing, is likely to generate ongoing training needs. Thought also has to be given to training employees for promotion, as well as with regard to the existing job. The willingness, as well as the ability, of employees to co-operate in implementing change may be considerably influenced by the extent to which they have been trained to handle any change. Unfortunately the degree to which managers are conscious of the need to identify the training needs of their subordinates varies enormously.

Great care has to be taken to ensure that training needs are realistically identified. The need for training can all too easily be used as a spurious alibi for explaining all shortcomings in performance. Furthermore, performance problems aren't always the fault of the individual concerned. What at first sight may seem to be a training requirement may, on closer examination, prove to be a case for changing work arrangements, amending policy, or even 'buying in' particular skills. Realism has to be used in judging whether a particular person will benefit from training — some individuals have a remarkable talent for emerging unscathed after the most rigorous of training. Cost issues that need to be worked out include the marginal costs of releasing an employee, the other things the employee could be doing in that time, and the time it will take for there to be a return on the training investment.

Meeting training needs

Training can all too often be seen as something to be handled entirely by external agencies, including an organisation's training department. However, there is only so much that can be handled externally, and even that may not be appropriate. People often have a tendency to offer themselves for training that is not related to their needs. This can be for a variety of reasons, including an inflated view of the level at which they require training. A person may opt for a seminar on corporate strategy when his needs may be much more basic, such as the need to develop supervisory skills. External training may also be sought because of its prestige, enjoyment or the prospects it offers for getting a job with a competitor. Not all external training is well handled anyway. One way of checking the relevance of what courses are on offer is to examine the objectives and to compare these with the actual, as opposed to imagined, needs of subordinates. If the objectives of courses are not clearly stated, that in itself may tell you something about the care, or lack of care, with which the course has been designed. The statement of clear objectives can also help to check if a person has benefited from a course — particularly if the objectives specified what changes in behaviour were anticipated as a result of attending the course. It is this, rather than just asking a person what he thought about a particular course, that is the acid test. When external training is appropriate the manager needs to help the subordinate to apply any relevant lessons, rather than let him suffer the frustration of seeing what needs to be done but being unable to do anything about it.

Yet another issue that managers will have to work out is the competence of their own training department. Effective training is literally disturbing, as the whole point of it is to alter existing patterns of behaviour. Some training departments help identify and facilitate such change, whilst others either opt out of mainstream activity or are never allowed near it. This can result in the activity of a training department being anaesthetised. An indication of this phenomenon is the preoccupation of a training department with soft options that do not contain a workshop element. Other indications are whether the training department is working in relative isolation from line management and engaging in training that is merely fashionable, random or token, or perhaps all three. Hopefully managers who want a genuine contribution from their training department will encourage them to become involved with real issues that are relevant to the needs of the organisation and not connive at their relegation to dealing only with peripheral issues.

Whatever formal training can achieve outside the line manager's department, the crucial issue remains of the extent to which the manager sees himself as a coach. If he systematically identifies opportunities to help subordinates improve themselves, the manager may find that, when performance of those subordinates is assessed, there is relatively little need for further improvement. Performance appraisal may seem to be the appraisal of subordinates by their manager, but the standards of performance of subordinates may reveal as much about the manager as they do about the subordinates.

COUNSELLING

Introduction

The techniques of counselling have already been covered to some extent in this chapter in considering appraisal. It is now appropriate however to deal with the subject in greater detail. The best point at which to start is to explain just what is meant by the term. Counselling can be defined as a purposeful relationship in which one person helps another to help himself. It is a way of relating and responding to another person so that that person is helped to explore his thoughts, feelings and behaviour with the aim of reaching a clearer understanding. The clearer understanding may be of himself or of a problem, or of the one in relation to the other. The point of all this is to enable people to work out how they will handle for themselves issues, problems or decisions that have to be made. The technique is necessary because it may be that it is only by this process that an issue can be understood and/or the commitment created that will lead to an appropriate course of action being taken by the person concerned.

The need for counselling can arise in a wide range of situations. Appraisal has already been mentioned and the requirement for these skills in grievance and disciplinary situations are explained later in this chapter. The need for counselling skills can arise whenever a subordinate or colleague has a work or work-related problem. As well as managers needing counselling skills themselves they also have to consider the extent to which their subordinates need these skills. It may be particularly important that any employee who has direct contact with clients or the public is trained in how to handle such contacts.

Usually counselling discussions are initiated by the person who needs the help. However, there will be occasions when managers need to take the initiative and encourage employees to face up to issues that are having an adverse effect on their work. Whoever initiates discussion, some interpretation of an employee's responses will be necessary. Care needs to be taken about the level of discussion and analysis that is attempted. In-depth 'Freudian' probing and analysis (for example) is better handled by those qualified to do it than by amateur psychiatrists. The requirement for counselling in work situations is usually for work-related rather than personal problems anyway. Obviously personal problems can affect behaviour at work and counselling may be given by one person to another in the capacity of personal friend. There may well be situations though where it is not appropriate for a manager to get involved or where the best help that can be given is to refer a person to an appropriate agency or service.

The value of counselling

The need to develop the techniques of counselling became rapidly apparent to me when I first started work as a personnel officer. I hadn't been trained in advance how to counsel, but was fortunate to have friends in the social work field who counselled *me* on how to deal with the flood of callers I received wanting help with a bewildering variety of problems, many of which I didn't even understand, far less have answers for. In my enthusiasm I had previously offered directive advice which often simply revealed my ignorance and increased the frustration of the colleague concerned. Eventually I was able to learn how to talk people through their problems so that often they came up with their own 'solution', or came to terms with the fact that there was no 'solution' and that they just had to put up with something. Once I had acquired this skill, I found that all manner of people, instead of viewing me as remarkably ignorant, thanked me for helping them resolve issues which I had still often barely understood. I realised in retrospect that previously I had all too often fallen into the trap of giving directive advice when I didn't know all the facts or, if I did, had recommended the course of action that I would have followed which did not of course allow for the different personality of the person who had come to see me. The non-directive style that I subsequently came to use enabled people to take account of facts that they had not explained to me, and also to take account of their own personal reaction to the problem. The further advantage of this non-directive approach was that the individual concerned was far more likely to be committed to a 'solution' that he had worked out for himself than to one that someone had sought to impose on him. The need that people had in these situations was not so much to be told what to do, but rather to have someone to calm them down and help them navigate their own way through the maze. In doing this they may have made their first systematic attempt to deal with the problem, and, with luck, found that they could see the appropriate course of action for themselves.

Specific skills

Having explained the general nature and purpose of counselling it is now appropriate to explain the skills in more detail. As has also been explained the choice of who counsels, and when, is much more in the hands of the person wanting this type of help than with the potential counsellor. A person may not choose to speak about his problems to some people and may refuse offers of help that are made. So the opportunity for counselling is likely to be determined by the person wanting help, but it is up to the manager whether he has the inclination and skill to respond. The counselling that is required may be easily dealt with in a few moments or involve several lengthy discussions. Those who have the opportunity to provide this type of help have to judge whether it is appropriate for them to give it and to assess if they are really likely to help, if they have the time to spare and whether there are other more appropriate ways of helping. A complication is that decisions on whether or not to counsel may have to be taken very quickly. If a person is rebuffed he may not ask again, or if counselling-type help is offered, it may be very difficult to stop once it has started.

The amount of direction given by the counsellor will vary according to the situation and the personalities involved. It is the essence of counselling, though, that the person is helped to work the problem out for himself. Not only may value judgements be inappropriate if made by the counsellor but, if they vary from the value judgements of the person requiring help, that person may see the counsellor as unsympathetic and consequently terminate any discussion. Nevertheless, even given all this, there can be a range of counselling styles. At the one extreme a person may be totally non-directive and just give sufficient response, perhaps by way of grunts, to let the other person know that he is actually listening. In other cases it may be appropriate for the counsellor to be rather more interventionist whilst at the same time avoiding imposing his own views. This can be done in a neutral but friendly manner by positively encouraging a person to elaborate on an issue. Further interventions can be to clarify what has been said and to ask questions that are designed to get the person to talk more. It may be necessary for a person to add information in such a way that the person being counselled feels free to make use of the information or ignore it. This of course represents a further stage in counselling intervention without sacrificing the neutrality of the counsellor. Another stage is to help the person concerned identify the options available to him — the critical point, of course, being that the choice has to be made by the person being counselled and not by the counsellor. This can involve a person taking a decision that is not necessarily in the interests of the organisation — for example to leave (or in some cases not to leave!). There is little point, however, in the counsellor seeking to impose the decision that is in the organisation's interests as the person would undoubtedly ignore it. If a person is going to decide to leave, for example, it may be just as well to help him come to that decision relatively quickly rather than let the issue drag on.

Throughout a counselling interview the counsellor needs to be aware of the need for eye contact when appropriate. That is not to say that he should spend all his time staring at the subject but such contact can be helpful in showing that the counsellor is actively listening. It is also necessary to be aware of signals that are being given by a person's 'body language'. This concept has already been explained in Chapter 8. Premature intervention by the counsellor can prevent further disclosure by the subject. A problem or issue may be the lead into another and perhaps much bigger area and the counsellor needs to be aware that the closing of discussion on a particular topic is by no means necessarily the end of a counselling interview.

The problem that a person raises may just be a lead-in or a pretext for going on to discuss much more serious issues. Often the stated problem is rather like the tip of an iceberg. The subject may want to test that he is going to get a sympathetic response before being prepared to reveal the next part of a problem. Sometimes a person may not even be aware that the problem is much deeper than that indicated by him initially. This shows the danger of trying to deal with just the 'tip'. The help that a person may need is to reason through the whole of a problem in such a way that he can cope with it, allowing for his own personality. It may be that there are also issues of which he is aware but which he deliberately keeps secret. This is yet another reason for the counsellor to beware of seeking to impose a solution, as it may be based on an incomplete knowledge of the facts.

Normally the whole basis on which counselling takes place is one of complete confidence. Sometimes however the counsellor will need to warn the subject that information that may emerge, or already has, cannot be treated confidentially. If, for example, an accountant is told that his cashier has been systematically embezzling money it is hardly likely that he can, or should want to, keep this a private matter between the parties.

Reference has been made in this section to the various stages that there are likely to be in a counselling interview. Part of the skill of counselling effectively is to identify the pattern an interview may take. The main stages are likely to be as follows:

1. Identification of the problem
2. Collection and exchange of information
3. Checking that all the necessary statements have been made
4. Establishing the criteria for a satisfactory 'solution'
5. Deciding on the appropriate 'solution'

6. Subsequently checking whether or not the 'solution' has worked

The issue of the different stages in a counselling interview is not quite the same as the different styles of counselling. Each person who counsels may have his own style, which may vary from that of other people in the level of intervention (or non-intervention) and the specific skills that are used. However, whatever basic style is used it will need to be varied according to the personality of the subject, the issue under discussion and the stage of the counselling process.

Given that managers spend most of their time in some form of communication and much of that is oral communication — as explained in Chapter 8, the need for counselling techniques can arise very frequently. The skills may not have the glamour of more high-status management activities but can nevertheless be one of the most critical of all management skills. The skills may also be constructively applied in one's personal life. Two of the situations where counselling techniques can be particularly necessary and useful are next examined — grievance and disciplinary handling. These are however but two of the many situations in which the skills may be appropriate.

Grievance handling

Grievance interviews are situations where counselling skills are particularly likely to be necessary. Many organisations have procedures that provide for the formal hearing of employee grievances. However, they tend to be little used, as the immediate boss is usually designated for the task of hearing the grievance, and he is invariably the cause of it. However, managers may handle many grievances quite informally and the range of situations will be much wider than just that of dealing with dissatisfied subordinates. Working relationships with colleagues may generate grievances as may contact with client groups, particularly the public.

There can be a variety of ways of handling grievances, including having a first-class row, ignoring it, referring it to someone else, or giving the person what he wants. Often, however, grievances cannot, and should not, be ignored, yet there may be nothing that the manager himself can do to resolve the grievance. It may be that a person has a perfectly justifiable grievance, but nothing concrete can be done about it. It is in situations like this that counselling may be not only desirable but the only course of action that can be taken.

Grievance handling skills may be needed by many levels of people within an organisation. Employees who have customer contact may need it in their handling of customers, though managers may of course also need it in this context as well as in handling dissatisfied employees. I have often marvelled at the way some airline staff cope with irate passengers who seek to hold them personally responsible for the weather, strikes or technical failures. This presumably is often because of the training they have received. In some of these situations the answer is simply to let people talk themselves out of their fury. Their frustration may require an outlet, and counselling techniques may enable them gradually to dissipate their anger. At the end of it an aggrieved person may actually thank the person at whom he has directed his anger for his help and go away reconciled to the situation. The dilemma for the person who has to handle the grievance is that, if he openly agrees with the complaints, he may compromise his employer and, if he rebuts the complaints, he may infuriate the complainant. Neutral, but sympathetic, listening in many cases is not merely the only option but may be a complete answer. It may even be appropriate for the person at the receiving end of the grievance to take the initiative as the anger subsides and probe to see if there is any more anger that needs ventilation — like poking a balloon with an open neck with a stick to see if any more air comes out.

In some cases the counselling of a person with a grievance will simply mark the end of the first stage of the 'discussion'. It may then be necessary to see what, if anything, can be done about the person's complaint. It may be that a decision has to be deferred or the answer given that, whilst you are sympathetic, nothing can be done. It is crucial, however, that, where feelings are high, this is only attempted after the counselling stage has been completed. It may be only then that a person can participate in a rational discussion of what can or can't be done. Even if he still expects some action, a hearing of his case may have gone some way, if not the whole way, to providing psychological restitution. It may also emerge that his anger has prevented him from properly explaining his grievance and that the cause of his dissatisfaction is rather different from that which first seemed to be the case. Clarification of the nature of the grievance may be crucial, as otherwise decisions cannot be sensibly taken about what action should, or should not, follow — yet it may only be at a relatively late stage in the proceedings that this is possible.

The processes I have just described can be very necessary in confrontations between managers and union representatives, or with other special interest groups for that matter. It may be impossible to communicate effectively with representatives until they have ventilated their feelings about a particular issue. It may be only then that representatives are able to listen to the management side of a case. The problem for whoever is chairing such joint meetings is to prevent anyone on the employer's side from retaliating and so inflaming a situation. This may be particularly necessary as the opposing interest group may have actually moderated their position after saying their piece.

Counselling in disciplinary situations

Counselling may also be applicable in disciplinary situations. As with grievance handling, it can be a necessary first, and even only, stage in resolving disciplinary problems. The best form of discipline is usually self-discipline and the attempt to impose a pattern of behaviour on an employee should normally only be considered if the employee is unable to show the appropriate self-discipline. If it is appropriate to 'bring an employee into line', one should normally seek to do this with the minimum amount of pressure consistent with that objective. If an employee's performance or conduct is inappropriate, it would seem sensible to encourage the employee to see this and work out for himself the required change in his behaviour. As was stated during the section on performance appraisal, people can often be their own harshest critics. It would seem far better, therefore, to give an employee the opportunity to mend his ways voluntarily rather than to try to impose one's authority. Apart from the greater commitment that this may create, it may also save the employee's face to be allowed to work out his own salvation. Again, as with grievance handling, even if counselling does not prove to be a complete answer, it may clear the way for appropriate action on any residual disagreement. The counselling stage may also be necessary to clarify the exact nature of the shortcomings, if indeed there are any. One of the problems of disciplinary handling is that there may need to be a considerable amount of discussion before it can be clarified whether there is a disciplinary problem or not. Counselling may, however, be just the first stage in the disciplinary process. The handling of further stages in that process is the subject of the next chapter.

NOTES

1. A. Savage, 'Reconciling your appraisal system with company reality', *Personnel Management*, May 1982, vol. 14, no. 5, p. 131.
2. Deirdre Gill and Bernard Ungerson, *Equal pay: the challenge of equal value* (Institute of Personnel Management, 1984), p. 47.
3. For a general and more detailed account of appraisal, see Gerry Randell, Peter Packard and John Slater, *Staff appraisal: a first step to effective leadership* (Institute of Personnel Management, 1984), third edition.
4. For a review of appraisal practice and more detailed information on rating and recording see Deidre Gill, *Appraising performance* (Institute of Personnel Management, 1977), Information Report No. 25.

APPENDIX I

Simplified and modified extracts from the documentation used for recording and rating the appraisal of sales staff in a department store.

Introductory comment

These extracts are given, not as a model appraisal form, but as an example. Other documentation that needs to accompany the following extracts includes:

1. Briefing notes for appraisers.
2. Sections for basic bio-data and a definition of the period under review.
3. Rating-factor definitions.
4. Signature sheet.

In practice a considerable amount of space would be allowed on the forms for the recording of comments.

Appraisal objectives

1. To facilitate any appropriate improvement in performance of the current job.
2. To identify training needs related to the current job.

Appraisal rating and report

Key tasks

Brief description of the six-to-eight key tasks of the appraisee. (This needs to be cross-checked with the job description and the appraisee).

Ratings

A Exceeds basic job requirements in most or all respects.
B Exceeds basic job requirements in some respects.
C Meets basic requirements.
D Fails to meet basic requirements.

Factor	Rating	Supporting comment

1. Job knowledge
2. Work effort
  (cross-refer to any sales
  data)
3. Appearance
4. Communication
  (a) with customers
  (b) with colleagues
5. Responsibility and
  initiative
6. Tact and diplomacy
  (a) with customers
  (b) with colleagues
7. Stability and reliability		

Summary of attendance record
(To be completed with reference to available statistics)

(a) Punctuality
(b) Sickness absence
(c) Unauthorised absence
(d) Other absence (e.g. compassionate)

Any other observations

Achievement report

1. Bearing in mind the appraisee's time within the company and present position, comment on his (or her) effectiveness in carrying out his duties and responsibilities. This should show the main strengths and any weakness of the appraisee within his existing job.
2. Can the appraisee's main strengths be better used and weaknesses remedied within the present job? If so please specify.
3. Is any training (formal or informal) or other form of support needed to maintain or improve performance? If so please specify.
4. *Overall rating of performance.* This judgement should be made in relation to key tasks, the ratings and other recorded comment. Use the rating key.

11

Disciplinary Handling

INTRODUCTION

The need to discipline subordinates can be unpleasant and embarrassing, but it is a necessary aspect of a manager's job. If everyone behaves in an appropriate way then the manager doesn't need to be concerned with disciplinary action, but sadly that isn't always the case. When managers are confronted with disciplinary problems they may handle them effectively, but often the problems are ignored, or dealt with unskilfully, too harshly or too leniently. Many managers would prefer to have nothing to do with discipline but, if they opt out, they are in reality opting out of what is an integral part of their job. The embarrassment that a manager can feel can affect the skill with which he handles disciplinary issues. This is an area, however, where he can develop some skills at least, without too much difficulty. Effective action can contain problems and prevent them getting out of hand. The effectiveness of a manager in this area can have a considerable impact on his relationships, not just with a person who may have to be disciplined, but with the other subordinates who may see particular incidents very much as test cases.

In this chapter attention is paid to the objectives of disciplinary policies which are often not clearly thought out. The legal position in Britain is briefly explained, partly because this is one aspect of discipline, but more importantly because of the impact that it can have on disciplinary action other than dismissal. The responsibility of the individual manager is considered, as are the procedures and procedural skills necessary for appropriate action.

THE OBJECTIVES OF DISCIPLINE

Just as with performance appraisal, so with disciplinary situations, a manager needs to work out quite carefully just what he is trying to achieve. Too often consideration of this topic simply consists of a discussion of an employer's track record at industrial tribunals. It may be that an employer has never lost a case at an industrial tribunal but that may prove very little. There is not much point in an employer always winning his cases at a tribunal if, in the meantime, his line managers have opted out of their disciplinary role, possibly with a catastrophic effect on standards of performance. Dismissal may be a necessary step to take and, when it is taken, it is undoubtedly best for an employer to be able to defend his actions successfully. However, it is no good just looking at the dismissal end of the disciplinary process. Dismissal is necessary only if other, more appropriate, means of dealing with a disciplinary problem, including attempts to alter a person's behaviour, have failed or are pointless. Any formal intervention can, to some extent, be regarded as a sign of failure — in that the more satisfactory approach of self-discipline may have failed.

Disciplinary action may only be appropriate if a person's behaviour is having a detrimental effect on his or other people's work. It follows from this that the objective is normally to try to get a person to mend his ways so that his behaviour is improved. If this is likely to prove impossible, then a manager has to make a judgement whether to put up with it or to consider following the avenue that could lead to dismissal. Judgements about when to intervene and about what issues may need considerable thought. People may have many irritating habits that they can't, or won't, change and it may be pointless trying to make them. Conversely, if a manager is too lenient, he may find that events get seriously out of hand: the analogy of a stitch in time saving nine can be highly appropriate with regard to discipline. A small issue discreetly checked at the right time can prevent escalation into something far more difficult to contain. That is why it is much better for a manager consciously to decide what intervention he makes, rather than to let things drift.

One particular horror story I came across recently concerned a woman who had two full-time jobs. She managed this by alternating between the sick-pay schemes of two companies. Discipline became a 'sick' joke in the departments of the companies concerned. Often employees prefer a tighter discipline than actually exists and may resent seeing colleagues being able to behave in an unconscientious way. This tends to devalue their own job and may lead to them leaving, or deciding that they may as well follow the lead that is given. Standards of attendance and punctuality can, for example, vary widely from department to department, even within the same organisation, acording to the lead given by the managers concerned. Employees can also object to too harsh a regime, which is why managers need to think carefully what standards are appropriate and how they should be achieved, rather than avoid thinking about the issue at all.

The political judgements that a manager has to make may be particularly difficult when dealing with professional-level employees. Some of them may find any concept of external control unacceptable, yet develop their work in a way that does not fit with the needs of the organisation. It is useful to distinguish between the professional's technical competence and his accountability for achieving objectives. It may be more effective, and acceptable, to make the point that discussion about the latter topic does not necessarily reflect on the professional employee's specialist competence.

There is a tendency for some managers to overestimate the extent to which standards in the disciplinary area are decided externally. It can be very convenient to assume that the responsibility for establishing and maintaining disciplinary standards lies elsewhere — either within the organisation or outside it. Organisations invariably have overall policies and procedures concerning discipline, but these provide a framework within which a manager should operate, rather than devices for passing the buck. It is only the manager in an individual department who can monitor and interpret the policies and procedures. If a person is not doing his job properly, it would seem to be a fundamental part of the manager's job to consider bringing the matter to the person's attention. The definition of standards within a department has to be undertaken, communicated and, when appropriate, enforced by the manager concerned. The existence of overall policies and procedures does not take away the individual manager's responsibility in this area, however much some managers would like to pretend that it does.

The primary objective of discipline is to identify and deal with inappropriate behaviour by employees which has an adverse effect on their work or the work of colleagues. It is implicit in this that disciplinary action will have a beneficial effect and not be counterproductive, and also that it is the most appropriate way of dealing with a particular problem. Another important objective is to demonstrate that discipline is administered fairly. It is necessary to try to demonstrate this, not only to the person who may be the subject of disciplinary action, but also to his colleagues, whose attitudes can be considerably influenced by the action taken. The emphasis in discipline usually needs to be on reform. The legal rights of an ex-employee to pursue a case for unfair dismissal do, though, have some impact on the disciplinary policies and procedures, so it is appropriate to explain the legal position in Britain before considering the skills involved in disciplinary handling.

THE LAW RELATING TO DISMISSAL

Since 1972 people who have been dismissed have had the right to claim before an industrial tribunal that they have been unfairly dismissed. This legal right was part of the 1971 Industrial Relations Act with the unfair dismissal provisions being implemented the following year. Since then there have been some modifications to the law, but the current legal provisions, mainly embodied in the 1978 Employment Protection (Consolidation) Act, do not differ greatly from the provisions that were first introduced. Further, relatively minor, amendments were introduced under the terms of the Employment Acts of 1980 and 1982. Before 1972 the only significant right of employees who had been dismissed was to take an action in the civil courts under common law, if they had not received their proper entitlement to notice. Such actions alleging 'wrongful dismissal' were restricted to considering the amount of notice, or money in lieu of notice, to which the ex-employee was entitled. Statutory rights to redundancy payments were first introduced in 1965, but the rights under the Redundancy Payments Act were restricted to the amount of compensation that an employee was entitled to, not whether or not he should have been dismissed.

Employers are still, of course, able to dismiss — the application for unfair dismissal is made only after the employee has been given notice. Normally any tribunal hearing will only take place several weeks after a dismissal has actually taken place. Industrial tribunals are obliged to consider reinstatement (or re-engagement) as a remedy, if an application alleging unfair dismissal is upheld, but this can only be recommended and not enforced. Although tribunals can award extra compensation if a recommendation to reinstate is resisted by the employer, the normal remedy is financial compensation and not reinstatement. Employers still have to consider the industrial repercussions of a dismissal. Irresepective of whether a tribunal judges a dismissal to be fair or unfair, or irrespective of whether a tribunal even hears a case, sanctions may be applied by the remaining workers to try to secure the reinstatement of a colleague.

Legal exclusions

Not all dismissed employees can take their case to a tribunal. The main exclusions are:

1. Employees who have not completed two years' continuous employment with their former employer;
2. Employees who have reached the normal retiring age;
3. Part-time workers employed for less than 16 hours a week (unless they have worked for eight hours a week for five years or more);
4. Employees engaged under fixed-term contracts who have signed away their rights to take an action for unfair dismissal.

Applicants also have to apply to a tribunal within three months of their dismissal. The length of service requirement does not apply to applicants who maintain they have been, or are to be, dismissed on account of their sex, race, trade union activity, or non-membership of a union. Employers are also required to observe the statutory procedures regarding consultation with recognised trade unions in the event of redundancy, regardless of the length of service of employees. Whilst these exceptions have not been subject to much variation the basic length of service requirement has been something of a political football. The latest change, which may of course not be the final one, was contained in the Finance Act of 1985. This increased

197

the normal length of service requirement from one to two years.

Grounds for dismissal

The grounds on which an employer can establish that a dismissal was fair are quite broad. The three main grounds, in practice, are capacity, conduct and redundancy. Dismissal also has to be reasonable in the circumstances. Dismissal on grounds of lack of capacity can be justified because of a person's poor performance or on medical grounds. Dismissal on grounds of misconduct can be either because of a single instance of gross misconduct, which can entitle an employer to dismiss without notice, or because of cumulative misconduct in which case the appropriate notice, or money in lieu, has to be given. Gross misconduct is not easy to define, the best definition perhaps being that 'you can't define it in advance but you can recognise it when you see it'. An employer will help establish his position on the matter, however, by including in any disciplinary rules predictable examples of what he considers will constitute gross misconduct. The employer will, however, need to demonstrate that he has sought systematically and fairly to enforce any such rules. His position at a tribunal would be weak if a former employee were able to demonstrate uneven application of any such rules. Erratic attendance and timekeeping are particularly common examples of cumulative misconduct and in cases like this the employer needs to be able to demonstrate to a tribunal that he has tried to operate policies fairly, and in such a way that the pressure on an employee was gradually stepped up, before any consideration of dismissal. In cases of redundancy, an ex-employee may argue that a redundancy was bogus or, if it was genuine, that he was unfairly selected for redundancy. The main test in establishing whether or not there was a redundancy is whether or not the person was replaced. Selection for redundancy has to be in accordance with an agreed policy or, in the absence of this, to be 'reasonable'. Length of service is a particularly important criterion in deciding who should be retained and who should be dismissed, but other criteria can also be considered.

Defences by the employer

In considering whether or not an employer has acted reasonably, a tribunal has to judge the employer's behaviour on the evidence available at the time. Even if evidence available after the dismissal proves that the employer was wrong, the dismissal may still have been 'reasonable'. Tribunals are also obliged to accept that there can be a number of different ways of handling a situation, all of which can be regarded as reasonable. An employer's judgement does not necessarily have to coincide with the judgement that the tribunal members would have made in the same situation for it to be regarded as reasonable. Regard also has to be paid to the procedure that an employer has followed in dismissing an employee. The Code of Practice on Disciplinary and Dismissal Procedures issued by the Advisory Conciliation and Arbitration Service (ACAS) provides the guidelines that employers are expected to follow. These guidelines are rather like the Highway Code — a breach in itself is not actionable, but in the circumstances of a dismissal a breach of the guidelines can lead to an application for unfair dismissal succeeding. The critical test is whether any decision to dismiss would have been likely to have been different had the guidelines been followed. Employers should have their own disciplinary procedures, which may or may not have been agreed with the appropriate trade unions, which follow the pattern recommended in the Code. The critical recommendations concerning procedures are reproduced as Appendix I of this chapter.

Appeals can be made against tribunal decisions, but only on points of law. Tribunals have three members — a person drawn from a panel submitted by the CBI, one from a panel submitted by trade union organisations (mainly the TUC), and a lawyer who acts as chair.

The freedom of action of the employer to dismiss is often greatly underestimated. This may be because of misunderstandings about the legal position, or because it may be a convenient alibi to maintain that the employer has much less discretion than he really has. One of the common mistakes that is made is for people to confuse the burden of proof in civil actions before a tribunal with the burden in criminal cases. An employer does not have to estabish his case 'beyond reasonable doubt', as is the case in criminal prosecutions. It is up to the tribunal to determine whether the onus of proof rests with the employer or former employee. Even so, the case has only to be established on the balance of evidence and the argument. At the risk of oversimplifying the issue, it is useful to liken the burden of proof to being 95 per cent at a criminal case but only 50 per cent at an industrial tribunal. Most applications alleging unfair dismissal are not in fact upheld. Of the 34 per cent of cases in 1986–7 that were not withdrawn, or privately settled, 66 per cent were decided in favour of the employer. The average (median) compensation awarded by tribunals in that year was £1,805.[1] The tribunals have proved to be more formal and legalistic than was originally intended. However, the fact that former employees can argue their case themselves, or be represented by their trade union, encourages people, perhaps quite rightly, to bring a case if there is just the remotest possibility of them winning. Lawyers do not have to be used and costs are usually only awarded against unsuccessful applicants if they have brought a vexatious or frivolous case.

Employers are much more likely to be defending the defensible rather than the indefensible if they appear before a tribunal. The requirement for them to be 'reasonable' sets a maximum standard for behaviour as well as a minimum — they do not have to have acted perfectly. Any well-organised employer should, almost by definition, be able to have a much better track record at tribunals than the national average. Successful applications against the employer occur particularly in the less well-organised sectors of the economy where managerial resources are limited. A convenient rule of thumb is for an employer to expect to win nine out of ten cases. A lower success rate may indicate weaknesses that need attention and a higher success rate the possibility that the employer is being too cautious. I am not suggesting that employers should be cavalier in their attitude to dismissal, but that it is in the nature of events that there will be occasional genuine differences of opinion between employers and tribunals. Employers can always consider reinstating if they lose a case at a tribunal. It is important to recognise that, if employers are seen to opt out of dismissing employees, unless the reasons are overwhelming, this can create a climate where nobody tries to tell anybody what to do, on the basis that nothing is likely to be done if the person refuses. The impact of decisions concerning dismissal needs to be seen in relation to the standards of performance in an organisation and not in isolation, or just in terms of the track record at tribunals.

The need for procedure

The Achilles heel of employers at tribunals often turns out to be their failure to follow a systematic procedure, even though there may be a clearly defined procedure within the organisation that the employer should follow. Individual managers may fail to deal with a disciplinary issue and then, when their frustration builds up, may dismiss in a moment of anger. The legal requirements are no so much aimed at preventing dismissal but at ensuring that, when it does take place, it is for appropriate reasons and in a manner which preserves the rights of the individual concerned to natural justice. The guidelines in Appendix I do not seem too difficult to follow but, as with so many areas of management, the problem is one of application of existing knowledge rather than having some magic wand for dealing with problems. One particularly apt quote from a tribunal illustrates this point: 'Mr G did not on that occasion give the applicant a serious reprimand, although he did mention that he would kill him if such a thing occurred again.'[2] The observance of appropriate procedures is not just a technical matter but one which can of course affect the actual decision which is taken. The decision to dismiss a person before he has, for example, had the opportunity to state his case is wrong, not just because it is a breach of justice but also because the fact-finding process is incomplete.

Consideration may also need to be given to separate procedures for handling performance or attendance problems that do not arise from any misconduct on the part of employees. There are, unfortunately, occasions when people can be trying their best but nevertheless still fail to meet minimum job standards. These, strictly speaking, are not disciplinary issues. In some organisations separate procedures are established to deal with such cases, whilst in others the cases are handled within the disciplinary procedure. Guidance on this and related issues is contained in the latest version of the ACAS Code of Practice on Disciplinary and Dismissal Procedures.

Sometimes employers try to circumvent the whole disciplinary process by putting so much pressure on an employee that he leaves. One of the dangers of this approach, apart from its doubtful morality, is that a tribunal could treat a forced resignation as a constructive dismissal. This can happen if the pressure by the employer amounts to a breach of the employment contract. The particular problem that the employer then has is to explain what opportunity the former employee had to state his case before being forced out. It is not sufficient for employers to have good procedures; it is also necessary for their managers to have the skills to operate the procedure appropriately. This is necessary for the handling of all disciplinary cases, not just the small proportion that result in dismissal. Consequently the skills involved in disciplinary handling are the next issue that needs to be considered.

THE RESPONSIBILITY OF THE INDIVIDUAL MANAGER

The first prerequisite for effective disciplinary handling is that managers accept their responsibility and discretion in this area. It is also important for them to encourage colleagues to do the same. There is a great temptation for subordinate managers to refer disciplinary matters upwards. It may be better to coach managers who do this to handle disciplinary situations for themselves, rather than take away their responsibility in this area.

Any form of action needs to be preceded by careful diagnosis. There can be many reasons for inappropriate behaviour including an inaccurate definition of what is appropriate. It is only when the facts have been checked out that one can begin to consider if disciplinary action is appropriate. Even if a person has behaved inappropriately, it may be that he sees this for himself and doesn't need to have salt rubbed in his wounds. This was the judgement made in one chemical works when a technician wrecked a particularly expensive piece of equipment. The manager concerned took the view that that was one mistake the technician would never make again. However, sometimes employees do need to have the error of their ways pointed out to them — either because they do not realise that they are in error or because they think that they can behave in a particular way with impunity.

Having established just who has the proper responsibility for dealing with such situations, it is important to stress that reform might as well be achieved with the minimum amount of pressure that is required to bring about the desired change in behaviour. If a quiet word will do the trick, there is little point in antagonising employees by using more pressure than is necessary. The oral warning may be the most important level in the disciplinary process. It may be convenient for people to argue that the only sanction is the sack, but the reality is that most people don't like being corrected, and that psychologically the oral warning is a sanction that the manager may find he can use effectively. Only if this doesn't lead to the required change in behaviour does the manager need to consider more formal measures.

The introduction of the law to protect employees against unfair dismissal has tended to concentrate attention on issues related to dismissal. Discipline is however a generic term and dismissal is just one aspect of the disciplinary process. Ideally policies and practices should be such that disciplinary issues are contained so that it is rare for a dismissal to be necessary. If there is effective supervisory and managerial control issues should be so contained. If this is not the case too many issues may be allowed to spiral upwards before being dealt with. The main volume of activity should be at the lower levels (see Figure 11.1).

Figure 11.1: The disciplinary pyramid

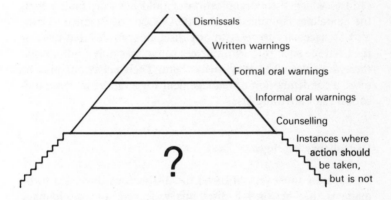

A heavy emphasis on severe penalties may be indicative of ineffective control at the lower levels of the pyramid. This can happen all too frequently and what can emerge is that 'disciplinary problems' can be the symptom of much deeper organisational problems. This can be the lack of effective supervision and management. Contributory factors to this can be a general opting out of the management process and poor selection and training of supervisors and managers. Sometimes supervisors either see themselves as not having any disciplinary responsibility at all, or are extremely vague about just what those responsibilities are. The area where greatest organisational attention and clarification is often needed is the responsibility for investigation and follow-up of minor issues and the administering, where appropriate, of low-level penalties. This involves more than just the drawing up of a clear procedure but also the training of supervisors and managers in how to handle their responsibilities. If these steps are not taken one is likely to have supervisors and managers intervening and getting it wrong or getting away with the potentially disastrous attitude that disciplinary control of their own subordinates is nothing to do with them but is some other mysterious person's responsibility!

DISCIPLINARY PROCEDURES AND PROCEDURAL SKILLS

When formal disciplinary proceedings appear to be appropriate, it is necessary for managers to refer to the disciplinary procedures which their organisations should have or, failing that, the guidelines contained in the ACAS Code of Practice. It may also be necessary to refer to any disciplinary rules that exist or the need for such rules. Employees sometimes only find out that there are rules when they break them. Their behaviour may be more a condemnation of management for a failure in communication than anything else.

Disciplinary hearings

Perhaps the most crucial of all the distinctions that need to be made is that between a disciplinary hearing and disciplinary action. A common failing, revealed by a Department of Employment survey, is for managers to assume that the outcome of proceedings is a foregone conclusion, and to 'sentence' the employee early in such proceedings.[3] The word 'hearing' is as important as the word 'disciplinary' and one cannot be sure that disciplinary action is appropriate until the hearing has been completed. A formal 'hearing' may not be necessary if relatively minor action is likely but, whatever the level of formality, it is important that the employee is given the opportunity to state his case before any action is taken. At a formal hearing it is normally appropriate for the managers conducting the hearing to recess before communicating any decision. This gives the managers time to discuss the position carefully, and to see if they have any differences of view, before any action is determined. Even if an employee's conduct seems quite inexcusable, there will be occasions when it turns out that an issue was not as straightforward as it first appeared. In any case justice needs to be seen to be done, as well as being done, not just for the benefit of the employee concerned, but for his colleagues as well. Although these points are obvious enough, my own experience has often been in line with the evidence revealed in the Department of Employment survey. On one occasion I found that an employee was listened to carefully, only to be handed a letter of dismissal which must have been typed *before* the hearing started. On another occasion an employee was asked to sit outside the room to await the decision of a disciplinary panel and was then given a letter of dismissal, which could have been typed during the recess apart from the fact that it was dated a week previously!

Suspension

A predicament which employers can face is behaviour by an employee which necessitates his leaving the employer's premises immediately. This could be for a variety of reasons, including fighting, apparent drunkenness or apparent theft. The appropriate course of action in such situations is to suspend the employee pending an investigation. Even if it appears that the employee has committed gross misconduct, which justifies summary dismissal, such a decision should not be taken without there being a disciplinary hearing. If the case against an employee is established at a hearing, then dismissal may be effected without notice from that point in time. If there is no such hearing, the employer will have fallen into the trap of prejudging the issue. Apart from giving an employee time to prepare his case, an interval between an incident and a decision can lead to a cooling of tempers all round and increase the prospects of a rational decision. This type of suspension is quite distinct from suspension, with or without pay, which is sometimes used as a form of penalty after a hearing has been completed. The distinction may need to be made to employees who are being suspended, together with an explanation that nothing is decided until the hearing is completed and that there is no loss of pay involved. The important point is that managers faced with the problem of needing to get somebody off the premises immediately should do this by suspension and not instant dismissal.

A further source of confusion can arise if a person has apparently committed a criminal action. It is a fallacy to assume that such action can only be handled by the police. If, for example, a person has apparently stolen something, it may be appropriate for the employer to institute disciplinary proceedings about the employee's apparent unauthorised possession of property belonging to the employer. Any decisions about whether or not there should be a prosecution should be handled separately. The option of letting such an issue be handled simply by the police may not be as easy as it seems. As has already been explained, the burden of proof in criminal law is much higher than in civil law. The procedural rules are much tighter in the criminal courts and it may be necessary to establish that a felony was committed or attempted. Added to this is the problem that, if no action is taken pending a court hearing, an employee may have to be suspended on pay for several months. In any case the employer may find that, if the case is substantiated, the primary remedy he wants is to be able to dismiss the person concerned. The point that needs stressing is that apparent criminal activity by an employee against his employer does not remove the employer's rights to handle an issue as a disciplinary matter.

An interesting illustration of the perils for the employer of relying on just the prosecution route was the case of Clive Ponting, a former senior civil servant in the Ministry of Defence. He admitted to having leaked information about British naval operations conducted during the Falklands War of 1982. Ponting was consequently charged under the Official Secrets Act but was able to convince the jury that, as the information was divulged only after the war was over and was in the national interest, he should be acquitted. The Government could still have initiated disciplinary proceedings after his acquittal in 1985 and pressed for dismissal on the grounds of misconduct — which would have been an easier procedural task. However, because this would probably have been seen as a case of 'sour grapes' on the part of the Government it could have been very counterproductive politically. As it was Ponting saved the Government further embarrassment by resigning.

Provided there is no specific procedural requirement that a prosecution should be resolved before disciplinary proceedings are taken, it is normally better for the employer to resolve the disciplinary issue in advance of a prosecution being resolved. Amongst other things, this avoids the dilemma of what to do if a person has already been acquitted in the criminal courts. Subsequent acquittal does not invalidate disciplinary action previously taken because the disciplinary action should be based on the rather separate issue of the extent to which the employee, or ex-employee, fulfilled his employment contract. People may nevertheless raise the issue of 'double jeopardy' forgetting that this is a concept to do with the criminal law only. Whilst it is not possible for a person to be charged twice with the same offence under criminal law, there is no prohibition on an employer taking the civil action of terminating a person's employment irrespective of whether or not prosecution is initiated based on the circumstances that led to the person's dismissal.

The role of the representative

Another critical issue concerning disciplinary procedures is the need for an employee to be accompanied by a representative. Sometimes managers see this as a sign of weakness, but ignoring the right to representation is far more likely to create trouble than prevent it. A representative who is denied the right to represent a colleague may see this as a breach of natural justice, the employer's disciplinary procedure, and the guidelines contained in the Code of Practice. The issue may then turn into the possibly larger issue of the right of a union to represent its members. In any case, a representative's function is to help a person put his case so that any decision is taken only after all the relevant arguments have been considered. The representative himself may have heard only the employee's version of events. A formal hearing can provide an employer with the opportunity to put over his version. This may influence the representative, whose views may be crucial if an issue is sensitive and likely to lead to industrial action. If an employer has a good case, it is appropriate that he should explain it; if the case is weak, then perhaps it should be dropped. Often managers fail to realise that the really critical audience in disciplinary proceedings can be the employee's colleagues.

The position of the representative has also to be considered. He may well feel that, whatever an employee has done, he has the right to have his case argued strongly, even if privately the representative does not condone the employee's behaviour. At the end of a hearing at least the representative can explain that he has done what he can for the employee concerned. If the representative does not agree with the action that an employer eventually takes, at least any subsequent disagreement need not be compounded by arguments about whether the man had a fair hearing. The crucial distinction is that, whatever an employee has or has not done, this should not affect his right to a fair hearing. Care should always be taken to ensure that employees know their procedural rights and it is preferable that they have a copy of any relevant disciplinary rules and procedures.

The need for a chair

When formal disciplinary hearings are held, consideration should be given to one of the managers acting as chair. A manager obviously will not be viewed as a totally independent person, but proper chairing can help ensure that proceedings are conducted as impartially as possible. One of the dangers of the senior manager present putting the case himself is that he may then be seen as judge, prosecutor, jury, executioner and possibly witness all rolled into one. A further problem is that, if the senior manager gets involved in an argument, which would not be surprising given such a load of conflicting roles, then it is difficult for anyone else to keep the proceedings in order. A more satisfactory procedure is for the senior manager to concentrate on chairing, leaving other people to present any case and evidence. This is not only necessary for form's sake but to see that the proceedings are conducted in a systematic manner, so that no decision is taken until the arguments have all been properly considered. This role of chair should continue during a recess. Consideration also has to be given as to who should participate in the discussions during the recess. In some organisations managers who have been involved in presenting the case against the employee are excluded from any further involvement. This is in order to reduce the possibility of collusion between those playing the roles of 'judge' and 'prosecutor'.

Conduct during hearings and appeals procedures

Perhaps the most awkward part of the whole disciplinary process is handling disagreements either about what happened or about what action should be taken. It is a fallacy that management is impotent unless an employee agrees to be disciplined, or that irrefutable proof has to be produced to substantiate any difference of opinion. The reality is that it is necessary for the managers carefully to hear and consider the relevant points and then to consider what action, if any, is appropriate. As with tribunals, the standard of proof, or the strictness of procedure, does not have to match criminal proceedings. The parties are in fact considering a civil issue concerning the degree to which an employee has fulfilled his contract of employment and not a murder trial. However, for proceedings to be handled effectively a clear, and preferably agreed, sequence of events needs to be established at each hearing. This should include arrangements for the exchange of any written documents and explanation of when each side should state their case, produce witnesses, cross-examine and sum up. The framework is essentially judicial but sometimes the parties can mistakenly adopt a negotiating approach. If that happens proceedings can degenerate into an unsystematic attempt by each side to browbeat the other which can aggravate an already delicate situation instead of 'defusing' it. Managerial representatives often also fail to realise the need for careful preparation and presentation of their case and evidence. The skills of advocacy are often much more part of the 'stock-in-trade' of union representatives than they are of managers. Consequently managers may lose cases, and their confidence, through poor preparation and presentation. To avoid this they need to develop their presentational skills so that they try to at least match those of the union representatives.

When any decision is communicated it is imperative that there should be no argument — if proceedings have been properly conducted all the relevant points should have been considered before anyway. If an employee disagrees with the decision, the appropriate way of handling that is to explain any rights of appeal. Often violent arguments can break out at this stage, simply because it is not made clear to an employee that there is an appeals procedure that he is entitled to use.

Thought has to be given to the stage at which appeals can be lodged. It may not be necessary to provide for appeals against informal warnings, for example, especially as an employee can always use the grievance procedure if there is no formal procedure for handling appeals against minor penalties. It would seem appropriate, though, to build an appeals procedure into a disciplinary procedure when warnings get to the stage of indicating that dismissal is becoming a possibility. Appeals should be to managers not previously involved in the case. The grounds for an appeal should be clarified — they should not involve a total re-hearing of a case unless that is clearly appropriate. If, for example, an appeal is just against the disciplinary action that has been imposed, it is just the level of 'penalty' that needs to be considered. An employee's right of appeal should always be made clear, regardless of whether or not he argues about the decision when he is told about it. Time limits need to be imposed, so that if an appeal is not lodged within a certain period of time it lapses. This can avoid subsequent disagreement about whether or not the employee agreed with the decision. In cases where employees are dismissed, consideration also has to be given as to whether or not they stay on the payroll pending the hearing of their appeal.

Communicating the result

Before any decision is taken after a hearing, there needs to be a careful review of the options and of the need to communicate accurately what has been decided. The options include stating that the employee has been cleared. In cases of cumulative misconduct it is appropriate to step up the pressure on an employee gradually so that he either mends his ways, or is made perfectly aware that failure to change his ways will result in more serious action next time. Care needs to be taken in deciding just what a person is being warned about. If the grounds of the warning are narrow, for example lateness, an employee may be able to maintain that his lateness record cannot be taken into account if he is subsequently disciplined for absence. Thus it may be appropriate to broaden the base of a warning from lateness to general attendance. Warnings about other matters may include a proviso that repetition of a particular action, or related misconduct, can result in more disciplinary action. It is not recommended that such broadening of the terms of a warning be extended to a bland statement to the effect that, if the employee does anything else at all, it will be linked to previous warnings. However, too narrow a definition of what the warning is about can lead to the possibility of a person getting a number of 'final' warnings, all for different offences.

Consideration also needs to be given as to whether or not there should be fixed time limits for any penalties imposed. According to the results of the Department of Employment survey, the conventional wisdom is that this may create undesirable rigidities in the disciplinary area. Holidays, sickness, staff changes and procedural delays can all eat into the 'life' of a warning. There comes a point when previous warnings have realistically to be ignored, but it would seem better to leave this to the discretion of a disciplinary panel rather than to predetermine when warnings have lapsed by pre-arranged time limits. It is also necessary to consider just what previous warnings can be taken into account. One union representative I discussed this with made the reasonable point that informal oral warnings should not be part of a person's record because that contradicted the concept of informality. The concept of a person receiving a copy of a formal oral warning may also be contentious. The most appropriate step in the early stages of discipline could be from informal oral warning to first written warning, with only the latter going on a person's record. A manager may however find it useful to keep a diary noting oral warnings that are given prior to the stage at which warnings are recorded on a person's file.

It may be necessary to put the first formal warning in writing, not just to create procedural clarity, but also to ensure that a person realises what is happening. It is all too easy for disciplinary interviews to be handled with so light a touch that a person comes away with the impression that he has been commended rather than rebuked. Ambiguities and carelessness in communicating just what has happened, as a consequence of a disciplinary hearing, can result not only in failure to achieve the desired effect, but also in confrontation, if a person is disciplined again, about what really was decided the last time. The representative of an employee should be given a copy of any written warning so that it is also clear to him what has happened. This may also help to prevent subsequent argument about whether or not an employee has received his copy. A further way of avoiding argument on that score may be to ask an employee to acknowledge receipt of a warning, making it clear that this is only an acknowledgement, and not meant to commit the employee either to agreeing or to disagreeing with a written warning. The importance and number of points to be considered in drafting written warnings is such that a checklist of the potential issues is necessary. Such a checklist is produced as Appendix II of this chapter.

CONCLUSION

If managers are prepared to accept that they have a responsibility for discipline, much can be done to give them the necessary support to handle this aspect of their jobs effectively. Clear objectives and policies are necessary, as are clear procedures and rules. It may also be necessary for an employer to dispel myths about the operation of the disciplinary process. In one health authority where I was involved it was a generally held belief that there was no point in taking disciplinary action against employees because such action would only be reversed on appeal. On investigation it emerged that in the last year there had been ten internal appeals against dismissal and that all ten appeals had failed. This simple statistic had not previously been established and the myth was what people believed, not the reality. People may actually want to believe such myths, which is why it may be necessary to communicate what really does happen, as opposed to what people may prefer to think happens. If appeals are upheld — either internally or at an industrial tribunal — it is important that employers do not engage in 'witch-hunting' exercises. If there are lessons to be learned from appeal decisions, it is best that these be quietly noted and applied rather than be used to castigate the parties concerned. 'Witch-hunting' may cause the rest of the managers to adopt a low profile and to opt out of the disciplinary process.

In giving an appropriate lead to subordinate managers, senior managers may need to dispel the myth that the immediate boss is powerless unless he has complete authority to dismiss subordinates. There are points on the spectrum between no authority and total authority. The right to institute disciplinary proceedings, and if necessary to recommend dismissal, can be a powerful sanction that also brings with it an element of protection for the immediate boss. If he has the right to recommend, rather than decide, it removes the danger of dismissal being seen as motivated simply by personality factors. It also means that, if a decision is subsequently reversed or criticised, then the immediate boss can point out that the decision was taken or endorsed by his superiors.

Much can be done by way of coaching and formal training to develop the skills of managers in this area.[4] I am much more optimistic about the ability of managers to benefit by training in this area than in the rather more complex area of appraisal interviewing. If managers have the will to accept the disciplinary aspect of their jobs, it is not too difficult to get across the basic concept that, whatever an employee appears to have done, he is entitled to a fair hearing. I have found in running internal company courses that, after about a day and a half using closed circuit television, managers can develop from a level of farce to one of considerable competence in handling disciplinary issues. The manager who stays out of this area, or who never has the process explained to him, is never going to learn. Exposure to the skills involved in handling disciplinary issues, whether for real or in training sessions, or both, gives the manager the chance to develop his skills and to realise that the processes are not that complicated. This in turn may give him the confidence to handle issues that he previously chose to ignore. A positive approach to this area won't resolve all problems — there will, for example, always be some behaviour that can't be changed and some people who master the art of operating always just within the limits of any rules. However, positive action can lead to many problems being contained by timely intervention, so that standards of performance are achieved rather than undermined by managers opting out of their responsibilities.

NOTES

1. Department of Employment, *Employment Gazette* (HMSO, October 1987), pp. 499, 500.
2. Incomes Data Services Brief, 99 (December 1976).
3. Department of Employment, *Manpower paper* No. 14, (HMSO, 1975), para. 99. pp. 33–4.
4. For an account of an in-company formal training programme see Bob Lee and David Rees, 'Disciplinary skills training at Canada Dry Rawlings', *Personnel Executive* (February 1983), pp. 41–5.

APPENDIX I: GUIDELINES ON DISCIPLINARY PROCEDURES CONTAINED IN THE CODE OF PRACTICE*

1. Management should ensure that fair and effective arrangements exist for dealing with disciplinary matters. These should be agreed with employee representatives or trade unions concerned and should provide for full and speedy consideration by management of all the relevant facts. There should be a formal procedure except in very small establishments where there is close personal contact between the employer and his employees.
2. Management should make known to each employee:
   (i) Its disciplinary rules and the agreed procedure;
   (ii) The type of circumstances which can lead to suspension or dismissal.
3. The procedure should be in writing and should:
   (i) Specify who has the authority to take various forms of disciplinary action, and ensure that supervisors do not have the power to dismiss without reference to more senior management;
   (ii) Give the employee the opportunity to state his case and the right to be accompanied by his employee representative;
   (iii) Provide for a right of appeal, wherever applicable, to a level of management not previously involved;
   (iv) Provide for independent arbitration if the parties to the procedure wish it.
4. Where there has been misconduct, the disciplinary action to be taken will depend on the circumstances, including the nature of the misconduct. But normally the procedure should operate as follows:
   (i) The first step should be an oral warning or, in the case of more serious misconduct, a written warning setting out the circumstances;
   (ii) No employee should be dismissed for a first breach of discipline except in the case of gross misconduct;
   (iii) Action on any further misconduct, for example final warning, suspension without pay or dismissal, should be recorded in writing;

---

*Source: Code of Practice No. 1, Disciplinary and Dismissal Procedures, Section 10 (HMSO, 1977).

(iv) Details of any disciplinary action should be given in writing to the employee and, if he so wishes, to his employee representative;

(v) No disciplinary action should be taken against a shop steward until the circumstances of the case have been discussed with a full-time official of the union concerned.

APPENDIX II: CHECKLIST FOR DISCIPLINARY LETTERS

1. Requesting attendance at hearing

Item	*Comments*
Specify charges.	The charges are allegations. They may or may not be proved as a result of the hearing.
Suggest the employee brings a representative if he or she wishes.	If a representative comes it gives you the opportunity to put your case over to the representative.
Refer to the disciplinary procedure.	The employee should have a copy. If there is doubt enclose a copy.
Indicate that disciplinary action could be imposed according to the result of the hearing.	

2. Disciplinary letter (given after the hearing)

State what disciplinary action, if any, is to be taken.	
State the nature of the offence(s).	You may wish to incorporate general terms, such as misconduct, in any warning letter. This may make it easier in the future to refer back to earlier offences.

215

Specify any conditions about future conduct. This may include any help you are prepared to give.

Alternatively you may warn an employee about future conduct and any repetition or 'related offence' may render him liable to further action.

Specify any time limits.

Sometimes procedures provide for warnings to lapse after a certain period of good behaviour. If you don't have to put in time limits it is probably best not to — they can be rather rigid.

Specify any appeal procedure. Also the time limit for invoking the appeal procedure.

The more serious the penalty the more important it is to give a person the right of appeal.

State if you want the employee to:
(i) Acknowledge receipt of the letter;
(ii) Register dissent about any part of the letter he considers to be inaccurate.

If suspension is involved, state if it is with or without pay.

If suspension is without pay, check you have the legal right to do this.

Send a copy of the letter to the person's representative. Also to any managers concerned.

216

12

The Manager and Trade Unions

INTRODUCTION

In the previous chapter consideration was given to the role of the trade union representative in disciplinary situations. Attention also needs to be paid to the other issues on which there may be a trade union involvement. Managers need to be clear what their objectives are in management–union relationships — there is rather more to it than just avoiding stoppages. Considerable diagnostic skills can be needed by the manager in the identification of the causes of problems in management–union relationships. Often problems can be created as a side-effect of decisions taken elsewhere in an organisation which, on the face of it, have nothing to do with industrial relations. Employers who recognise unions will normally have formal policies, procedures and agreements that the individual manager will need to know and understand. Even if trade unions are not recognised by the employer, the manager will need to consider the effect of managerial decisions on the attitudes and behaviour of his subordinates. It may be irrelevant if employees are union members or not, if they refuse to co-operate with particular managerial decisions.

Special consideration is given in this chapter to the skills necessary for negotiation. These skills may be just as relevant in the conduct of other types of negotiation — for example in the general commercial area. The widespread coverage that white-collar unions have achieved, especially in the public sector, means that managers, as well as often having to deal with trade unions, may well also be trade union members themselves. This can create conflicts for them in reconciling their managerial and trade union roles. Detailed attention is given to the interrelationship between industrial relations and other management functions. This is because of the need for managers to develop a 'systems approach' (as explained in Chapter 3) to industrial relations. Finally current trends in industrial relations are identified and examined. These include the impact of chronically high levels of unemployment, legal developments and the erosion of union power.

OBJECTIVES IN INDUSTRIAL RELATIONS

The primary aim of managers in the industrial relations area is likely to be to obtain the co-operation of their subordinates in achieving organisational objectives. It is just as well to specify what those objectives are likely to be:

1. Cost-effective performance (resulting in low unit labour costs)
2. Control of change
3. The avoidance of stoppages and other sanctions

The pursuit of these objectives needs to be balanced as they may conflict with one another. This can also be the case with the objectives of trade unions which are likely to be:

1. The maintenance and, if possible, improvement of their members' terms and conditions of employment
2. Job security
3. Control of change
4. The avoidance of stoppages and other sanctions

The terms under which people work are negotiated either individually or between union representatives and the employer. The negotiated agreements represent a balance which provides sufficient incentive for both parties to come together. The parties will, however, take a continuing interest in the extent to which their concerns are being met. This may be done quite amicably — the resolution of areas of conflict through negotiation does not mean that sanctions have to be applied. Often the term 'conflict' is used in an industrial context synonymously with strikes, ignoring the point that the application of sanctions is a way of trying to resolve conflict only when negotiation has broken down.

Managers need to try to prevent strikes and the use of other coercive tactics by employees, but they will have to achieve other objectives as well. It is no good a manager or employer maintaining that he has no industrial relations problems because in his organisation there are no strikes and he has no trade unions, if employee co-operation is poor, performance low and costs high. 'Good' management–union relations are not an end in themselves, but a means for the respective parties to achieve their objectives. The individual manager wants to have a relationship with his employees such that he achieves his overall objectives. This is likely to involve him in elements of negotiation with his employees so that they find it sufficiently worthwhile to co-operate in achieving these objectives.

The responsibility for negotiating with employees is likely to be distributed within an organisation. The determination of overall wage and salary structures is likely to be centralised, with the personnel department, if it exists as a separate function, being considerably involved. External agencies may also be involved, such as employers' associations, external trade union organisations, parent or associated companies, the Government and legislative requirements. Internally there may need to be considerable co-ordination between individual managers, often facilitated by personnel departments, so that decisions form an integrated pattern and not a set of conflicting precedents. However, the individual manager is bound to have some responsibility within this framework. Even if all the financial and other formal agreements are determined outside his department, he has, as a minimum, to see that employees keep their side of the bargain. This means monitoring performance and wage costs and may also involve retaining sufficient control over work arrangements so that the employer's interests are protected.

Much of the media coverage of industrial relations focuses on wage claims, but the ongoing maintenance of managerial influence at shop-floor level can be just as critical. The historic problems of the British national newspapers, for example, stemmed much more from the lack of managerial control and influence at shop-floor level than from the problems of annual wage bargaining. The individual manager's primary responsibility in industrial relations is likely, then, to be the monitoring

219

of work arrangements within his own department. These work arrangements are likely to be subject to change and, in addition, the manager will have the responsibility for implementing any changes in the work arrangements effectively.

DIAGNOSTIC SKILLS

It has been necessary to spend some time in clarifying the objectives and involvement of managers in industrial relations because the key issues are not always self-evident. Also appropriate objectives need to be identified before managers can establish a proper basis for decision-making in industrial relations. The nature of the problems can often be easy enough to recognise — some of the most likely ones being interruptions to work, poor performance, resistance to change and restrictive practices. What can be much more difficult is establishing the actual causes of these problems and working out what, if anything, can be done about them. The emotional nature of the subject can hinder accurate diagnosis — if one has come to hate the sight of a particular representative it can be very tempting to go along with a stereotyped view to the effect that all 'troublemakers' should be sacked or, according to some, imprisoned or shot! The reality is, of course, that, whatever one's feelings, one usually has to live with particular representatives, and they with their managers, about whom they may have equally strong views.

Bad personal relationships can exacerbate management−union relationships and in some cases conflicts can be no more than personality clashes. However, even if all the people involved were angels, they would still have to resolve issues where the interests of the parties are in conflict. One of the skills that managers need in this area is the ability to identify the basic conflicts that lie behind any personal issues. It is important, too, for the manager to judge the extent to which a representative is reflecting the views of his colleagues. Getting rid of the representative, even if this was possible, would not do much good if someone else then replaced him and made the same representations on behalf of his colleagues.

Recognising conflicts of interest

Perhaps the most critical ability needed by the manager is that of being able to recognise when managerial and employee interests come into conflict. Some people adopt a unitary perspective of the organisation and simply don't accept that this can happen. The line of argument can be that what is good for the organisation is automatically good for all of its employees. Whilst this approach may present a simple and comforting philosophy for those who hold it, it does not help equip managers to deal with the conflicts of interest which can manifest themselves — for example, about wage levels, working arrangements and job security. Managers may be so preoccupied with the various pressures upon them that they neglect to consider the implications for their employees of particular decisions. If their employees see their interests being threatened in any way, they are likely to take action to protect those interests. It may, for example, be highly inconvenient for an employer to find that employees resist the introduction of new processes because the changes are seen as a threat to career opportunities and job security, but decision-making needs to be based on an accurate assessment of the employees' views and not wishful thinking.

Resistance to change can blandly be ascribed to the innate conservatism of the work force, but such an analysis may miss the point that employees may resist a particular change because it represents a threat to their interests. Other changes, such as pay increases, may be eagerly accepted. It is the nature of the change, and its impact on their interests, that employees are likely to consider. In a study of restrictive practices, carried out for the Donovan Commission, it was concluded that 'there must be few restrictive labour practices which are not genuinely thought by at least one of the parties concerned to be defensible in terms of their own interests'.[1] If diagnosis has been accurately undertaken, it is at least possible for managers to consider what, if anything, can be done. Acceptance that one just has to live with some problems may be much more constructive than time, money and effort being wasted on false solutions that won't work because the diagnosis was faulty. With some problems remedial action can be taken. It may be that effective communication can remove misunderstanding, or that it can pave the way to a negotiated answer which gives sufficient concessions to both parties to make a deal worthwhile. Anticipation of problems can lead to their being avoided or reduced in scale. If labour-saving processes are to be introduced, it may be best to time their introduction so that it coincides with a time when job security fears will be low rather than high.

Much can be achieved simply by managers thinking through the implications of their decisions as far as the employees are concerned. Managers may, for example, make apparently simple technical decisions blissfully unaware of the problems their decisions can create in other parts of the organisation. If product schedules, for example, are to be altered in such a way that people's earnings are affected, it is best to anticipate the likely reaction of employees, and to take that into account at the decision-making stage, rather than to take the decision in ignorance of its likely effects. The importance of identifying the interrelationship between industrial relations and decisions in other areas of management is such that a separate section is devoted to this topic later in this chapter. Diagnosis also need to take account of the power relationships. If a clash of interests is identified it is then necessary to calculate the extent to which the respective parties are able to impose their views. It may seem regrettable that conflicts are determined by power relationships as well as by intellectual, technical and moral criteria, but it is hardly prudent for a manager to try to impose a particular decision if it can easily be resisted. Conversely the mere fact that employees protest about a proposal doesn't automatically mean that the employer is not able to implement it.

Consideration also needs to be given to the frame of reference of the union negotiators. Usually they are likely to operate with a pluralistic frame of reference and to try and get the best bargain that is possible in the circumstances. However, some representatives may instead have a 'radical' frame of reference. This view is outlined by Alan Fox in a critique of the pluralist approach,[2] written by him after his initial identification of the unitary and pluralistic frame of reference (explained in Chapter 2). He explains that those with a radical perspective of society see the pluralists as advocates of 'enlightened managerialism' who simply try and make the existing (capitalistic) system work more effectively. This however leaves the existing fundamental distribution of power and control basically undisturbed. The radicals would argue that what is required is a dismantling of the existing structures and their replacement by more egalitarian arrangements. This can have very practical implications in negotiating relationships. If managements are confronted by a radical group they need to recognise that the group's objective may be to precipitate the collapse of existing insitutional arrangements by making unacceptable demands. If concessions are made which make agreement seem possible this may simply lead to fresh demands. An appropriate tactical response to such a challenge may be to seek to negotiate 'over the heads' of the radical representatives to check if they really have the support of their constituents.

Understanding union hierarchies

Consideration of the realities of management–union relationships needs also to take into account the fact that power within trade unions lies at the bottom of the organisation rather than at the top. The fact that unions have an organisational hierarchy can cause people to believe that they either do, or should, behave like organisations where power is much more at the top — as is the case with employers generally. Control in unions is ultimately in the hands of the lay members who pay their subscriptions and who elect their leaders. Elected groups of lay members have the ultimate formal authority in unions but, in any case, unions have to move in line with their members' wishes. It is no good an official calling a strike, or failing to call a strike, if his views are out of step with those of his members. Admittedly officials at all levels of a union can develop a considerable amount of influence, and they can bring considerable pressure to bear on individuals, or small groups, who do not follow the union line. However, there is little in the way of sanctions that a union can apply against a sizeable section of dissidents who, in any case, may threaten to join a rival union. This point has been amply demonstrated, since being made in the first edition of this book, by the establishment of the Union of Democratic Mineworkers in 1985 as a breakaway from the National Union of Mineworkers. The mistake that some people make is to see union officials as being akin to policemen with the responsibility and ability to 'bring their members into line'. Even if union officials were to accept this debatable view of their role, their power to discipline members is extremely limited.

223

JOINT AGREEMENTS

Relationships between employers and employees may to some extent be regulated by joint agreements. Collective agreements may be about substantive or procedural issues. Substantive agreements cover matters such as the wages and conditions of employment; procedural agreements can be likened to the Queensberry rules for boxing — there can at least be rules regulating the manner in which arguments about substantive issues are conducted! Procedural agreements may be about the resolution of differences over individual or collective issues. Consideration has already been given to the individual procedures that may exist concerning grievances, disciplinary issues and dismissals. Collective differences may be handled by a disputes procedure, which may also be used for handling wage claims. On the other hand, there may be a separate procedure for dealing with such claims. Sometimes there are also substantive agreements about redundancy payments and procedural arrangements for negotiating the implementation of possible redundancies. Obviously managers need to know the details of any agreements that may affect them. It is necessary for them not only to honour any substantive agreements but also to avoid making concessions that could have embarrassing repercussions in other parts of the organisation.

Procedural arrangements can provide a very useful framework for handling differences when they emerge. Managers and stewards can both be somewhat at a loss as to what to do when discussions end in failure. They can have a common interest in defining the area in dispute and agreeing on the next step and what, if anything, is to happen in the meantime. In this way a dispute can be processed without either party having had to give way, with the issue normally being referred to the next level so that it can be tackled afresh. The definition of the area of disagreement, and time thus bought for fresh thought, may help in the subsequent resolution of a dispute. If nothing else, procedures can get the immediate parties to the dispute off the hook, at least for a while. Ultimately, of course, if discussion at higher levels does not produce agreement, the thorny issue of what happens next has to be considered. Either side may give way or consider imposing their will, which in a way is the final stage of procedure. Managers will have to weigh up carefully the disadvantages of risking union resistance against the disadvantages of giving way. This needs to be a consciously taken decision. In some organisations the view is taken that management should never seek to impose unpopular decisions, but this can have disastrous consequences in terms of managerial control at shop-floor level. There is litte point, however, in trying to force an issue or series of issues if failure is likely.

Although the handling of differences via an agreed disputes procedure won't guarantee a satisfactory resolution, it does at least provide an alternative to an immediate 'shoot-out', and gives the parties the opportunity to explore the possibilities for an agreed solution. Knowledge that, if there is no agreement, there may be resort to 'other means' can in itself have a sobering effect on the parties. Sometimes arbitration is seen as the answer to unresolved differences, but if it is too readily available it may relieve the parties of the responsibility for settlement and lead to exaggerated claims and counter-claims with no movement towards a negotiated settlement. One of the advantages of agreed procedures is that the parties can at least limit the area of disagreement by agreeing what is in dispute and how the difference should be resolved, even if resolution can ultimately be one side trying to coerce the other. A further way of limiting the area of dispute can be the use of a 'status quo' clause in a disputes procedure, which provides for the continuation of work on the basis that existed before a dispute began. This can be a useful device, but there can be occasions when it is difficult to identify just when a dispute arose and therefore what the 'status quo' position was. Sometimes, too, managements feel that they are conceding too much opportunity to unions to block change which is not to the unions' liking, if such a clause is part of a disputes procedure.

One of the main advantages of agreed disputes procedures is that work interruptions are avoided whilst disputes are being discussed. If disputes procedures are to be respected, it is necessary for employers to demonstrate that they take any discussions seriously. If the discussions are seen to be unnecessarily long, and particularly if this forms part of a consistent pattern, union members may try the more direct method of interrupting work immediately in order to force serious consideration of their views. If employers then respond by making concessions, they can unwittingly be indicating that, if the employees want results, they should apply pressure and not route differences through a disputes procedure. If, on the other hand, they take discussions in procedure seriously and route concessions through the union officials who participate in such 'constitutional' discussions, the credibility of the procedure is enhanced for future occasions.

SUPERVISORY CONTROL

Care needs to be taken to ensure that those with direct responsibility for the supervision of work groups do not take the easy way out of all this and avoid doing anything which might meet with any opposition. I have seen factory situations where control at this level had degenerated to the extent that the supervisors asked the stewards' permission to do anything that was out of the ordinary. If the permission was not granted, that was the end of the matter. Consequently the stewards came to be seen as the authority figures on the shop floor and controlled any patronage that was going, such as overtime distribution, remission of discipline and dictation of the terms on which new work arrangements would be accepted. This in turn meant that the supervisor's lot became so unenviable that no-one with any ability wanted to be a supervisor, which increased the spiral of the shop stewards running the shop floor.

A crucial aspect of industrial relations in any organisation is the extent to which managerial interests are safeguarded at shop-floor level. This may involve considerable time and thought being given to the viability of the position of those with direct supervisory responsibility. As was discussed in Chapter 3, considerable attention may have to be given to the identification of the rewards which can be given by those managing at this level, so that supervisors are not in the position of only handing out penalties. Responsibilities need to be clarified and discretion in decision-making given where appropriate. The selection and training of managerial and supervisory staff are also important. When all this has been done, it is important that those who have been given responsibilities are integrated into the management team, listened to, and not bypassed. It is no good managers at very senior levels taking tough stands if in the meantime they have let managerial influence at shop-floor level be quietly eroded over the years.

NEGOTIATING SKILLS

Contact with trade unions can involve managers in negotiations. These may be informal or routed via an agreed disputes or negotiating procedure or other joint arrangement. The process of negotiation may be very similar to other types of negotiation in which a manager can be involved — for example, commercial negotiations. Negotiation may be seen as a mystic art which is only learned through practice. Whilst perhaps there is no substitute for experience in negotiation, there are basic skills which it is perfectly possible to identify and for people consciously to develop. There are also complexities in the process of negotiation which are not always appreciated but which will be explained in this section.

Defining objectives

As with so many managerial skills it is essential that people with responsibility for negotiation clarify their objectives. The pattern of reaction and competition in negotiation can be so ingrained that it is possible to lose sight of the exact purpose of negotiations. Usually the objective is to see if a mutually advantageous bargain can be struck. This may involve taking initiatives to ensure that there is something in a proposal which is of benefit to both sides, rather than just trying to outwit the other side. Whilst in some negotiations one side can only gain at the other's expense, this is not always the case. There is no point in failing to agree just because the other side would do better than you if agreement would mean that both parties would have gained. Success needs to be judged against the achievement or non-achievement of overall objectives, not just by relative comparison with how well the other side did.

One of the problems of identifying objectives in negotiations is that there may be considerable differences within a management team as to what the objectives should be. Short-term problems may conflict with long-term aims and the pressures to give concessions in a particular department may have to be balanced against the repercussions this action might have elsewhere in an organisation. Managers may also differ in the risks they are prepared to run. This often means that it is crucial for agreed objectives to be hammered out before there can be any

227

question of meeting the other side. Managers may be so caught up in considering their personal response to a particular union claim that they may fail to realise that the reaction of other managers may be quite different. If negotiations are conducted before any reconciliation of differing managerial views, the results can be disastrous: the wrong points can be conceded, managerial disunity advertised and managers feel that their colleagues have been disloyal to them. The device of adjournment may be both necessary and useful as a means of avoiding such problems. This can enable the management group to consider fresh points or to re-examine their position if new differences emerge within the group. It may also be appropriate, at times, to suggest that union negotiators adjourn so that they can properly consider new points.

A further advantage of clearly identifying objectives is that it can help managers avoid developing 'tunnel vision' during negotiations. This can happen when, during a complex negotiation, there is obsessive attention to a particular point, which may turn out to be of only marginal importance.

Identifying power realities

The identification of appropriate objectives needs to be accompanied by a sober assessment of the power realities in any negotiations. It is all too easy for parties to examine only the intellectual aspects of a case and ignore the fact, sad as it may be, that one's own particular moral outlook isn't the only factor that can determine the outcome of negotiations. To put the case somewhat dramatically, a man with a knife at your throat may have a poor moral case for taking your wallet but it may be as well to consider giving it to him. In industrial situations it is necessary to consider just what will hapen if a union claim is rejected. The Post Office workers fared badly in their national stoppage in 1971 compared with the miners in their two national stoppages in 1972 and 1973–4, not because their case was necessarily any less strong than that of the miners, but because the nation was much more able to cope without the postal services than with disruption to its energy supplies caused by the miners' strikes. However, power relationships may well vary over time and in 1984–5 it was the National Union of Mineworkers who disastrously misread the power balance. They underestimated the care with which the Government had prepared for a long industrial struggle with them and overestimated their ability to maintain unity within their own union and to obtain support from other unions.

A further example of the employer 'learning the hard way' concerns British national newspapers. Thomson newspapers failed miserably to introduce new technology and new disputes procedures at *The Times* and *Sunday Times* in 1978–9. The lockout of employees lasted a year and cost the owners a vast amount of money. It was a very different story in 1986 when new technology was introduced by the new owner — Rupert Murdoch's News International (also owner of the *Sun* newspaper). He carefully established alternative high technology production facilities at Wapping together with an alternative labour force and distribution arrangements and crushed the resistance of the print unions in an admittedly different economic and technological climate.

The negotiating ritual

The ritual of negotiation with its claim, offer, counter-proposal and ultimate compromise agreement seems to many people a waste of time. Such a judgement is to ignore the very necessary functions that such a ritual can fulfil. Even if the parties directly involved in a negotiation could come to a quick settlement without such a ritual, it is necessary to remember that they both have audiences to consider. If either side accepts too quickly it may leave the suspicion that a more favourable settlement could have been achieved. A union official is hardly going to enhance his credibility with his members if he develops a reputation, however unjustified, for settling too easily. Apart from the 'show' element in the ritual, however, considerable skills can be needed by the parties in handling the ritual so that an appropriate settlement can be achieved.

The 'pitching' of an initial offer can have a crucial effect on the ultimate outcome. If an offer is too low it may so antagonise the union side that they resort to direct action and escalate their real demands. This is what appears to have happened during the national steel pay negotiations in 1980. The initial offer of two per cent infuriated the steel workers and it seems likely that this not only helped cause a national stoppage, but also led to a

229

higher settlement than might have been achieved if there had been a more 'reasonable' opening offer. Much the same seems to have happened during the national negotiations over miners' pay in 1972, but in 1973–4 the reverse mistake seems to have been made. On that occasion a generous 'take it or leave it' offer was made, which left the leaders of the National Union of Mineworkers little opportunity to demonstrate their negotiating ability, and the miners with the feeling that the Government was holding something back. It seems quite possible that both strikes could have been averted had more skill been demonstrated in the use of the negotiating ritual.[3]

A general point which needs stressing about the negotiating process is the need to consider a case from the other party's point of view. It may help to have someone play 'devil's advocate' in order to understand what the other side really wants and is likely to do. This may help identify any area of common interest and also avoid forcing a party into a corner. If one has the edge in a negotiation, it may be best to find a way of letting the other side back down with dignity — especially as the positions could be reversed in the future. It is particularly important to be seen to bargain in good faith. If management develops a reputation for being untrustworthy, this can bedevil negotiations for years. Negotiations have to be conducted with a view to the long-term relationship as well as short-term advantage.

The conduct of negotiating meetings

Preparation for negotiating meetings needs to involve consideration not only of the substantive issues, but also of the roles that managers will assume during negotiations. A common mistake is for one manager to try to negotiate, chair and record what has happened. This can be too much for any one person and such an overload can be quite unnecessary if there are other managers present with relatively little to do. A manager who tries to combine all three tasks may all too easily find that the control of the meeting suffers and that there is misunderstanding about what has actually been agreed. The chairing process may need to be identified before a meeting begins — at, for instance, a management pre-meeting. As has already been explained, there may be a need for considerable discussion amongst managers to try to reach agreement about just what the managerial objectives should be. For this to be done there may need to be a systematic attempt to establish the views of the interested parties — which necessitates some type of chaired meeting — whether the chairing be formal or informal. When the two sides meet to negotiate, it can be of advantage for one person to chair the management team with the responsibility for co-ordinating the presentation of the management view. Given that there can be conflicting objectives on the management side, it can be appropriate for one person in particular to watch that the team does not depart from its agreed brief. It may also be necessary to see that the ritual is handled skilfully and not clumsily, as lack of skill could jeopardise the chances of a satisfactory settlement.

The number of problems that can arise if the process is not handled carefully strengthens the case for one person concentrating on chairing and another on presenting the substantive case for management, if negotiations are at all complicated. This can also free the person handling the substantive presentation to concentrate on that, without having to alternate between dealing with procedural and substantive issues. In the chapter on counselling it was explained that in negotiating meetings it can be important to let the union side lead, so that they have an opportunity to ventilate any anger they have about a particular issue. It is only after this has been done that union negotiators may be properly ready to hear what management has to say. It is important for the management chair to see that his colleagues do not engage in unproductive recriminations, particularly if the union anger may have subsided. If the person presenting the management case shows signs of anger, it can be very useful to have the chair on his side to come in and cool a situation. This emergency arrangement can hardly work if it is the chair who is arguing the case and who is the one who gets angry!

The concentration by one manager on a process role can enable him to chair the meeting as a whole as well as chairing the management side. This is sometimes provided for formally, but whether it be on a formal or informal basis, it is important that the chair sees that the union expectation that everyone has a fair opportunity to state his case is met, and that the procedure is not manipulated to give the management side any unfair advantage. The greater the disagreement, the more the need for someone to see that each side has the opportunity to present its case in a logical way, and to feel that, if nothing else, the case has been properly communicated. Sometimes the issues are not at all obvious and the real nature of a union claim may not surface until there has been much patient listening and clarification.

The skill of listening can be particularly critical in negotiations. It is all too easy for parties to fail to follow the track of what the other side is saying because of preoccupation with their own views. It is also very easy for people to come away from negotiations with much clearer views of what they have said than of what the other side has said. The chair needs to pay particular attention to the need to clarify what is really being said at each stage and to check that the other side has grasped the point at issue. This is particularly necessary when any agreement is reached. I have conducted a number of experiments when people have been asked to write down what they think has been agreed after a simulated negotiation. The norm is for there to be a significant amount of misunderstanding about just what had been agreed. Written records of agreements can help reduce the possibility of such subsequent disagreement, but written records should be a record of what really was agreed and not the point at which it becomes apparent, for the first time, that the negotiations were not resolved.

Written reports can also be subject to conflicting interpretations. There are powerful pressures that can create the illusion rather than the reality of agreement. People may remember only what they built into an agreement and fail to recall — or have never realised — what the other party was building into an agreement. Ambiguous terms can be used which increase the possibility of this happening. One side may interpret an ambiguous term in their own favour, whilst the other side may place a conflicting interpretation on the same term. It is much better to face up to such problems during negotiations rather than have arguments afterwards, with the possibility of accusations of bad faith. Parties may feel that they have been tricked into an agreement when the reality was that the possible conflict in interpretation was simply not clarified at the time. Sometimes, however, ambiguous phrases are necessary — but as an open device for deferring some differences until another day, not as a way of pretending there is agreement when there isn't.

The problems of achieving accurate communication during negotiations can be compounded by the pressures and problems that can arise during the report-back process. People who have not been exposed to the pressure and argument of negotiations may be critical of any concessions that have been made, both on the management and the union side. This can lead to the front-line negotiators playing down the concessions they have made, or even neglecting to mention them at all. In some cases, it can even change their perception of what really was agreed. If there is such distortion at one or both ends of a negotiating chain, there can be obvious problems when an agreement is implemented contrary to the expectations of the other side. Care then needs to be taken to give any help to stewards to explain just what has been agreed at a negotiation.

It may be just as well to see that any 'hardliners' are included in negotiations so that they have a front-seat view of what is really happening. Even if some stewards do not actually participate in negotiations, their presence during negotiations, as observers, may help considerably with the report-back process. Managers who receive 'report-backs' need to be prepared to coax an accurate summary out of the negotiators. If they jump down the throat of the negotiators when the first concession is mentioned, negotiators may, whether consciously or subconsciously, refrain from revealing all the concessions which were made.

THE MANAGER AS TRADE UNION MEMBER

One of the implications of white-collar unions is that managers may have to give serious thought as to whether or not they join a trade union. If they are in a union, they may find that the possibility of industrial action by their own union leads to their greater involvement in union affairs. The sheer size of an employing organisation may mean that union membership is the only way in which there can be proper discussions about a manager's terms and conditions of employment. The use of job evaluation schemes and fixed incremental scales for managerial grades are further reasons for managers combining to affect their terms of employment, rather than relying on the individual relationship. An argument against this has always been that an individual manager may have looked to promotion for his salvation. If a company is growing this can be a powerful disincentive for joining a union, but private companies in particular are much less able to grow now compared with the days of greater economic expansion. Contraction and mergers can be powerful reasons for managers joining unions so that they can seek to obtain protection against redundancy or, at least, separation on the most favourable terms possible. The legal insurance that unions provide, and the services they provide at industrial tribunal hearings, can also be selling points to the potential managerial recruit.

One of the decisions that a manager may have to make is just what union he should join. A specialist union, because of its specialised appeal, may not have many members and therefore lack comprehensive support services. Larger unions, whilst not perhaps offering the same degree of understanding about the individual manager's problems, may have a comprehensive range of services and specialists and the negotiating strength that can come from having a large membership, particularly if this membership includes groups of key workers. Whilst some specialist unions thrive, others fail to last and merge with larger unions, often to the relief of the employer , for this reduces the number of different unions with which he has to deal.

Whilst it may be to the advantage of the individual manager to join a trade union, membership can bring with it a fresh set of problems. The manager may find that it is not always easy to reconcile his union and managerial roles. Sometimes the accommodation is fairly easy. The manager may join a managerial union, or the white-collar section of a manual workers' union. On the face of it there may be no problem in negotiating as a representative of the employer with employees who are in other unions, or even the same union but in a different section. However, sections of the same union can be bound by common policies and also some union branches can take in a large vertical section of the white-collar workers with a particular employer. This can lead to role conflict, such as a manager wanting to pursue a grievance against his boss who may not only be in the same union branch, but also one of its officers! The militancy of some white-collar unions, particularly in the public sector, may mean that members find that there is a conflict between a desire on the part of management to keep services going during an industrial dispute, and a union desire to interfere with services. The individual may find that he is damned by his employer if he doesn't keep services working, and damned by his union if he does. There is no easy answer to the conflicts that can arise for managers within unions. However, if the individual manager recognises the problems that can arise, this should help him make careful judgements about whether or not he should join a union, which union it should be, whether he should hold office within that union, and the way in which role conflicts that occur for himself and his colleagues within the union can be resolved.

THE INTEGRATION OF INDUSTRIAL RELATIONS WITH OTHER MANAGEMENT FUNCTIONS

The emphasis in this chapter so far has mainly been on looking at industrial relations as a subject on its own. However, for there to be any real understanding of the area it is vital to see the way in which industrial relations interrelates with other management functions. This is because often the causes of industrial relations problems, and by implication any 'remedies', lie in these other areas. This basic point is often missed because of departmental boundaries. This may be compounded by lack of knowledge of those inside the industrial relations area of what goes on outside it and conversely lack of knowledge of those outside the area of what goes on within it.

This crucial interactive relationship is best explained by way of relevant examples. A particularly neat one concerns a bag manufacturing company in one of the Caribbean countries. The company endured a strike of several weeks over a redundancy. The organisation had invested in equipment and labour to meet a large order from a sugar producer. The order was not met on time and was then cancelled. Subsequent investigations revealed that delivery had been promised at the time of peak seasonal demand for bags and there had never been any prospect that the order could be delivered on time. A contrasting example — but which makes the same basic point — concerns the causes of industrial relations problems in the National Health Service. An ACAS investigation[4] concluded that the prime causes of the problems were deficiencies in basic organisational structure. These included weak links in the structural chain, consensus management, a poorly defined personnel function and poor communications between NHS disciplines.

Examples from the construction industry are equally revealing. The notorious pattern of industrial disruption that occurred during one phase of the development of the Barbican site in the City of London led to the establishment of a Court of Inquiry. It emerged that the contractor's view was that they had been seriously hampered by:

The unusual number of inconsistent and late instructions from the architects and other consultants responsible for the contract. This had led to severe difficulties in adhering to the planned programme of work. In many cases design changes had led to the taking down of work already done. Work had also to be executed to standards substantially higher than those normally required in the building industry. These factors in combination had a serious effect on site morale and in particular upon the operation of the bonus scheme, by making it difficult for operatives to earn reasonable bonuses and creating an imbalance between earnings on different parts of the site . . . These circumstances had in turn given ample opportunity for those who wished to foster discontent to do so.[5]

An investigation into delays on large industrial sites in Britain[6] revealed that at some sites construction workers could spend more time idle than working because of factors such as shortages of materials and late design changes. There are other examples. Karen Legge[7] gives an illuminating account of an ill-conceived attempt at a children's clothing firm to switch the product range from long-run 'bread-and-butter' production runs to a wide range of small-batch fashion garments. This came to grief because of the failure to take into account the learning problems for the production employees together with the impact of the change on their bonus earnings. A former industrial relations manager at British Leyland (now the Rover Group) has explained how production targets were set eleven per cent above capacity at one particular plant. He claimed that this 'inbuilt loss of production . . . had nothing to do with industrial relations problems, except to create them'.[8]

It is necessary to make this crucial point about the inter-relationship of industrial relations with other functions by way of example because of their illustrative value and the lack of systematic study in this area. Unfortunately the tradition has been to view industrial relations as a self-contained activity, both by those within organisations and those outside but who either write about the area or have sought to promote reform. The danger of a lopsided emphasis is that attempts to secure improvements in industrial relations may focus on too narrow an area. The Donovan investigation, for example, concentrated entirely on the need for improvements within the industrial relations 'system'. The main thrust of the Report was that the way forward was the formalisation of procedures at plant level. The 'central defect in British industrial relations'[9] was identified as being disorderly bargaining at factory level. The narrowness of this approach may have been why so little was apparently achieved as a result of the Donovan recommendations.[10] This may also have been the case with the work of the Commission on Industrial Relations, with its strong emphasis on — but limited achievements in — promoting procedural reform.[11] Subsequent attempts to 'improve' industrial relations by altering the legal and institutional framework may also turn out to be of limited benefit.

The implications of this analysis for the individual manager is clearly not to look for or expect progress in tackling industrial relations problems to come just from initiatives in that area. The argument is not that some procedural arrangements and industrial relations expertise is not desirable or important, but that one has to look elsewhere as well. Unfortunately the training and background of those in industrial relations is sometimes such that they may not understand that the causes of many of their problems lie outside their sphere. Conversely those outside the industrial relations area may know so little about the area that they don't appreciate the need to work out the industrial relations implications of decisions they are taking. One answer to this problem is general management training for all managers. The case for this is all the more powerful when one realises that the way in which industrial relations problems can be created by decisions or failures elsewhere is but one example of the way in which problems can be transmitted into any area of management. To push the analysis further it is not just a question of getting managers to see the implications of their decisions in other areas but recognising that plain incompetence in one area can easily precipitate crises elsewhere. To return to the example of industrial relations, the development of a sound management team throughout an organisation may do much more to improve industrial relations, as well as being desirable in its own right, than following the latest fashion in procedural arrangements. Hopefully such a preventative approach will ensure that the minimum number of industrial relations problems arise in the first place.[12]

CURRENT TRENDS IN INDUSTRIAL RELATIONS

The pattern of industrial relations, as ever, is evolving. One of the most significant recent developments has been the impact of chronically high levels of unemployment on the behaviour of employers and trade unions. This had the effect of shifting the balance of power more in the favour of the employer. This is a phenomenon affecting many countries, not just Britain. A particularly dramatic demonstration of this was when in 1981 President Reagan broke the strike of air traffic controllers in the USA by permanently sacking all the strikers. The fall in demand for air transport, and the availability and willingness of other air traffic controllers to continue working, or be recruited during the strike, were key factors affecting the outcome of this dispute.

The same shift in the power balance has been very obvious in Britain. Employees in the private sector have become very reluctant to strike because of the fear that it could force an employer to reduce his labour force because of lost orders, or even close down altogether. There has also been a great reduction in the volume of industrial action in the public sector, particularly since the peak during the 1978—9 'Winter of Discontent'. The miners' strike of 1984—5 was against this general trend.

There are other factors, also, which have contributed to the shift in the power balance towards employers. In Britain one of these has been the reduction in the legal immunity, under the provisions of the Employment Acts of 1980 and 1982, for trade unions who take industrial action. The legal protection of unions has been further eroded by the 1984 Trade Union Act. This requires unions to hold secret ballots prior to taking industrial action, as well as for appointing all voting members of national governing bodies and for authorising the establishment of a political fund. The impact of all this however may well be relatively minor compared with the continuing high levels of unemployment and excess manufacturing capacity.

Employers in general seem to be using their industrial muscle to impose their will rather than to take legal action against trade unions, which may prove to be counterproductive. This was certainly the line taken by the National Coal Board (now British Coal) in its dispute with the miners in 1984—5. There are other factors, too, which are contributing to the reduced level of industrial action. These include the deteriorating financial position of unions because of falling membership, the legal presumption that strikers receive some strike benefit from their trade unions (even if they don't) and privatisation of some public services. Privatisation has a triple effect. First, former public sector employees may be transferred to work for relatively small commercial organisations. This presents more difficulty for trade unions in terms of organisation and negotiation. Secondly, the threat of privatisation may undercut the bargaining position of unions with regard to pay rises and manning arrangements in the public sector. Thirdly, the private contractor will go out of business if he gives in too readily to union demands.

The Conservative Governments led by Mrs Thatcher also set out to systematically reduce the impact of institutional arrangements on the conduct of industrial relations and to increase the impact of market forces. As part of its general programme of deregulation the Fair Wages Resolutions were rescinded and the provision for reference to the Central Arbitration Committee for comparability awards ended. Other deregulatory measures included the abolition of the Civil Service Pay Research Unit, the reduction in the scope of Wages Councils, the abolition of the provision for unilateral reference to arbitration, for example, by teachers, the discontinuation of the official London Weighting index and the removal of restrictions on the hours of work when women could be employed. The intention was to make pay more related to market needs and less to considerations of equity. The need for employees to 'price themselves back into jobs' was stressed repeatedly. This was also reflected in the Government's role as employer and funder of other bodies. There was less use of third-party involvement in disputes involving the Government and a clear message to public and quasi-public employers to take a hard line in negotiations about pay and efficiency. A related development was the acquisition of powers to limit the spending of local authorities by rate-capping and the abolition of the Metropolitan Authorities and the Greater London Council. All this meant that not only was the institutional framework of industrial relations altered but a harder line was also taken within that changed framework.

The harsher climate of industrial relations had also had an impact on the effective use of labour as well as on pay issues. There has been a considerable shake-out of labour in parts of the public sector — for example in steel, as markets have contracted and technology advanced. There has also been considerable pressure to use existing labour more effectively. This is also apparent in the private and quasi-private sector. There has been a revolution in relationships and efficiency at Austin Rover's (the car division of the Rover Group). One of the key issues has been the introduction of change. Instead of having mutually agreed change, Austin Rover's management has now introduced a 'ten-day rule' which operates rather like a Parliamentary guillotine. If the management considers that discussion about a particular change has gone on long enough, it reserves the right to announce that the decision will be implemented in ten days. It then offers to continue discussion on the basis that the change will be introduced as announced, unless there is some other prior agreement. Trade unions have logically tried to control the pace of technological change in the country by obtaining New Technology Agreements, but have been unable to get more than a handful of agreements and even those which they have obtained have not always been honoured.

Further, and important, examples of the reduced union ability to control change include the defeat of the National Union of Mineworkers in 1985, over the issue of pit closures, and the introduction of new technology in some of the national newspapers in 1986, particularly by Rupert Murdoch. This has both encouraged other employers to take a harder line about the introduction of new technology and working arrangements and put these other employers under competitive pressure to cut their costs. There are though other important, if less obvious, ways in which unions have been losing their influence to control events. New technologies have created demands for new skills and new organisational arrangements. Many unions are aligned to dying technologies and their structures are often not geared to cope with the 'sunrise', as opposed to the 'sunset', industries. The flexible firm (discussed in Chapter 3) and the multinational corporation are also much more difficult to organise and influence than conventional national companies.

There have been other important changes in the climate of industrial relations. Proposals for industrial democracy, with their connotations of joint regulation, have perhaps not surprisingly received little recent attention. There has also been a grudging, if direct, compliance of trade unions with the laws restricting their freedom of action. In the case of balloting arrangements there even appears to be enthusiasm amongst trade union and Labour Party moderates who have seen these requirements as strengthening their position within the labour movement. No doubt the legal and institutional arrangements in industrial relation will continue to be a political football. However, even if there are future changes in favour of the unions these can hardly counter the strength of the forces that have reduced their power. It is not a swing of the pendulum that has occurred but a significant reduction in power that is likely to remain so into the foreseeable future.

These developments may lead some managers to the view that they need not worry about thinking out strategies and developing skills in the industrial relations area. However, autocratic unimaginative managerial styles can cause unnecessary aggravation and on occasion a fierce backlash. One imaginative approach is that used by the Plessey Company, which estimates what manpower it will require in five years' time as part of its corporate planning activity. It then gears its industrial relations strategy to its overall plan so that industrial relations is more than just a set of tactical *ad hoc* responses. The relentless progress of technology is such that organisations continuously need to try to identify what manning levels and permutations of skills they are going to require.

Genuine worries about job security by employees are problem enough without such issues being exacerbated by managements who don't think ahead. There is also always the danger of a sudden surge of industrial unrest — either within an organisation or within a country. One of the lessons of the 1978–9 'Winter of Discontent' was that many people in senior positions within organisations were caught flat-footed by sudden outbreaks of industrial action. Often such senior people, in trying to cope with industrial action, perhaps for the first time in their lives, reacted without skill and with poor judgement and created an escalation of industrial action. A dramatic example of this from another country concerned the late Shah of Iran. He commented on the British Government's inability to cope with one of the national mining strikes, but was quite bewildered when his own oil workers went on strike prior to his downfall.

There are other reasons why it should not be taken for granted that it is now an easy matter for managements always to impose their will. Social changes are such that there is a continuing challenge to previously accepted authority relationships. Some technological change may restore the initiative to management, but technological change often has the effect of making economic systems more and more interdependent. This increases the number of points at which the economic chain can be broken — both within an organisation and within a country. If a key group of workers in, for example, the electricity industry goes on strike, the existence of a large pool of unemployed labour will be irrelevant if those key workers have a monopoly of an essential skill. An example of how the Government miscalculated with an emergent group of key workers was the dispute between the Department of Health and Social Security and the computer staff at Newcastle.[13] Proposals were made for the introduction of new shift-working patterns and the bulk of the economies management wanted were achieved. However, there was deadlock about an estimated £44,000 worth of further annual economies which led to a seven-month dispute. The closure of the central computer facility necessitated the hiring of large numbers of clerical staff throughout the country at a cost estimated as being £178 million.

Industrial relations aggravation in the public sector is also likely to be a continuing feature. The sheer size of the public sector is such that the days are long gone when a Government could regard itself as a relatively neutral party in industrial disputes, primarily concerned with ensuring fair play. Any Government is bound to get sucked into public sector disputes, and often indirectly into private sector disputes, because of the impact of these disputes on its economic policy. A further feature that is here to stay is the impact of size on industrial relations in the private sector. As the size of private companies increases, particularly through mergers, so is the myth of individual bargaining between employer and employee exposed. Large companies cannot treat even senior managers on an individual basis because of the danger of setting precedents that have to be followed with other employees. A realisation of this, coupled with fears of job security — perhaps because of further mergers — means that, even if the negotiating power of unions has been reduced, there continue to be good reasons for those still in work to join trade unions.

A further perspective is that increasingly managers need to have a negotiating style in dealing with their colleagues. The pace of technological change in organisations is such that managers need to develop collaborative styles because the dispersal of expertise is such that knowledge has to be pooled.

Social changes reinforce this. The negotiating style that managers need to develop in dealing with their colleagues may be much more in tune with the relationships that are appropriate with trade unions whose co-operation may still be more valuable than a 'take it or leave it' attitude. The impact of all these changes and trends will vary from one country to another, and it is dangerous to assume that there is a common approach that is appropriate in all countries and cultures. However, change is certainly no respecter of frontiers and the forces making for change identified in this section are likely to be at work to a greater or lesser extent in all countries.

NOTES

1. Royal Commission on Trade Unions and Employers' Associations, *Productivity bargaining and restrictive labour practices*, Research Paper No. 4 (HMSO, 1967), p. 52.

2. Alan Fox, 'Industrial relations: a social critique of pluralistic ideology', *Man and organisation* (ed. John Child), (George Allen & Unwin, 1973), Ch. 7, pp. 185–234.

3. Stephen Fay and Hugo Young, 'The fall of Heath', *The Sunday Times Weekly Review*, 22 February 1976, 29 February 1976 and 7 March 1976.

4. Royal Commission on the National Health Service, *ACAS evidence*, ACAS Report No. 12, May 1978.

5. *Report of a Court of Inquiry into Trade Disputes at the Barbican and Horseferry Road Construction Sites in London*, Cmnd. 3396 (HMSO, 1967), para 74.

6. National Economic Development Office, *Large industrial sites in Britain* (HMSO, 1970).

7. Karen Legge, *Power, innovation and problem-solving in personnel management* (McGraw-Hill, 1978), pp. 45–6.

8. T. I. Richardson, 'What Sir Don Ryder didn't say', *The Guardian*, 3 June 1975.

9. Royal Commission on Trade Unions and Employers' Associations 1965–8, Cmnd. 3623 (HMSO, 1968), para 1019.

10. Norman Singleton, *Industrial relations procedures*, Manpower Paper No. 14 (HMSO, 1975), Ch. 8.

11. J. Purcell, 'The lessons of the Commission on Industrial Relations: attempts to reform workplace industrial relations', *Industrial Relations Journal*, Summer 1979, Vol. 10, No. 2.

12. See also W. David Rees, 'Industrial relations: the need for liaison', *Personnel Executive*, April 1985, pp. 49–51.

13. ACAS, *Annual Report* (1984), pp. 28–9.

13

Meetings and Chairing

INTRODUCTION

Attendance at meetings can occupy a considerable part of a manager's time. There is often much flippant comment about the pointlessness of meetings, such as the description of a camel being 'a racehorse designed by a committee'. However, meetings, whether formal or informal, are increasingly an integral part of organisational activity and it is naive for people to suggest that meetings are unnecessary. What is important is that meetings be conducted effectively and that people distinguish between meetings which are unnecessary and those which need to be properly organised.

The people who most need to develop skills related to the effective conduct of meetings are those concerned with their organisation — particularly the chair, and secretary if applicable. Ordinary members may also need to develop skills, such as working out just what they want to achieve at meetings. An appreciation of what is happening at meetings may also be educative in terms of understanding how organisations work, or don't work. Understanding in this area may also be a useful preparation for the day when an ordinary member has to chair a meeting. Some of the skills have already been considered in the section of Chapter 12 concerning industrial relations negotiations. However, this whole area requires treatment in its own right, which is why it forms a separate chapter. The need for meetings and the consequences of ineffective meetings are considered. The various types of meetings are identified and particular attention is given to the role of the chair. His role will be affected by the amount of conflict that has to be resolved and the way he handles this issue. An underlying theme in many of the sections is the way in which the procedural and substantive roles of the chair can conflict. There is a need for considerable preparation prior to meetings and once meetings have started they need to be chaired with skill. The skills required include the need to optimise the contributions by the various members. These topics are all covered and finally an appendix is provided which explains the main rules relating to formal committee procedure.

The term 'chair' is used throughout the chapter rather than the alternative expressions 'chairman' or 'chairperson' — this seeming to be the most fluent way of making the point that the chair can be a man or a woman. As the 'chair' is nevertheless often referred to as 'he' in the chapter it is as well to repeat the point made in the Introduction, that the pronoun 'he' is used in the generic sense and refers to women as well as men.

THE NEED FOR MEETINGS

Meetings can be an indispensable part of an organisation's structure. In some organisations — for example in local government — policy decisions must be taken with a committee-type structure, with various committees, or sub-committees, reporting to the council as a whole. In commercial organisations the need for meetings, below the level of shareholders' and directors' meetings, may not be obligatory, but may still be very necessary. Meetings may be necessary as an aid to the running of departments. They can also be vital in promoting interdepartmental co-operation which otherwise might not be achieved. The growing complexity of decision-making, caused partly by the diffusion of knowledge within organisations, means that very often decisions can only be taken effectively by groups of people coming together and pooling their knowledge and expertise. If meetings are ineffective it can mean that a vital aspect of organisational structure is failing.

The consequences of ineffectiveness

There are many reasons why attention needs to be paid to the effective conduct of meetings. The decisions that are taken in meetings can be very important. The quality of decision-making may well correlate with the skill with which meetings are conducted. Small improvements in the effectiveness of meetings can lead to considerable savings in managerial time because of the multiplication of the time saved by the number of people present. Meetings can also have functions other than decision-making — such as providing briefing for those present, or ensuring that decisions are taken in an open way. The quality of decision-making and the efficiency with which business is conducted can also affect working relationships outside meetings, and the credibility of the role of meetings for future occasions.

TYPES OF MEETINGS

Meetings can vary in importance and formality, from the proceedings of the House of Commons to the informal discussion of a temporary problem between colleagues. Whatever the type of meeting, it is necessary for the participants to be aware of the process by which the business is conducted, as well as the substantive content of the meeting. The procedural arrangements may be formally embodied in the constitution or terms of reference of a committee, or agreed by the parties present, or, in some cases, imposed by one party on another. Even in very informal situations, there is always a procedural aspect to the discussions and the skill with which this is handled can affect the quality and acceptability of any outcome. Behavioural scientists often distinguish between process leadership and task leadership. In this chapter the difference between these two aspects will be identified in terms of procedural issues and substantive issues.

As well as the level of formality varying, so can the purpose and decision-making arrangements. Meetings can be part of a constitutional decision-making process, for briefing purposes only, for negotiation, for consultation, or for the mutual exchange of views. In some meetings, decisions are taken in accordance with the views of the majority of the members. In other situations the decision-making power may be vested elsewhere — for example in a management structure with the most senior manager, or in the armed services with the most senior officer, present. In some cases there may be no decision to make, or if there is it may be by a manager in his own right and not by virtue of his membership of a particular committee. This basic classification is necessary because people may fail to distinguish between the different purposes and decision-making arrangements of meetings. If the members of a meeting fail to see the distinction it can lead to confusion, whilst if the chair does not see the differences it can lead to chaos. This can happen if people have a stereotyped view of meetings and start applying the wrong conventions in a particular situation. Managers may assume that they have to operate by consensus or majority vote, when the reality may be that an organisation has vested them ultimately with the sole decision-making responsibility within a particular area. Management chairs at joint consultative meetings can, and sometimes do, use voting procedures and short-circuit established management structures because the chair has not appreciated that a consultative meeting literally means just that. It is an aid to decision-making via established management procedures — not a substitute for those procedures. In negotiating meetings there can be three different centres of decision-making and therefore of chairing — what each party can agree and what they can jointly agree.

THE ROLE OF THE CHAIR

The variety of aims and nature of meetings mean that those responsible for arranging meetings have to consider just what their particular aims and procedures should be. It follows that they must devote time to this and that it is no good them spending all their time considering the substantive aspects of a particular topic. A chair needs to understand the substantive issue under discussion, but needs also to devote some time to a consideration of how the meeting is to be handled effectively. A common error is for the chair to be so immersed in the substantive issues that he neglects the procedural side. This is especially likely to happen if the chair is particularly involved in the substantive issues, and if there are controversial issues where he has a vested interest in securing particular results. This can lead to a further complication, which is that a chair may seek to manipulate, or cut through, any inconvenient arrangements about decision-making to secure a particular outcome. He may or may not get his way in securing a particular outcome, but this may be at the expense of reducing the quality and/or acceptability of a decision. If the case for a particular decision is that strong, it may be that there is little to fear from open and fair discussion. The danger is, though, that the manager concerned is so involved technically and emotionally that he fails to consider the process side adequately.

Poor quality decisions, to which there is little commitment, may stem not so much from a desire to manipulate decision-making processes as from a failure to consider the relevance of those procedures to the business in hand. If the decision-making process requires the pooling of information, and elements of negotiation amongst colleagues, the chair needs to ensure that just that takes place. If conflicts have to be resolved, the chair may also need to ensure that discussion takes place in an atmosphere in which those with opposing views each feel they have at least had a fair opportunity to state their case. Whilst a chair will need to understand the substantive issues, it may be best if he refrains from taking a partisan line as far as possible. There are those people who have the skills to referee a football match in which they are also playing — but it does require a high degree of ability and it is best for a chair to avoid doing this to the maximum extent practicable. The person with the greatest knowledge of the substantive issues will not automatically have either the time or the aptitude to chair discussions.

It is critical to recognise that there needs to be a division of labour at meetings. Otherwise, for example, a group of people may be invited to a meeting and find that their views are not sought or are ignored. The chair will need to ensure that he obtains the necessary contributions from those present at a meeting, and may want them to concentrate on resolving, as far as possible, the substantive issues at hand. He, assisted sometimes by a secretary, is the one who has to concentrate on the procedural side so that there is a framework within which the group can operate. It is only when the chair has satisfactorily created the framework for a meeting that he should consider taking time off from his procedural role to get involved in the substantive issues. Even then it may be best to do that to the minimum extent, as, if the framework of the meeting is right, the rest of the group may be able to resolve the business, looking to the chair only for procedural and specialist guidance when appropriate. Meetings don't automatically keep on the rails and, if the chair becomes so involved in the discussion that he neglects to consider how the meeting is handled, the discussion may be inadequately guided. The division of labour, whereby the chair spends perhaps most of his time on procedural matters and the other members concentrate exclusively on the substantive issues, does not seem unreasonable. A meeting where no-one concentrates or even bothers about the procedural aspects is the one most likely to be ineffective.

A complication concerning the chairing of meetings is that the chair may be the person with the greatest knowledge of the substantive issues. Even if that is the case, the chair still needs to recognise that he must find time to give adequate attention to procedural issues. The chair may find that he is also fiercely committed to a particular outcome. In such cases he needs to pay considerable attention to seeing that his commitment to a particular view does not prevent him from giving those people who have a different view a fair opportunity to state their case. Some people have, or can develop, the skill to explain a partisan line yet at the time chair a discussion fairly. It may be important that they do both, so that the substantive decision is based on a consideration of all relevant views, including the chair's. If, however, the chair finds that he cannot combine these two tasks, then it could be that he should consider letting someone else take the chair, at least for the duration of discussion of a particular topic. That may be an alternative way of seeing that all relevant points of view are considered fairly. Both tasks may need to be accomplished so that the decision is appropriate and conflict resolved in the least damaging way.

Resolving conflict

One of the key roles of meetings can be as a way of resolving conflict. The problem may be how to do this in such a way that the mechanism for resolving conflict is not destroyed in the process. Sometimes there is little or no conflict and the exchange of specialist information leads to a decision to which all contributors are equally committed. On other occasions the conflicts can be so bitter that the decision-making process collapses. The range of potential conflict within the House of Commons is such that they do not risk having a chair who is not neutral: the Speaker, who chairs the proceedings, has a neutral procedural role. The mayor fulfils the same function in meetings of local government councils. Many trade unions appoint a president who will fulfil a similar function.

The conflict between providing procedural and policy leadership is more obvious within the British Cabinet. Prime Ministers have to do both, but run the risk that, if they fall out of step with the majority of Cabinet members, their position will become threatened. The problem of achieving balance may influence the choice of party leader in the first place. It would seem that Clement Atlee was preferred as Prime Minister in 1945 to some of the more powerful personalities within the Labour Party leadership, partly because he was seen as being the person most likely to 'hold the ring' between the more powerful personalities in the Cabinet such as Bevin, Cripps, Dalton and Morrison. Any one of those other members would probably have been less acceptable, and less effective, because their dominance might have prevented them from providing acceptable procedural leadership. Party leaders have to be careful not to be identified with too extreme a position for fear that they are seen to frustrate the democratic process within their party — particularly in countries which pride themselves on their democratic traditions. It is also necessary for party leaders to demonstrate that they can distinguish between their own views and those of the party, particularly as the views of the party which they will have to present will sometimes differ from their personal views.

Examples of the problems of reconciling leadership on procedural and substantive issues are particularly easy to give from the world of politics because of the blaze of publicity that surrounds political activity in democratic countries. A balance still has to be kept within less democratic structures, as few leaders have so much power that they can afford to ignore the views of their supporters. In any case, a balance is necessary so that decisions are taken after the relevant information has been considered, and not imposed by one person regardless of what information is available from others.

One of the ways in which the chair can retain credibility and acceptability when he is involved in securing a particular outcome is by avoiding getting involved in controversial discussion unless it is as a last resort. He may then find that the conflict resolves itself satisfactorily without his involvement, or that the residual conflict between himself and the majority of those present at a meeting is so small that accommodation between the two views is relatively easy. Even when the residual conflict is large, the chair may then preserve his position by demonstrating that, after providing for fair discussion of a particular point, he will resolve the outstanding conflict by whatever method is agreed. If the decision-making process is democratic, this may mean that the chair is outvoted, but the defeat on the substantive issue need not affect the chair's credibility to lead procedurally if he has shown that his views have not affected the quality of his procedural leadership. In a more hierarchical structure, the chair may ultimately say 'I have heard you all but disagree' and impose his own decision. Resolving conflict that way means at least that the chair is fully aware of the arguments against his particular decision and has demonstrated that colleagues have had a fair opportunity to state their case before the final decision is taken. What is likely to be counterproductive is the chair appearing to be willing to listen, or to share decision-making powers, when he has decided what to do anyway. What is then likely to emerge is that the members have complete freedom to come to the decision that the chair has already determined!

The need for procedural leadership may exist even in informal discussions between relatively few people. Sometimes the level of informality, the competitive nature of relationships, or the sensitivity of the issues being discussed is such that it is inappropriate for a formal chair to be appointed. It may nevertheless be both useful and necessary if one person, perhaps quite informally, deals with the procedural aspects of discussion. This may involve taking a purely neutral role and asking such questions as 'What is the problem?', 'What are everyone's views?' The other parties may be quite prepared to let one person emerge as the informal chair, particularly if it is seen that he is confining himself to a neutral role. It may later be possible for that person to enter into the substantive discussions, but only so long as he demonstrates that this is not going to endanger the procedural arrangements that have evolved. Otherwise the person may find that his substantive contributions are not welcome or that his procedural leadership is challenged.

PREPARATION BEFORE MEETINGS

The amount of preparation required before all meetings will vary according to the type of meeting — its formality, importance, predictability and the role that the individual who is

251

attending the meeting is going to take there. There can be few meetings, however, where people do not need to give some prior thought. Perhaps the most important issue to consider is what your own objectives are going to be at a meeting. It is only when these have been clarified that it may be possible to establish what other prior preparation is required. It is also necessary to consider what is likely to be expected of you at a meeting. This may indicate the preparation you need to make so that other people's needs can be satisfied. At formal meetings it will be necessary to see that the agenda and papers are distributed well in advance. Any procedural rules or constitutional statement about the powers of a meeting needs to be not only to hand, but also thoroughly understood, so that such issues can be dealt with immediately and reassuringly if they emerge during a meeting. One would not be reassured by a football referee who had continually to refer to a book on the rules of football whilst a game was being played. The more formal the meeting, the more a chair may rely on the secretary to handle procedural matters before a meeting, and to be a source of information during it. It may be expected that the meeting will be run not just in accordance with its constitution, but by the normal conventions of committee procedure. Consequently a list of these conventions is included as an appendix to this chapter.

Who should attend meetings?

Thought may have to be given to who should be invited to a meeting. This may be totally prescribed by the constitution of a committee but, when the constitution is first established, the matter has to be examined. In any case, constitutions sometimes need amending, people may need to be specially invited to attend meetings and, on occasion, people may need to be excluded from meetings, or for part of the proceedings, because of conflicts of interest. A balance usually has to be struck between having the interested parties present and not involving too many people because of the varying levels of interest and the costs involved, particularly in terms of time. A system of subcommittees can be a way of getting the optimum balance between representing parties and maintaining economy of time. Sometimes it will be appropriate to establish *ad hoc* subcommittees that can enable the detail of a particular issue to be examined, without holding up the main business of a meeting. It can be particularly dangerous to exclude a person from a meeting primarily because he is likely to take a controversial position, or controversial as far as the chair is concerned. To exclude on this basis may lead to charges of unfair chairing, which may then mean that the chair is under procedural challenge, as well as being challenged on a substantive issue. Controversial issues tend to surface anyway and it may be best to see that this happens via the established machinery for resolving conflict rather than in another way, particularly if the chair would otherwise lose respect in the process.

Other preparation

Other issues that may require forethought include the exact nature of information that people attending meetings need to have beforehand so that they can contribute effectively, and the seating arrangements at a meeting. The type of room and layout can affect discussion, as can seating arrangements. Seating arrangements can be controlled by providing name plaques, which has the added advantage of identifying those present. The chair will also need to understand the substantive issues and their history sufficiently well to guide the discussion effectively.

It is only realistic to add that there may be pre-meetings before the main meeting. This may be part of the established procedure — for example it may be customary for the chair and secretary to go through the items before a meeting so that they are *au fait* with the issues. Other pre-meetings may be of a political nature, with one or more subgroups within a committee caucusing to try to agree the line that they will take during a meeting. A small minority, who prepare in this way, can have a powerful influence on the outcome of any discussions. They will be primed and create a certain amount of momentum for the views that they express during a meeting. If they vote *en bloc* at a meeting, they may find that the natural divisions amongst the other people present make it relatively easy to get a majority in favour of their point of view. This may lead other subgroups to have pre-meetings as well, in an attempt to counter such tactics, or to copy the tactics in order to establish supremacy for their subgroup. One way of dealing with an attempt to bulldoze a minority point of view through a committee, or other meeting, is simply to alert other members as to what is happening beforehand. The chair, or for that matter any member of a committee, may wish to forestall a particular proposal. It may be a matter not so much of converting others, which is often very difficult, but of alerting people as to what is happening, so that they are on guard as far as their own interests are concerned. This may also be necessary when there is an attempt to conceal information.

The importance of preparation before meetings was confirmed for me by a study I was able to undertake into the operation of joint consultative committees within one of the regional Gas Boards in Britain.[1] Eight out of the 19 consultative committees collapsed, ostensibly because the employees were not prepared to continue sending representatives to the meetings. This was attributed by some to apathy, but raised the question as to whether or not the Gas Board was in breach of its statutory duty to consult with employee representatives. A detailed analysis of the committee proceedings revealed that the key variable was the managerial style of the chair. Some worked out what they wanted from the meetings and also considered what the employee representatives expected. Other managers clearly saw the meetings as an unnecessary chore and went through the motions of holding meetings without thinking of the uses to which the meetings might be put, or what the employees wanted. The pattern that emerged was remarkably clear. The managers who prepared carefully for their meetings found their committees survived and made a constructive if not dramatic contribution. Invariably there were more items initiated by the management side than the employee side. The other committees all collapsed, and it emerged on studying the committee minutes that with the collapsed committees invariably more items were raised for discussion by the employee representatives than by the managers. The last meeting of one committee ended somewhat dramatically when, after repeated requests for clothing lockers had been turned down, the employee representatives commented acidly that it was strange that an employer who could not afford clothing lockers could afford to build new gasometers at the same site. Ironically it also emerged that the consultative meetings tended to operate efficiently where they were least needed — the need for open communication being greatest at the undertakings where the local managers were unwilling or unable to make their joint consultative committees effective.

CONDUCT DURING MEETINGS

The job of chairing a meeting effectively obviously depends a great deal on prior preparation and on the ability of the chair to distinguish between procedural and substantive issues. Consideration will now be given to some of the potential problems that may arise during a meeting. A key job of the chair is to see that he actually uses the knowledge of the people who are present. It is up to the chair to see that the appropriate issues are identified, and then to see that the collective knowledge and skill of the members are used to resolve the issues. The chair may contribute to the substantive discussions, but should only do so when the issues have been properly identified. He should not use his position as chair to exclude members from discussion who may have important contributions to make, or who may feel neglected if they are not given the opportunity to contribute. This may seem an obvious enough point to make, but in practice chairs vary considerably in the skill with which they use the abilities of the people present. Good and bad examples are obvious on radio and television programmes, just as there will be good and bad examples of chairing in most organisations. Some chairs are very adept in drawing out the views of those who have been invited to speak and in controlling subsequent discussion. Others lack this skill, invite people to contribute to programmes and then use their procedural position and studio confidence to grab the limelight — and in so doing wreck any discussion.

The danger of over-involvement

It is very easy for the person chairing a meeting to underestimate the extent to which they involve themselves in discussion and to overestimate the extent to which other people are involved. This is a problem that can confront lecturers who have responsibility for leading discussions. At the college where I work, one system for training lecturers in the technique of discussion-leading is to chart the pattern of contributions during a discussion. The resultant chart, or sociogram, can reveal a pattern of which the discussion leader was unaware. A typical pattern is shown in Figure 13.1. An examination of the flow of discussion shows that most of it was centred around the chair (or discussion leader). There was little cross-discussion and one person did not contribute at all. If this was appropriate, and the chair was

Figure 13.1: Chair-centred discussion

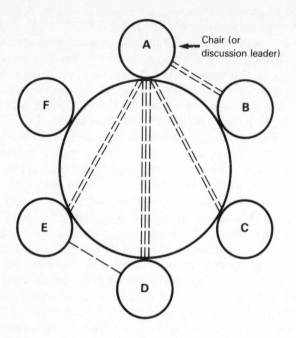

aware of what was really happening, this may be perfectly satis-factory. However, it is very easy for a chair to assume that, because he was involved and interested, so was everyone else. This is not automatically the case. It is possible for a person to sit through a meeting, seething with frustration, but not con-tributing. Others may remain passively silent though able to con-tribute. Meanwhile the chair may be quite unaware of all this. It can be instructive for a chair to be shown a flow chart (or socio-gram) of a meeting he has chaired and mentally to try to build up a picture of the actual pattern of discussion during his next meeting. Regular checks on the expressions on people's faces can provide important clues as to their feelings about particular topics and about the conduct of the meeting generally.

Involving members

Often the flow of discussion that is actually needed is more like

Figure 13.2: Group-centred discussion

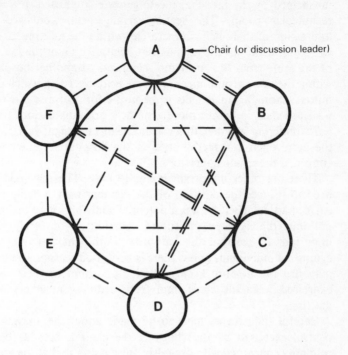

that shown in Figure 13.2. In this second chart it is much less obvious who is the chair. Everyone has contributed and there is more cross-discussion than was the case in the previous chart. The flow of discussion may need to be routed more through the chair in large formal meetings, but even in that situation it may be appropriate to allow some cross-discussion provided it is not disruptive. In large formal meetings it may still be necessary for the chair to check out the attitudes of members to the way meetings are handled.

I was once able to compare the attitudes of the various members of a hospital management committee towards the way in which meetings were handled and found that there were some surprising differences in perception. The chair and secretary appeared convinced that everyone had ample opportunity to contribute, whilst the senior member of the nursing staff who was present at the meetings was clearly of the opinion that she was only permitted to speak when invited to do so. I, as an outsider, seemed to be the only one aware of these differences in perception. In this particular case openness of discussion was not helped by the fact that meetings were conducted in a long rectangular room. The seating arrangements conveyed an impression of there being a hierarchy within the meeting, and it was significant that the nursing representative sat at the far end of the table from the chair and secretary. At another hospital, within the same group, meetings were held in a room which permitted seating arrangements to be in the form of a semi-circle, which seemed to permit more genuinely open discussion. I was left wondering whether this was accident or design, in view of the more open managerial style of the hospital secretary who convened those latter meetings.

There are other important points to note. These include the need to protect the position of the member who is being ridiculed, particularly if he has a potential contribution to make, if not immediately then on future occasions. Conversely it is important to see that the authority of the chair is not used against an individual, unless there is very good reason. Members may feel much more keenly about opposition to their views expressed from the chair than from ordinary members of a meeting.

Careful judgements have to be made about the amount of control exercised by the chair. If the chair is seen as being primarily concerned with organising discussion so that the group can resolve its differences and proceed with its business, control by the chair is much more likely to be accepted, compared with a situation where there is suspicion that the control is being used to establish particular policy decisions. If exchanges become too heated, that may be the time to insist that all contributions are routed through the chair, even if subsequently that convention is dropped. The routing of all contributions through the chair may only be necessary when the group lacks the self-discipline to evolve a means of taking it in turns to speak. If the chair is ignored, or if people talk whilst the chair is speaking, the pointed silence may be a more appropriate way of re-establishing control than by the more formal means of raising the voice.

Chairs also need to strike the right balance concerning the pace of discussion. People may be very concerned to state their own views but impatient of the right of others to do the same. Too quick a pace may leave many people with the feeling that they have not had adequate opportunity to state their views, whilst too slow a pace may leave many people with the view that their time has been unnecessarily wasted. The ease with which points at issue can simply be misunderstood should never be underestimated. It is important that the chair clarifies and summarises whenever there appears to be any doubt or whenever decisions are taken. Formal minuting can help with this process, but one does not want misunderstandings about what was really decided to be left to surface when the minutes are distributed. The responsibility for action needs also to be carefully noted, so that any decisions that are agreed are actually implemented.

CONCLUSION

The theme that has been continuously developed in this chapter is the need for chairs to recognise that substantive issues cannot be considered properly unless there is an appropriate procedural framework. This need is reflected in the procedural convention that points of order take precedence over other issues during meetings. What is crucial is that the load on the chair is clearly recognised, with a view to seeing either how the load can be handled or, if necessary, if part of it can be redistributed. There is often a dangerous assumption that the procedural leadership can be left to look after itself — rather like the quaint notion that in sports teams the choice of captain involves no more than picking the best player.

Emphasis has been placed on the procedural role, because that is common to all meetings. This chapter should provide a basic understanding of the key issues, but should be seen as a starting point only. Much can be learned by observing the way discussions, meetings and committees operate — both within employing organisations and elsewhere including within the family. This in turn can be a basis for practising the skills of chairing when the opportunity presents itself. If a person has the ability to learn in this way, he may find that he increasingly assumes the chairing role in a variety of situations. This in turn can provide opportunities for further practice and development, and also help ensure that meetings are run more effectively.[2, 3]

NOTES

1. W. David Rees, 'The practical functions of joint consultation considered historically and in the light of some recent experiences in South Wales', MSc (Econ) thesis (University of London, 1962).

2. For an excellent account of the rules of meetings procedure see Michael Cannell and Norman Citrine (eds), *Citrine's ABC of chairmanship* (NCLC Publishing Society Ltd, distributed by the Fabian Society, 1982).

3. For a further account of this subject, see Michael Locke, *How to run committees and meetings* (Macmillan, 1980).

APPENDIX I: DEFINITIONS AND EXPLANATIONS OF SOME TERMS USED IN FORMAL MEETINGS

Ad hoc: This Latin phrase means, literally, 'to this'. Its meaning has been extended to 'set up to serve a particular purpose'. Thus an *ad hoc* committee is one which has been set up to serve a particular purpose and which will cease to exist as soon as this purpose has been served.

Agenda: This is a Latin word meaning 'things requiring or deserving to be done'. It is really plural in form but is now used as a singular word and means simply 'a list of the items of business to be dealt with at a meeting'.

Amendment: When someone moves that a proposition should be altered in some way, he is moving an amendment. It should be noted that an amendment proposes an *alteration* of a proposition, not a direct negation of it nor a completely different proposition.

Ballot This means simply 'a secret vote'. Members register their votes on paper and not by a show of hands.

Casting vote: The chair is allowed an ordinary vote as a member of the meeting. Sometimes, however, the standing orders allow him an extra vote which is called a 'casting vote' because he may, if he so wishes, use it to decide an issue on which the voting is equal.

Co-opt: If a committee feels that it would benefit from the services of some person possessing, for example, special qualifications or experience, it may decide (if it has been given such powers) to co-opt that person, i.e. to make him an additional member of the committee. The committee has exercised power of 'co-option' and the person has been 'co-opted'.

Ex officio: A person may claim to be a member of a committee, not because he has been elected but *ex officio*, that is 'by virtue of his office'.

Minutes: This word means 'a brief but accurate record of what took place at a meeting'.

Motion: This is a general term which means 'anything that is moved or proposed at a meeting'. Thus a proposition is a motion but also an amendment is a motion.

Nem. con.: This is an abbreviation for the Latin phrase *nemine contradicente* and means 'no one speaking against'. Thus 'carried *nem. con.*' does not mean the same as 'carried unanimously' which means that every one present voted for the motion.

Next business: When a motion is being debated it may appear to some member or members that it would be unfortunate for the meeting to reach a decision on the matter in question or that it would be a waste of time to continue the debate. One device to stop the debate is for a member who has not already spoken to stand up and say 'Chair, I move next business'. If this motion is seconded it is put to the vote immediately, without discussion and if it is carried the meeting does in fact move on to the next business. If the motion is defeated, the meeting then resumes the debate on which it was already engaged.

Nominate: This means 'to propose someone for election to an office'. Usually a nomination does not need to be seconded.

Any other business: This may appear on the agenda of a meeting to allow members to raise items which have come to light after the agenda has been prepared. However, any items the chair allows under this heading must be agreed by the meeting to be urgent and to have come to notice so recently that there was no time to have them included in the agenda.

261

Point of information: Sometimes a member who does not wish to take part in a discussion or who is preparing to speak later may wish to ask a question on relevant facts. He may do this by saying 'Chair, on a point of information, can you tell me, etc.'

Point of order: A member may rise at any time and say something 'on a point of order' — but he will soon be told to sit down if what he says is not in fact 'on a point of order'. The member must be able to prove that, or reasonably to question whether, another member has spoken or acted, or something has been done, or is going to be done, not in accordance with the rules, standing orders or terms of reference or other regulations which govern the conduct of the meeting. A point of order relates only to procedure: if the point raised is really part of the subject under discussion, it is not a point of order.

Previous question: This really means 'that the question be *not* now put'. If the motion is carried, no more discussion of the main question can occur, and it is shelved. If it is not carried, then the original motion must be put to the vote at once. Previous question can only be moved for an original or substantive motion.

Quorum: This a Latin word meaning simply 'of whom'. Its meaning in meeting procedure is extended to 'the number of members who must be present before the proceedings can be valid'. The quorum for a meeting is usually laid down in the rules or standing orders which apply, but if it is not laid down it is generally taken to mean a minimum of approximately one-third and never less than three.

Reference: When a task has been delegated by a meeting to a committee or by a committee to a subcommittee, the committee or subcommittee will eventually report to the main body and will probably recommend some action. If a member of the main body does not agree with any action reported or recommendation made, he should 'move the reference back' of the report or of the relevant section of the report. This motion is discussed and if it is carried it means that the committee or subcommittee must reconsider the subject in question and report again later.

Resolution: It is wrong to talk of moving or proposing a

resolution. One can move or propose a motion or proposition and either of these becomes a resolution if it is passed. In other words a resolution is something that a meeting has resolved to do.

Right of reply: It is customary to allow the mover of a proposition (but not of an amendment), who will have spoken first in the debate, the right to speak again at the end of the debate. In this second speech, however, he must not introduce any new material but merely reply to points already raised by other speakers.

Standing orders: Organisations which hold regular formal meetings (e.g. trade unions, councils, clubs) often have rules which stipulate the manner in which the business of their meetings shall be conducted. These are called 'standing orders' and they deal with such things as: for how long speakers may speak, the order in which speakers shall speak, the manner of conducting elections of officers, the order in which items shall be taken. Standing orders may be in addition to, or even override, the general rules of meeting procedure. If there are any, the chair and the secretary should be very familiar with them.

A member may at any time move 'suspension of standing orders' and have this motion debated. For instance, if standing orders stipulate that a speaker may speak for only five minutes, it may occasionally be desirable to allow someone to exceed this limit in order to complete an important statement. Suspension of standing orders, if carried, will allow him to do this.

Substantive motion: When any amendments to a motion have been passed, the motion has its wording altered accordingly and is then called the substantive motion.

Teller: This means a member who has been appointed to count the number of votes cast on any question.

Terms of reference: These are instructions given, generally to a committee, defining clearly the nature and the limits of the task which it has been set.

That the question be now put: This may be moved at any time during the debate on a motion, but must be moved by someone

263

who has not already spoken. If it is carried, the matter under debate is immediately put to the vote; if it is not carried, the debate is resumed. Clearly this is a useful device to stop unnecessary or useless discussion.

Conclusion

The aim of this book has been to help those who have, or expect to have, managerial responsibilities. Readers may have found that the content is relevant to the problems they see or face to a surprisingly large extent. The reality is that many other people have had to face similar problems and one may as well profit from their experience. There is little point in rediscovering the wheel on your own if such rediscovery, or its managerial equivalent, is unnecessary. The coverage of the book is not intended to be exhaustive, but anyone with managerial responsibilities must be confronted with many of the problem areas that have been identified and needs to have or to develop the complementary skills.

The skills of management are not a mystic art which people either do or don't have. Neither is it a pattern of behaviour which can only be acquired in a mysterious way which defies analysis. As with so many skills, careful study and practice can lead to substantial improvements in performance. Admittedly some people may have more potential than others, but perhaps the most important requirement for the conscious development of managerial skills is the realisation that this is possible.

Many readers are likely to have had little in the way of formal management training, and even those who have received such training may have found that it has not always helped in the development of their performance. This book is intended to provide a sound base for the development of a range of critical managerial skills. The conceptual understanding of what is required is the vital first stage. That needs to be followed by the conscious development of skills, and evaluation by the reader of the extent to which he is actually able to apply these skills. It is hoped that this book will serve not only as a starting point for the conscious development of skills, but also as a way of monitoring the extent to which those skills have actually been developed. It may well be of course that readers are already very proficient in some of the areas that have been identified. But it is also likely that there are other areas of relative weakness that need particular attention.

A key element in the book has been to stress the need for

managers to develop their diagnostic skills. The book is not intended to provide a set of prescriptive remedies to be applied without thought. The individual manager has not only to identify the problems that confront him, but also to determine the priority in which they must be tackled. Implicit in many of the chapters is the need to clarify just what the nature of a problem is before the fund of information about techniques is applied. It is only after careful diagnosis that the right tool can be selected for a particular job.

The self-development of the individual manager and improvements in job performance may hinge on the identification of realistic objectives. This may necessitate not just concentration on one or two key areas but also the setting of attainable standards. It may be quite counterproductive for a person to set out to change the world in managerial terms, either in the range of improvements he attempts, or in the level of performance at which he aims. Setting unrealistic standards of performance may confirm the adage that the 'excellent' is the enemy of the 'good'. It is far better to achieve a good improvement than to fail in attempting the impossible. A gradual approach to the development of managerial skills may also help in the assessment of what improvements are politically possible. It is no good a manager identifying improvements in an organisation, however necessary, if these are not politically attainable. It may also be appropriate to identify short-term and long-term objectives for improvement — both in oneself and in the job.

The development of the reader's managerial skills is likely to result in an advance up the 'managerial escalator'. This in turn is going to lead to a need to pay even more attention to the managerial aspects of the job and to the relevant areas of skill. This also emphasises the constantly changing pattern of work in organisations. Just as the individual is not a static creature with fixed characteristics, so do organisations change and the environments in which they operate. Individuals may also move from one organisation to another. The reader may not only have to cope with a fairly continuous pattern of change, but may find that much of his job is concerned with implementing change that affects other people. This is likely to be both the continuous everyday changes and the more spectacular one-off changes caused by, for example, the development of specific new technologies or markets. In short the manager will find that he is continuously having to adapt to changed circumstances and also to help other people adapt. The realisation of this, and the development of appropriate skills, should help the individual not only to handle such change more effectively, but also to influence events as well as simply be influenced by them.

One of the particular problems likely to be encountered as a person acquires increasing managerial responsibility is greater exposure to criticism. 'Back seat' advice can be very annoying, particularly if it comes from people who are neither particularly well informed nor competent. It can be all the more annoying if sometimes the advice turns out to be correct. As the importance of the decisions that the manager has to take increases, it is inevitable that those affected will comment on these decisions — either openly or indirectly. This is a cross that just has to be borne — hopefully somewhat more easily if it is recognised in advance. It is the price to be paid by almost anyone who accepts responsibility. What is particularly needed is the ability to react sensibly to criticism — neither over-reacting to ill-informed comment nor ignoring what may be sound advice.

This book is not intended as a substitute for decision-making but as a means of helping managers develop the ability to take appropriate decisions for themselves, and to acquire the ability to implement those decisions effectively. The more that managerial problems are consciously identified and tackled, and the more that the individual works at his managerial skills development, the more effective he is likely to be. This may give confidence and create the opportunity for even further development. Ironically one of the ways in which managers may learn most is when they make mistakes. This can cause them to question their pattern of behaviour with a view to improving their performance. The critical need is for managers to use such incidents as opportunities for learning, instead of letting them affect their self-confidence. One of the biggest adjustments that a successful manager may have to make is that of continuously outgrowing his job. In coping with that, however, he may not only gain substantial material rewards, but also make a powerful contribution to the particular organisation that he works for and to society in general.

Index